From Charity to Enterprise

From Charity
to Enterprise

The Development of American
Social Work in a Market Economy

**Stanley Wenocur and
Michael Reisch**

UNIVERSITY OF ILLINOIS PRESS

URBANA AND CHICAGO

First Illinois paperback, 2001
© 1989 by the Board of Trustees of the University of Illinois
Manufactured in the United States of America
1 2 3 4 5 C P 6 5 4 3 2

This book is printed on acid-free paper.

The Library of Congress cataloged the cloth edition as follows:
Wenocur, Stanley, 1938–
From charity to enterprise : the development of American social
work in a market economy / Stanley Wenocur and Michael Reisch.
p.   cm.
Bibliography: p.
Includes index.
ISBN 0-252-01556-8 (alk. paper)
1. Social service—United States—History. I. Reisch, Michael,
1948–   . II. Title.
HV91.W49   1989
361'.973—dc19   88-18836
                                                                CIP

Paperback ISBN 0-252-07073-9 / 978-0-252-07073-0

To our wives and children,

Amy, Jennifer, and Nikki,
and
Gail, Eric, Jonathan, and Jaimie

Contents

Preface

During our many years as educators, we have met relatively few social work students who entered professional training with a clear sense of what a profession is about and how professionalization might affect their practice or the lives of their clients. They come mainly seeking practice skills and knowledge and usually a credential which will provide access to an employment market; sometimes they seek an opportunity to help some needy population. They seem only dimly aware that they also are joining an extremely complex enterprise organized to promote their economic and political interests. They have yet to learn that much of the legitimacy of this professional enterprise has rested, and still rests, on a historic commitment to serving and advocating for the victims of modern industrial society, and that professionalization may in some ways hinder that mission.

The issues surrounding professionalization tend to be addressed only haphazardly in social work schools, if they are addressed at all, due to a crowded curriculum that stresses technological mastery. When professionalization is finally discussed, it often involves an intellectualized discourse on "the attributes of a profession" (Greenwood, 1957), or some variation on this, after which students are left with the impression that social work's status as a profession is precarious due to the lack of a well-developed, scientific knowledge base. This technological bias is also transmitted in other ways throughout the "socialization into the profession" experience, especially through an emphasis on research for building professional knowledge. Political and economic forces that have shaped social work's development and practice, past and present, are generally not explored.

The uncritical transmission of the idea that social work's uncertain professional status stems from a lack of scientific rigor in its practice borders on the ideological. And, through this bit of ideology, social work educators unwittingly reproduce social workers who harbor a vague sense of professional inferiority which they can do little to correct. This is unfortunate for many reasons, not the least of which is that social workers continue to suffer from lower salaries and prestige than their important occupational roles warrant.

The notion that a lack of scientific knowledge best accounts for precarious professional status has little, if any, empirical support (a statement which should also tell the reader that we ourselves value scientific research, lest we are suspected of the opposite). Yet, if support is lacking, then why is the notion so widely held? The answer is complicated, requiring both investigation into the sociology of professions in general and specifically into the history of social work's efforts at building a profession, which is what this book is about.

This book was written, then, partly to reopen the question of how aspiring occupations become professions and, in particular, to examine how social workers historically went about this profession-building process and with what consequences. It is not a book about the history of social work practice per se, nor about the history of social welfare policy, though both practice and policy developments enter into the account. Given the challenges that the social work profession is facing in the 1980s and 1990s, an historical perspective on its profession-building activities may be of some use.

The book is targeted at social work students and educators, social historians interested in social work, and students of the sociology of the professions. Social workers who are active in professional associations beyond their employing organizations may also benefit from an historical overview of their activities.

Chronologically, the book covers the years between 1880 and 1950. In part, we stopped at 1950 because the end of the 1940s marked a significant turning point in social work's development. By then all of the main themes and issues affecting current social work conflicts and practice had been sounded, such as the nature of professional practice at the baccalaureate level, the place of professional social work in public welfare, and the difficulties of certification. We stopped at 1950 also because we believe that modern social work history requires extensive interviewing of living social work leaders, past and present. Such an endeavor exceeded our limitations of time and resources.

The historical perspective which informs this book is explicitly political and economic. That is, we have viewed professionalization as an organized effort by subgroups of occupational entrepreneurs to develop and attain monopolistic control over a specialized competency. We do not suggest a conspiracy by any segment of the social work community. We recognize that the motivations of social work activists to build a profession were seldom simple and often quite unconscious. We all act in some sense in response to our historical context without being aware of how much that context is shaping our behavior. In fact, this is one of the chief disadvantages of an ahistorical practice that we seek to counter.

Thus, it is no accident that since the mid-1850s, members of numerous occupational groups in the United States actively engaged in profession-building projects, e.g., physicians, lawyers, teachers, engineers, architects, dentists, nurses, and social workers. All were responding to the opportunities and demands of the rapidly expanding, competitive market economy that accompanied industrialization. To the extent that they faced similar political, economic, social, and ideological requirements, professions as a form of social organization have evolved similar structural and ideological characteristics.

At the same time, aspiring groups also developed individual features and gained varying degrees of occupational prestige and rewards. Many factors account for these variations, including the nature of the service "commodity" offered to the public, market conditions, internal and external political machinations, and the availability of talented and influential occupational entrepreneurs.

Much of the uniqueness of social work has stemmed from its singular commitment to advocacy and social action on behalf of its traditionally disempowered clientele. Sometimes this commitment has translated into a deep concern for large-scale social reforms, sometimes into more narrow tinkering with small groups and organizational structures. In either case, social work's effort to convert its historic commitment into a reproducible technology has created unusual tensions in its profession-building project. Besides adding conceptual complexity and undermining occupational unity, at times it has also forced social workers to question the role of professions themselves in creating basic structural inequities in American society. While individual members of other professions have often shared these concerns, social work is unusual as a profession in attempting to incorporate a method for environmental change. This distinction makes the development of professional social work an especially interesting focus of analysis.

The study of professionalization through a political-economic lens has not been entirely neglected in historical investigations of social work and/or discussions of professional issues. Yet, it has seldom formed the central analytic frame of reference. A noted exception is Roy Lubove's book, *The Professional Altruist* (1965), a landmark because up to that point professions had seldom been scrutinized in this light. Our book attempts to extend Lubove's work in several ways.

In our first section, we have outlined a theoretical model of professionalization which serves as the framework for the analysis in the chapters that follow. Although such theoretical writing is necessarily abstract, the theory section makes the historical case study more comprehensible in the long run. It also helps readers to formulate their own analysis of some of social work's current internal professional struggles and activities and its responses to external competition and pressures such as the movement to "deprofessionalize" various job classsifications in some settings. We do not claim that our theoretical model is entirely original, but do believe that it is useful in organizing, synthesizing, and extending a political-economic perspective on professions found in numerous writings.

After Part 1, we provide a short introductory chapter on historical context at the start of the other sections. This will orient the reader to the social, political, and economic events of the larger society that shaped the opportunities, beliefs, and limitations of the activist profession-builders. We believe this material may also help the reader, as it helped us, to avoid the danger of attributing importance to past events based on present-day knowledge. In the introductions to the various chapters that follow the historical material, we have also tried again to make the connection to the theoretical model.

Our second section briefly covers the time span between 1880 and 1916, which others, including Lubove, have reviewed. Working from primary historical documents, we have added some new information and, we hope, imparted some additional insights. Parts 3 and 4 of the book move respectively from World War I to the Depression, and from the Depression through World War II. These sections extend our analysis into new ground and provide information which we believe is crucial to understanding the dynamics of social work practice in postindustrial American society. We conclude with a sketch of some of the issues that social work as a profession is currently grappling with and which derive from its political-economic history.

Acknowledgments

This project took many years from inception to completion. Without encouragement from families, friends, and colleagues, we would never have persevered. We are particularly grateful to Professor Clarke A. Chambers of the University of Minnesota for his careful reading of various versions of the manuscript, for his steadfast and unselfish support, incisive comments, and good humor. As founder and first director of the Social Welfare History Archives at the University of Minnesota, as teacher and scholar, Dr. Chambers has inspired productive scholarship on the history of social work and social welfare for more than a generation. David Klaassen, curator of the Social Welfare History Archives, also provided able and patient assistance, as did the research staffs of the New York Public Library and the Columbia University Libraries.

A grant from the Graduate School at the University of Maryland at Baltimore made our archival research possible. Along with the grant, we received a wonderful dose of intellectual stimulation and regular encouragement from Dr. Ross Kessel, then acting Dean of the Graduate School—a physician, a microbiologist, truly a man of letters, and now a good friend.

Dr. Harry Specht, Dean of the School of Social Welfare, University of California–Berkeley, an early mentor, read and commented thoughtfully on the entire manuscript and provided timely advice and assistance with the publishing process. We are deeply appreciative of his support. Our colleagues at the University of Maryland, Dr. Paul Ephross and Dr. David Hardcastle; Dr. Harold Lewis, Dean of the Hunter College School of Social Work; and Professor Steven Stowe of Indiana University all provided valuable comments on various chapters as well.

We are, of course, indebted to our wives and children, to whom this book is dedicated, for their patience and understanding throughout.

PART I

A Political-Economic Perspective on Professionalization

. . . There are two kinds of inequality among the human species; one which I call natural or physical, because it is established by nature, and consists in a difference in age, health, bodily strength, and the qualities of the mind or of the soul; and another, which may be called moral or political inequality, because it depends on a kind of convention, and it is established, or at least authorized by the consent of men. This latter consists of the different privileges which some men enjoy to the prejudice of others; such as that of being more rich, more honored, more powerful, or even in a position to exact obedience.

Jean-Jacques Rousseau, 1754

CHAPTER ONE

A Political-Economic View of Professionalization

INTRODUCTION

Modern professions in the United States arose in response to opportunities created by the industrial revolution, during a two-generation time span, roughly 1825–80 (Larson, 1977). During these years of societal transformation, technical and scientific knowledge and specialized skills of all sorts developed at a rapid rate, transforming many older occupations and creating some entirely new ones. These highly specialized, skilled occupations, however, should not be equated with professions. The concern for professionalization which accompanied this occupational elaboration, and which has continued to the present, represented something more, namely, an institutionalized effort to gain occupational prestige, security, and financial rewards.

In our view, some occupations have been able to achieve the special status accorded to professions because of the entrepreneurial activities and structures which their members developed to advance their interests during the growth of modern capitalism. The central idea is that "a profession is not an occupation, but [an institutionalized] means of controlling an occupation" (Johnson, 1972: 45).

So, for example, if we look at health care, we can find an array of occupations and subspecialties that provide the necessary services. In addition, we find that the members of these occupations have organized themselves into distinct groupings which have developed institutional lives of their own in the form of professional associations, schools, journals, and so on. It is this institutionalized order surrounding a given occupation that constitutes a profession. Its main purpose is to regulate the service commodity through which the members of the occupation earn their livelihoods.

In more formal terms, then, we view a profession as a quasi-corporate enterprise whose members have obtained a substantial degree of control over the production, distribution, and consumption of a needed service commodity. Or, as Freidson (1970a: 71) has put it, ". . . a profession is distinct from other occupations in that it has been given the right to control its own work." The degree of control is never complete; its nature and extent vary over time with socio-political, economic, ideological, and technological developments within the enterprise and the society. This control involves to a greater or lesser extent:

(1) the definition of the commodity which its specialized practitioners produce and distribute;
(2) explanations of the relationship of the production and distribution of the commodity to the broader needs of the total political economy;
(3) delineation of the organizational parameters in and through which this commodity will be produced and distributed, including some ability to define the relationship between the workplace and the commodity producers, the commodity users, and the concept of the commodity itself;
(4) definition of what constitutes efficient and effective production and distribution of the commodity (i.e., how its production and distribution are to be evaluated);
(5) control over resources required to produce and distribute the commodity;
(6) control over demand (i.e., consumer need) for the commodity, and over the number (supply) of specialized practitioners who are sanctioned to meet it—that is, a quasi-monopoly over production and distribution involving control over education, training, licensing (legal sanctions), and cultural sanctions (values, beliefs, customs, etc.).

Structurally, the professional enterprise can be viewed as a loosely ordered system of occupational control, consisting of: (a) certified individuals who perform roughly similar specialized functions, primarily as a means of earning a livelihood; (b) associations to advance the interest of these specialized practitioners and promote occupa-

complish several tasks. Ideologically, they had to construct a "monopoly of credibility" with the public to secure a clientele, and they had to conquer "official privilege" so as to obtain "a set of legally enforced monopolies of practice." The precondition for successfully managing these external ideological tasks encompassed two internal tasks: the development of a distinctive competency and "the unification of the corresponding areas of the social division of labor under the direction of a leading group of professional reformers." The heart of the unification project was the creation of a training system which would help to fashion this distinctive competency— the professional commodity—and standardize and centralize its production, namely, the professionals themselves who gained the specialized expertise (Larson, 1977: 16–17).

The tasks by which members of an aspiring occupation construct a professional enterprise are further refined in the outline below. Although we have divided the tasks into separate categories, they overlap and are frequently carried out simultaneously. For example, producers may create and/or shape a service commodity to take advantage of an emerging market opportunity, but also as a commodity is developed—perhaps a new way of dealing with truancy in the schools—its producers may seek to expand the market for this new service commodity.

Economic Tasks

A. Create a marketable (needed) commodity
B. Ensure sufficient production of the commodity
   1. Secure and train a production force
   2. Secure production sites
   3. Institute centralized systems of product control to maintain a commodity of standardized quality
C. Acquire control of outlets for distribution and sales
D. Establish and negotiate an acceptable rate of return for investors
E. Create a consumer market or clientele for its commodities

Political Tasks

A. Induce individuals and groups of potential providers and other resource holders or managers to invest labor and capital in developing and producing the commodity, providing workspace, distribution outlets, etc.

B. Define the boundaries of the new enterprise so as to include and exclude desirable and undesirable members
C. Establish the domain of the enterprise by overcoming competitors for resources and markets
D. Negotiate favorable agreements with regulatory bodies to protect investments in the enterprise (preferably a monopoly)

Ideological Tasks
A. Convince the potential members of the enterprise that they share a joint mission
B. Convince legitimating bodies—including relevant segments of the ruling class—that the enterprise is worth sanctioning
C. Convince the public of the superior quality of and necessity for its commodities

Though similar to other entrepreneurial ventures, some aspects of profession building are (and were) unique because of the unusual type of commodity to be marketed. Also, given a comparable social context, the differential success of particular professionalizing occupations can be accounted for by variations in the commodity and in other strategic resources and their management. We can divide these variables into three sets:

Economic Variables
A. Intangible quality of the commodity
B. Patterns of consumer demand, consumption, and distribution
C. Ability to attract producers to join the enterprise

Political Variables
A. Social status of the founders and other members of the enterprise and the strength of their ties to members of the ruling class

Ideological Variables
A. Ideological justification and the capacity to communicate it

These variables may, but do not necessarily, operate independently of one another. For example, the social status of the founders affects their ability to attract other producers as does the political ideology of the enterprise. In addition, the political process is always a function of skillful negotiation among multiple opportunities, contingencies, and ideological constructions. The analysis of individual professionalizing efforts ultimately involves sorting out these variations and determining the effects of combinations of multiple interactions on the outcomes. In the remainder of the chapter we will explain how these variables may affect the profession-building project.

The Intangible Quality of the Commodity

Professionalizing occupations have a unique set of production and distribution problems that derive from the nature of the commodity they seek to exchange in the marketplace. For most professions the commodity is an abstract, intangible service of uncertain worth—"an intellectual technique"—rather than a tangible good whose ultimate utility (use value) is immediately visible or apparent to a potential consumer or investor. In Larson's words (1977: 14), "professional work, like any other form of labor, is only a *fictitious* commodity; it 'cannot be detached from the rest of life, be stored or mobilized,' and it is not produced for sale. Unlike craft or industrial labor . . . most professions produce intangible goods; their product, in other words, is only formally alienable and is inextricably bound to the person and the personality of the producer." This intangible quality makes it difficult to attain a degree of market security sufficient to offset high investment and production costs. The main problems revolve around issues of *visibility* and *cognitive superiority*.

For a commodity to be marketable, potential consumers and investors must be able to identify it as something valuable because it will solve a real problem or meet a real need. "Professional" commodities vary in their ability to demonstrate visible benefit. Some are inherently more "useful" because they can be defined by the producers in terms of individual, clearly articulated needs for a large group of potential consumers, such as legal services to obtain a favorable contract or a judgment regarding disputed life, limb, and property, or medical care to treat common afflictions or specific maladies. The benefits of other types of "professional" commodities may not be as readily apparent because they are bound up with conflictual societal values and/or more ambiguous individual needs, such as psychiatric treatment or social work services.

The utility of some commodities also may be easier to demonstrate because the relationship between the applied technology and a beneficial outcome may be dramatic and direct rather than indirect, close in time sequence rather than protracted, or empirically more capable of support. Medicine has had many of these advantages in its profession-building efforts. When a commodity controlled by a professionalizing occupation is also, in fact, demonstrably superior to its competitors, e.g., sulfa drugs by physicians, the construction of a professional enterprise may be greatly advanced.

As with more tangible goods, standardization of an intangible commodity may enhance its visibility. It allows the commodity to be recognizable to a wide public; it facilitates claims to a definable professional domain; it makes commodity production possible in dispersed locations but identifiable with the same occupational group; it facilitates production of sufficient quantities to meet market needs. In a situation where new professional markets had to be developed altogether during the industrial revolution, standardization was a major requirement.

But standardization also poses some unique problems. Since the "professional" commodity is not separable from the producers, the ability to reproduce it uniformly in sufficient quantity and quality requires that "the producers themselves be reproduced," that is, "sufficiently trained and socialized so as to provide recognizably distinct services for exchange on the professional market" (Larson, 1977: 14). In industrial terms, in effect the situation requires quality control over the mass production of human beings whose skills can be marketed as a distinct and recognizable service. This degree of control necessitates highly selective screening of applicants and rigorous education and socialization in a standardized setting where the producers can closely supervise and regulate the training process. Institutions of higher education, programmatically controlled by producers, lend themselves to these needs better than apprenticeship arrangements in diverse settings. During the formative years of profession building in the United States, the growth of the modern university and the prominence of science made this possible and helped to legitimate the higher status attached to professionalizing occupations (Larson, 1977).

The difficulties of securing a professional market are compounded by the abstract, cognitive nature of the "professional" commodity.

Internal battles over cognitive superiority may be quite intense (Turner and Hodge, 1970: 26), but colleagues can still make a reasoned, even scientific, assessment. Laypersons, who do not ordinarily share the specialists' universe of discourse, find evaluation more baffling. Consequently, the professional cannot easily establish the authority that will make a client seek out and follow his or her advice. As a result, cognitive superiority must be partially established through ideological means.

Some commodities have greater potential for ideological exploitation than others, and some occupations by their nature can make better use of institutionalized ideological supports to advance their claims for functional authority. The trappings of educational credentials, expensive office furnishings, prestigious associations, high social status, and legal regulation often substitute as supportive data for any public evaluation of cognitive superiority (Freidson, 1970b). When a legally protected monopoly of practice can be established, the professional enterprise gains official sanction for its expertise which then does not have to be continuously proven.

Patterns of Consumer Demand, Consumption, and Distribution

Successful professionalization could not occur without sufficient demand for its commodity from a large, fairly heterogeneous consumer body (Johnson, 1972: 51). In an environment with only a small number of powerful clients, a professionalizing occupation would lack the broad base of support necessary to secure its sizable market investment and/or it would be highly dependent upon meeting the needs defined by the group paying for its services.

Profession building also benefits from consumer disorganization because collective consumer action may lead to greater regulation of the profession by external sources. For example, the development of Health Maintenance Organizations (HMOs) and third-party payment systems has led to significant shifts in the control of professional medical services in the United States.

Services provided to consumers on a fee-for-service basis through solo or group partnership arrangements also strengthen professional control. Consumer power is decreased when the consumer population is large and heterogeneous, and the provider group is carefully restricted, and when large inequalities exist in the ability to pay for services. Furthermore, the individual approach reduces consumers' potential to collectively define their problems, needs, and roles, and thereby to alter the demand for certain kinds of benefits or services.

The professionalizing efforts of both law and medicine at the turn of the twentieth century benefited from the nature of their clientele—an expanding, urban, middle-class market—which sought and paid for "professional" assistance on an individual basis, whether privately or through corporations. Engineering, on the other hand, suffered because its technical and economic consultation could be better assessed by its consumers and because engineers were generally salaried employees of large-scale economic enterprises rather than independent entrepreneurs (Larson, 1977: 27). In a still different pattern, social work services at this time were neither sought out nor paid for by the direct users of the services, the urban poor. The real clientele of social workers were the philanthropists, and eventually the state, who actually paid for the services and thereby restricted the collegial control that social workers could establish in their sphere of occupational expertise (Leiby, 1978).

The need for professional services is also affected by sociocultural patterns and is distributed differentially according to socioeconomic status. Need itself is therefore elastic—subject to custom, economic capacity, and ideological manipulation. Consequently, the struggles to build a profession and a corresponding professional market have involved not only the identification of need, but also its creation, a twentieth-century American trend that led one alarmed critic to lament the veritable "disabling of the citizen through professional dominance" (Illich, 1977: 27).

Consumption patterns and demands may affect the ability to control the distribution of a specialized commodity. In situations where the definition of and demand for a commodity are much less strictly regulated by the producers or the marketplace, as for example with public school education, the distribution of services is also much less subject to producer control. This lack of autonomy may contribute to crises of legitimacy for a professionalizing group (Baum, 1978).

Additionally, the nature of the specialized commodity or service itself affects the ability of producers to control its distribution. For example, routine medical examinations can be performed in a private office, but non-routine medical care often requires other facilities, e.g., the hospital or nursing home, and/or other specializations. For economical and pedagogical reasons, educational services do not lend themselves well to individualistic arrangements. Thus the distribution requirements of specialized commodities vary as to size and complexity of physical facilities, machine implements and hard technologies (computers, X-rays, etc.), ancillary labor, interdependencies with other specialized groups (heteronomy), legal sanctions, and legitimacy. All of these distribution requirements represent sources of dependency (hence less autonomy) that a professionalizing occupation must deal with successfully to gain collegial control. These dependencies may also change for many reasons, as for example, newly organized demands by consumers for more control over the commodity, or the need for new and sophisticated technologies controlled by other specialized groups, or competitive professionalizing occupations. The relationships between production and distribution, as well as production and consumption, then, may become major sources of tension for an aspiring occupation or an existing profession.

Ability to Attract Producers

The construction and continuation of a professional enterprise requires a steady stream of recruits able and willing to pay for the protracted education (and overhead set-up costs in some cases) to become its specialized experts. Since investment costs in time and money are high, potential recruits have to be convinced that their endeavors will be worth it. The attractiveness of professionalized occupations has usually involved the promise of high social status, high income, career security, autonomy over the conditions and content of one's work, social class socialization to the value of intellectual or "genteel" vocations, and/or a persuasive mission or ideology.

Clearly, professionalizing occupations have varied in the past, and still vary, in their ability to manipulate these rewards and hence in their ability to attract producers. Aspiring occupations with a core of elite producers trained in already prestigious universities—the older "learned" professions of medicine and law—had the advantage of prior social standing and accepted mission to lend to their attractiveness. In the nineteenth and early twentieth centuries, physicians in the American Medical Association, for example, were able to use their social advantage to establish the reforms necessary for monopolistic market control, that is, to professionalize the field of medicine as they defined it. This control, in turn, enabled medical schools to restrict entry to members from elite groups, to exclude women and minorities, and to promise highly remunerative and socially prominent careers to their recruits (Larson, 1977: 164).

Newer aspiring professions or those whose status, financial promise, and autonomy were less certain because of the clientele they served or the organizational context of their work, relied more on ideological persuasion to attract recruits. These occupations benefited from the ideology already attached to the professional concept in general, such as an association with "science" and education, as well as the substantive ideological potential of the particular aspiring vocations, such as the nobility of public service, moral reform, or social justice. These professionalizing occupations, such as nursing, social work, and teaching, already in a disadvantageous position in the occupational hierarchy, remained much more open to women, minority-group members, and working-class persons who were excluded from the older "professions" by the ostensibly neutral meritocratic criteria that masked sexual, racial, ethnic, and social class discrimination.

Founder Status and Ties to Power Structure

Occupational groups whose members are connected to societal elites have a competitive advantage in the political and ideological struggle to establish a monopoly of practice. Wealthy elites command the resources to define and legitimate knowledge, values, priorities, social problems, and needs, and different ways of meeting them. They can sanction a professional enterprise, invest resources in its development and upkeep, and help it to fashion and control its consumer market.

Members of the "learned" professions of law, medicine, and theology brought a preindustrial inheritance of wealth, aristocratic traditions and ties, political title, and university education (with little technical expertise) with them into the competitive nineteenth-century period of professional expansion and development. In medicine, to use an example from the archetypical profession, this inheritance gave American physicians a competitive edge over other healing occupations to establish themselves as the controlling segment within the health care field (Freidson, 1970a; Larson, 1977).

Nineteenth-century America was a society with a spacious frontier and an egalitarian ethic. As one form of healer on the scene, physicians did not have a demonstrably superior technology, nor could they regulate producer or consumer markets. For the elite of physicians, connected to the most prestigious medical schools, urban hospitals, and public offices, this situation was temporarily worsened by the reform of higher education in the 1860s which brought technological and professional training and scientific research into the universities and set off an era of tremendous expansion (Ben-David, 1964; Bledstein, 1976). The new middle classes now had access to credentials and legitimacy for a broad range of healing practices.

As medical specialties developed within the physician group and outside it, e.g., nurses, midwives, chiropractors, homeopathic doctors, and surgeons, the medical field also became confused and overcrowded. To oversimplify a complex history for the sake of a point, ultimately, through their connections to the corporate and university power structure, the elite specialists from the most reputable Eastern medical schools prevailed over the medical domain. As enforcement of licensing became more feasible through an expanding network of county medical societies, the Flexner Report of 1910, also promoted by the AMA and funded by the Carnegie Foundation, spurred the reform of medical education and the consolidation of the medical field under the "scientific doctors."

Flexner's recommendation, essentially for "fewer and better doctors" grounded in thorough scientific training, was not the most significant aspect of this history; high-level commissions commonly make recommendations that are never followed. Rather, it was that the recommendations were sanctioned and implemented through resources controlled by societal elites, such as the Rockefeller and Carnegie foundations (Larson, 1977: 164; Starr, 1982).

Ideological Justification and Communication Capacity

As part of their political struggles for monopolistic privileges, professionalizing occupations must engage in several ideological tasks. These involve convincing relevant segments of the ruling class and the public of the merits of their demands for autonomy and privilege, and that once granted, neither will be abused, but on the contrary, will benefit society. Successful exercise of these ideological tasks in the main requires two kinds of ideological resources: the construction of a persuasive rationale or justification and an effective capacity to communicate proof of the occupation's merit.

The justification for monopolistic advantage that aspiring occupations developed in the nineteenth and twentieth centuries fit with the tenets and values of industrial capitalism and helped to shape its development. Eventually this justification became an ideology of professionalism still used by aspiring occupations today. The content of this professional ideology centered around the cognitive superiority of specialized knowledge/technology based on science as a method, and the norms of impartiality, objectivity, and noncommercial advantage embodied in a service ideal. This ideology was responsive to, and promoted at the same time, such dominant values as individualism, free competition, the application of science (as a method and a world view) and technology to human endeavors and social progress, and the rationalization of the economy and community life to secure a stable environment for business and industry (Kolko, 1963; Wiebe, 1967). It supported and received support in turn from such major developments as the reform of the university to be more compatible with the industrial world and its rise as a status-transforming and status-conferring institution, and the growth of large-scale bureaucracies in the public and private sectors of the political economy. At least one observer has situated this professional ideology as the centerpiece of an entire culture of professionalism that permeated middle-class life in the United States between 1840 and 1915 (Bledstein, 1976).

Professionalizing occupations vary in their capacity to use the ideology of professionalism strategically, either because they cannot convey an image sufficiently consistent with the ideology or because their capacity to communicate the proof of their claims is in some way deficient. Ideological resources to communicate justification include: *symbolic resources*, the status of the aspirants as a symbol itself, and the special language and dramaturgy of their practice; and *formal and informal vehicles of communication*, such as journals, textbooks, conferences, conventions, occupational associations, and the mass media.

The symbols associated with an occupation can convey or reinforce persuasively a belief in the unique knowledge and skills of its
practitioners. "The more abstract and ambiguous the language, the
more superhuman the practitioners and their challenges are por-
trayed, the more exclusively the occupational dramaturgy is enacted
with clients (who must assume the good faith of the practitioners)
rather than customers, the more convincing these symbols are . . ."
(Nilson and Edelman, 1976: 24). A familiar illustration of the power
of symbols to justify occupational prestige has been the successful,
long-running, and stereotypical television portrayal of the ethical
sensitivity, drama, and skill of physicians and lawyers at work. Similar efforts to portray social workers and nurses have been largely
unsuccessful (Andrews, 1987).

Summary

In this chapter we have viewed professions, not as occupations
that have attained special status in the division of labor, but rather
as the institutionalized means for controlling certain occupations.
As Western societies were transformed by the industrial revolution,
modern professions arose like other corporate ventures to take advantage of newly forming economic markets. In the United States,
within a competitive and rapidly expanding capitalist economy,
workers who had information and services to sell—an intellectual
technique—needed to find a means of protecting their labor. Those
workers who could garner resources by virtue of individual talent
and the advantages of institutional ties to the structure of power—
through family, education, and social class positions—were able to
consolidate occupational functions in a given sphere and control
them by building a professional enterprise. Thus, as we have defined
it, professional status rests on the degree of control which the members of an occupation have been able to achieve over the production,
distribution, and consumption of their defining commodity.

Occupations have differed greatly in the degree of professional
status they have been able to attain. The struggle is ongoing.
This political-economic perspective suggests a number of variables
which are important to consider in accounting for these differences.
They include variations in the intangibility of the commodity, pat-

terns of consumer demand and consumption, the ability to attract producers, the capacity to communicate a justification for monopolistic control, and access to elite resources.

In the chapters which follow, we propose to analyze the development of the social work profession along political-economic lines. In so doing, we intend neither to glorify professions nor to denounce them. We do, however, believe that in order for professionals to be able to look at their work critically, they must be able to understand it in political and economic terms. Technological and cognitive understanding alone does not go far enough.

For social workers, this fuller understanding is particularly important, because their profession has historically concerned itself with ameliorating social distress through institutional change. Since its professional status partially rests on this concern, and its members are often attracted by its humanitarian and democratic ideals, the concern for social reform cannot be easily excised. Yet professions by their nature tie their members into ongoing structures of power and privilege, and serve them, through their expertise, in order to advance their own class interests and status aspirations. This latter concern limits the former. How much it may do so, whether or not change is possible and desirable, and what the options are for making any changes are all questions which require the development of greater class consciousness. These are also the kinds of questions which we hope will be considered anew in light of the analysis in the following chapters.

PART II

The Emergence of a Professional Social Work Enterprise: 1880–1916

Charity in cities may rear her monumental piles, and endow them with the munificence of princes. Yet, she, too—warm, impulsive, heaven-born Charity—may degenerate into a cold, mechanical, political economy. Her life may be crushed beneath a system.

Anon., The Knickerbocker, 1840

All modern industrial life tends to concentrate as a matter of economy.

F. G. Kingsbury, 1895

CHAPTER TWO

Historical Context

INTRODUCTION

In March 1865, the U.S. Congress established the Bureau of Refugees, Freedmen and Abandoned Lands under the auspices of the War Department to provide unprecedented services in such diverse areas as health care, education, and civil and criminal justice (Olds, 1963; Osthaus, 1976). More than half a century later, the American Red Cross, under the direction of a professional social worker, Homer Folks, distributed relief to wounded soldiers and their families and engaged them in counseling to deal with the psychological effects of war. In 1865, the term "social work" was not yet part of our national vocabulary. Fifty years later, an organization of paid social workers reacted with considerable dismay and indignation when informed at their national conference by the leading authority on professional education in the United States, Dr. Abraham Flexner, that the full-time work in which they were engaged did not constitute a full-fledged profession.

What factors account for this transformation of social work "from a part-time avocation to a full-time occupation" (Lubove, 1965: 1)? What made the drive for professional status so critical to social workers, and how did this drive influence the character of their emerging profession? We believe the answers lie in the economic and social transformation of the United States within the context of capitalist modes of production, organization, and ideology. To understand the political economy of professionalization in social work, therefore, we must briefly examine the historical context in which this phenomenon began.

The Economic and Social Transformation of the United States

The enormous industrial expansion of the late nineteenth century produced an uneven pattern of economic and social development, new cultural "rules" and new ideologies which explained and justified the dramatic changes underway (Gutman in Frazier, 1974: 32). This transformation was rapid and painful, producing social problems which existing social institutions seemed incapable of solving, such as the widening gap in the distribution of income and wealth. By 1900, a relatively small number of families and corporations owned most of the nation's wealth, while much of the worst poverty was concentrated in the newest and least powerful social groups: industrial workers, immigrants, and rural Southern blacks.

In an effort to preserve economic stability, most governmental and industrial leaders tried to play down the widespread disruption of the social order by maintaining the appearance of social harmony (Schwartz, 1976: 192). Thus they sought to reestablish "organic and natural relations" based upon the "belief that unity is the natural state of the community" (Bender, 1975: 132, 136) and to bridge the widening social gap by creating "a new order of instrumentalities . . . to raise up the degraded class of the city" (Brace, 1872: 18; Bender, 147–48; Buder, 1969: 39–45).

Most of these efforts were targeted at the nation's burgeoning urban centers, safety valves for the surplus rural population and havens for the 23 million new immigrants who came to the United States in the half century following the Civil War, largely from eastern and southern Europe (Kessner, 1977: viii; Karp, 1976: 212–13). Immigrant families, who soon comprised over 50% of the population of most major cities, lived in incredibly squalid environments with population densities as high as 1,700 persons per acre, or 15 to 16 people per dwelling unit, in "dumbbell tenements," an architectural innovation which the editor of *Sanitarium* called "an ingenious design for a dungeon" (Kessner, 1977: 21; Lubove, 1962; Carlton, 1982; Dinnerstein, Nichols, & Reimers, 1979: 157ff). They transformed neighborhoods, physically expanded city boundaries, and altered the nature of community life (Boroff, 1975: 38; Kessner, 1977: 39).

The average immigrant had great difficulty escaping the trap of scarce assets, few occupational skills, and little education. Moreover, twelve major depressions between 1870 and 1915 made available work as precarious as it was dangerous. Most salaries ranged between $7 and $15 per week, and many groups such as steelworkers, women in garment industry sweatshops, and blacks earned far below the average for longer hours (Brody, 1980). Each year, 35,000 workers died in industrial accidents; a half million more were injured without compensation (Maddow, 1979). In 1910, only one-seventh of foreign-born families earned the U.S. "standard" of $900 per year for a family of five; two million children still worked at wages as low as 50 cents for a 16-hour day (Dinnerstein, Nichols, & Reimers, 147–49; National Child Labor Committee Records, 1913). Seasonal employment, chronic unemployment, and broken employment compounded the economic insecurity of the poor. For many families, child labor and prostitution provided the only recourse to starvation.

There seemed little prospect of improvement. Even after the introduction of compulsory public education, two-thirds of the children in urban slums did not go to school, and adult illiteracy remained high. Chronic and endemic diseases such as tuberculosis, industrial accidents, and inadequate diets sapped the energy of the poor. In New York, deaths of children under five increased 22% between 1885 and 1892, while between 1885 and 1896 overall mortality rates increased 50% and suicide rates leaped 85% (NYC Health Department Records, 1900; Felt, 1974: 13, 1965). Infant and adult mortality rates for urban blacks were 50% higher than for whites of similar social class (Carlton, 1982).

Many reformers such as Henry George (in Cook, Gitteland, and Mack, 1973) argued that the growth and transformation of cities broke down the social fabric of village and town life in the country and threatened the quality of U.S. civilization. Josiah Strong (1898) implored his readers "that we cannot shut our eyes to the fact that the foreign population as a whole is depressing our average intelligence and morality in the direction of the dead-line of ignorance and vice." In New York, an 1880 report of a leading charitable organization stated, "Our city, operating like a sieve, lets through the enterprising and industrious, while it retains the indolent, the aged and the infirm . . . to become a burden, and often because of their vices, a nuisance to the community" (AICP, 1880: 1).

These comments reflected longstanding anti-urban and anti-European prejudices, particularly against Catholics and Jews, and produced "reform movements" which stemmed as much from fear of political power shifting to the ethnic, non-Protestant masses as they did from moral outrage over the corruption of political machines like New York City's Tweed Ring (Boyer, 1978; Hershkowitz, 1978). Education and religious conversion were two major components of this reform strategy (Boyer, 1978; Atherton, 1975). The development of social services with educational or religious overtones was a third.

The Professionalizing Impulse

Most histories of social work regard the phenomenon of professionalization in modern, industrializing America as inevitable. Yet there is nothing inevitable about the efforts of members of the same occupation to establish a monopolistic hold on the distribution of a particular service commodity with concomitant material and status rewards. The emergence of a social work professional enterprise reflected instead a powerful tendency throughout U.S. society since the advent of industrialization in the mid-nineteenth century to concentrate economic, political, social, and cultural power for competitive advantage in a market economy (Larson, 1977; Poulantzas, 1976). Around the turn of the century, the experience of doctors in building an organized medical enterprise served as an influential model for other occupational groups seeking professional status.

Medicine achieved its dominance within the U.S. occupational hierarchy because of the success of its practitioners in defining a uniform service commodity, recruiting and maintaining powerful political and institutional sponsorship, and selling this new conception of medicine to other physicians and the general public (Starr, 1982). The successful synthesis of more scientifically based medicine with business practices suited the needs of powerful corporate interests by placing medical care within the institutions they already dominated—hospitals and universities. It also served the interests of many doctors who feared the further erosion of their status and power by the uncertain progress of industrial development and transformation (Markowitz & Rosner, 1979; Brown, 1979; Wiebe, 1967).

The American Medical Association (AMA), which grew to 70,000 members by 1910, played a key role in this process through its promotion of restrictive state licensing laws and public health legislation which confirmed the preeminent role of the physician. Powerful corporate sponsors such as Andrew Carnegie and John D. Rockefeller helped the AMA eliminate the competition of alternative forms of medicine and ensured that prevailing institutional forms of medical practice would dominate the profession. By placing training schools under university auspices, admissions requirements were made more restrictive, medical school curricula were lengthened, and the total "production" of physicians was reduced (Kunitz, 1974).

In contrast, the professionalization of social work had its roots in the formation of voluntary charitable associations that proliferated by the 1870s in every city in the United States, organized by groups as diverse as feminists and Protestant clergymen, for reasons ranging from benevolence to social control (Reisch & Wenocur, 1984). Despite the democratic vision of many proponents of voluntarism, upper-class white men soon dominated voluntary organizations and shaped them in their interests. This control enabled a continuous and permanent upper class to strengthen its hold on the nation's capital resources and extend its power to all areas of cultural and social life, including the administration of major social welfare organizations and the credential-granting apparatuses of the emerging professions (Hall, 1974–75).

New, multipurpose reform organizations such as the League for Social Services and the American Institute of Social Services first appeared in the early 1870s as a reaction to the inability of existing private charities to deal adequately with the individual and social deprivation produced by the depression of 1873–77 (Bremner, 1980: 197ff). They "reflect[ed] an interesting blend of religious zeal, social scientific detachment and organizational efficiency" (Walker, 1976: 617). Some reformers optimistically believed that such associations were symbolic of "the general tendency of modern development . . . toward . . . political and legal equality" (George, 1976: 119). Other, more skeptical observers like William Graham Sumner attacked the reform spirit.

Most reformers came from the respectable, educated middle and upper middle class. Born into privilege, they confronted an uncertain future in which their academic training, social skills, and political connections appeared of little value. They solved what Richard Hofstadter (1955) termed their "status anxieties" by accepting an urban, industrially centered society and embracing a technological future which emphasized the importance of scientific expertise organized and implemented through bureaucratic means (Wiebe, 1967: 166).

SOCIAL WORK AND WOMEN'S WORK

The problem of "status anxiety" was particularly acute for middle- and upper-class women, who comprised the vast majority of the staffs of late nineteenth-century charitable organizations. Two notable examples are Josephine Shaw Lowell, the principal fundraiser for the Freedmen's Relief Association in New York, the first woman appointed to the State Board of Charities in New York, and a founder of the New York Charities Organization Society, and Louisa Lee Schuyler, founder of the New York State Charities Aid Association shortly after the Civil War and a dominant force in shaping the professionalization of social work for the next several decades (Frederickson, 1965; Vandiver, 1980; Bolin, 1973; Schuyler, 1915). Such women were attracted to social activism and charity work by a curious combination of feminism and noblesse oblige and by a view of charity work as an extension of their domestic roles into the community (Kusmer, 1973; Becker, 1964; Philadelphia SOC). These factors played a critical role in how social work emerged as a professional enterprise in the United States.

In the late nineteenth century a slow but significant shift occurred in society's view of women's potential. While women's occupational horizons broadened, this development was limited largely to the daughters of wealthy families. Yet the increase in female workforce participation from one-sixth to one-fourth between 1860 and 1920 was greatest among black and foreign-born white women, ages 15–44, primarily in unskilled factory and service jobs (U.S. Dept. of Census, 1904: 10–15; 1930: 45).

Even the apparent growth of middle-class, female employment in the professional/technical sector, (from 5.6% of all employed women in 1870 to over 13% in 1920) is a misleading statistic. While women in 1900 made up 35% of the professional/technical workforce, they were largely restricted to the lowest-paying, lowest-status, and, generally, least-skilled jobs. The sex-typing of occupations within the U.S. workforce was also found in the professional sphere where clear demarcations between so-called "masculine" and "feminine" professions were already firmly established. Fewer than 1% of all lawyers and 6% of all physicians were women; correspondingly, nearly 94% of all nurses and 75% of all social workers were female (U.S. Census, 1904, 1930; Adams, 1921).

The "opening" of the workforce to women, therefore, involved neither a major transformation of American values, nor a dramatic shift in economic, political, or social power. While more women of all classes worked, most were limited in their choice of occupations to the jobs considered too low-paying or too demeaning by men. While more middle- and upper-income women joined the ranks of professionals, this occurred largely through the development of newly emerging "feminine" professions such as social work, nursing, and teaching whose requirements mirrored the attributes deemed desirable for women by the dominant culture (C. Chambers, 1986).

The evolution of these professions created a peculiar contradiction for potential professional women. They could move out of their traditional social roles only via those occupations which perpetuated female stereotypes and which were structured to ensure continued male dominance of the occupational hierarchy and the political-economy as a whole. Any attempts by such women to restructure their professional domain along lines which deviated from preconceived notions of femininity jeopardized their tenuous professional status. Yet professions like social work could not establish themselves or survive in a competitive environment unless their members developed those very attributes which contradicted prevailing conceptions of appropriate sex roles.

Since the establishment and sustenance of social work within the professional hierarchy required the maintenance of a delicate balance between acceptable feminine attributes and more "masculine" traits of assertiveness and activism, the types of women who were attracted to the profession and were able to lead it successfully exhibited a unique synthesis of traditional female characteristics and qualities which had historically been associated primarily with male behavior. The first-generation leaders within the social work profession could realistically emerge, therefore, only from the educated middle- and upper-income, native born, white population (Becker, 1961; Vandiver, 1980; Kessler-Harris, 1982). (Mary Richmond, self-educated and of modest background, was an exception to this general pattern.) Their importance meant that, in its critical early stages, social work had to contend with traditional societal attitudes about such women even among their allies in the broader Progressive movement. "Middle class progressives relied upon [the] expertise [of] . . . a well-trained occupational sector that could apply scientific thought to family, civic and economic problems. In a rough way, this kind of expertise fell within the province of women, who guarded the nation's morality" (Kessler-Harris, 115).

The breadth and vagueness of this social-housekeeping function encouraged the incorporation of an expanding and diverse range of interests into the field of social work, but made it more difficult for social workers to define specifically what their particular service product was—an acute problem in a social environment in which the values of specialization, rationality, and efficiency were ascendant.

One by-product of this problem and the marketplace division between "masculine" and "feminine" professions was the "semiprofessional" status of social work (Etzioni, 1969; Toren, 1972). While professional *men* were encouraged to strengthen their professional enterprises by increasing their spheres of expertise and power and limiting access to their ranks, *women* professionals were instructed that their first priority was the satisfaction of the needs of others. Specialized knowledge was less important to women, therefore, and certainly could not be used to establish greater independence and power. Consequently, "whereas the masculine professions used special knowledge to claim autonomy from hierarchical authorities, the feminine professions did not seek autonomy, nor [did they] have the special knowledge to substantiate such a claim. Feminine professions [were as a result] easily integrated into administrative hierarchies and placed under the power of supervision of men professionals" (Matthaei, 1982: 177).

While women provided the vast majority of line workers in elementary education, nursing, and library science, the managers of these institutions were usually men. In addition, women lacked access to the "high professions" of medicine, law, and ministry, as well as to careers in business and engineering. Only in social work did men and women play roles of equal significance in shaping and managing agencies.

CONCLUSION

Prior to the 1890s, social work and social reform were generally viewed as inseparable components of the tasks of social service organizations. Yet the diversity of these organizations made it increasingly difficult to articulate a coherent definition of social work to potential supporters and members alike (Bartlett, 1976: 284). In a competitive economic environment particularly receptive to marketplace arguments and unreceptive to other non-traditional roles for women, a primary task of social work leaders was to develop a comprehensive and comprehensible definition of the commodity which social workers produced; *comprehensive* so as to garner the widest possible sphere of control and *comprehensible* so that the knowledge and skills required to produce it could be demonstrated to sponsors and the general public and communicated to future generations of practitioners. The growing strains within the ranks of social workers—between those who emphasized "social treatment" and those who stressed social justice—can, to a great extent, be attributed to the pressure to establish occupational control over a particular sphere of "helping activities."

CHAPTER THREE

The Earliest Definitions of the Social Work Commodity

INTRODUCTION

The economic crisis of the 1890s stimulated a reappraisal of prevailing attitudes toward the "Social Question." By traditional standards, a large number of the new poor were undeserving: the products of mental instability, environmental conditions, or racial and ethnic inheritance. Old-style charity was designed to reinforce the work ethic, but how could it affect this population? Ironically, those who sought to preserve the status quo and those who sought to reform it both searched for means to harness the forces of "progress." Given the climate in which this search occurred, it was not surprising that defenders and critics of American society embraced technology "as a principle of order and preserver of union, [as] the harbinger of peace and guardian of prosperity" (Kasson, 1976: 186).

While corporate and political leaders applied technology to strengthen their control over the direction of society, social workers compensated for their lack of scientific theory by creating a new technology based on a generation of practical experience and the theoretical formulations of the other professions with whom they came into regular contact. This integration of a "technological approach" into what had been viewed as a practical field moved social work into the economic and political mainstream in terms of the problems it addressed, the clients it served, and the institutional forms it created. In other words, the definition of the service commodity as "social treatment" made social work more attractive to potential sponsors, and, ultimately, to the larger pool of potential consumers. While the economic and political forces that shaped these developments were already in place by the early 1890s, the emergence of casework as the primary form of social work practice and the professional dominance of its East Coast practitioners were by no means foregone conclusions.

THE CHARITY ORGANIZATION SOCIETIES

The antecedents of social casework were the friendly visiting and scientific charity practiced by the Charity Organization Societies (COS). Friendly visiting—a peculiar synthesis of evangelical community service, positivism, Social Darwinism, and social control—reflected the views of social philosophers like William Graham Sumner and corporate leaders like Andrew Carnegie. Scientific charity helped shape the evolution of the social work profession by defining social work in the language of science, order, and efficiency which was compatible with parallel organizational efforts by U.S. industry.

The COS flourished because they claimed to offer solutions to previously intractable individual and social problems, couched in terms of the ideology of the dominant classes they sought as sponsors (Boyer, 1978). By emphasizing science and secularism, the COS broke in significant ways from the tradition of U.S. charitable provision as practiced earlier by church-affiliated charities, urban missions, and especially the Association for the Improvement of the Condition of the Poor, or AICP.[1] COS leaders, therefore, attempted to fuse the traditional American emphasis on individualism and individual responsibility with the application of the scientific method and a business-oriented philosophy. This fusion had the "latent function of further individualizing the stigma of poverty" through the primary utilization of the casework approach (Waxman, 1977: 83).

In a speech to the business community of Philadelphia in 1899, Mary Richmond (then secretary of the Philadelphia Society for Organizing Charity) tried to "sell" the COS definition of social work to potential sponsors by validating the business community's view of the poor: "I know that there are a great many people born lazy who will never do one stroke more of the world's work than direct necessity forces them to." [Charitable expenditures are] "hopelessly wasted . . . encourage idleness, vice, crime and disease. . . . Heretofore, we have encouraged the lowest and worst [characteristics of man], let us now try to arouse the better instincts of his nature: Teach him industry, sewing, cleanliness, self-control" (Richmond, 1899a: 17).

Firm in the belief that the scientific organization of charitable work represented an enlightened mode of social intervention which would benefit both the poor and their benefactors, the COS developed as their guiding principles the enhancement of the productivity of the individual and the refusal "to support any except those it [could] control" (Lowell, 1889: 68). They implemented these principles by restricting access to services and by giving clients no voice in the determination of the outcome goals of service (Archives of New York COS; Bolin, 1973: 6).

Many supporters of the COS movement also felt that organized charity represented "the real answer to the Socialistic and Communistic theories now being energetically taught to the people" (Kellogg, 1880). It is significant, therefore, for the development of the social work profession that it was largely through the COS that organized social work first began the self-conscious process of professionalization.

Who Were the Earliest Social Workers?

Both the men and women of the COS came from roughly similar urban, upper-class backgrounds and possessed comparable educational credentials. Although well educated, some male COS volunteers were "leisured," i.e., gracefully unemployed; most were lawyers or retired businessmen. Paid agents tended to be former teachers or ministers. Most were over 30 and married, although a higher proportion of men were single than in other professions. Their primary motivation for engaging in social work activities appears to have been a sense of noblesse oblige, in a few instances stemming from their family's history of community service (Becker, 1968; Rauch, 1975).

In their early years, these men dominated the COS as board members, directors, supervisors, and paid agents, while women comprised virtually the entire corps of "friendly visitors" and unpaid office staff (Rauch, 1976). Although they earned less than male professionals in other fields, male COS employees were paid the highest salaries within social work (Rauch, 1975). Recent evidence also suggests that the paternalistic and often punitive approach of the COS was also the product of male domination and class bias (Cumbler, 1980; Rauch, 1976; Vaile, "The Denver Bureau of Public Welfare," n.d.). While many women in the COS deeply resented their subordinate role and actively fought to overcome persistent male dominance (Rauch, 1975), other women leaders regretted the lack of more such men. Josephine Shaw Lowell, for example, remarked, "What we need are more men of leisure with the tradition of public service like so many of the nobility and gentry of England. Our young men, those that we catch, are very good, but usually too busy" (Stewart, 1911: 129).

Women COS volunteers tended to come from what we now term "two-career" families, in which their fathers often held political office and their mothers were unpaid community or social activists. Such families not only encouraged their daughters to seek a college education, but instilled in them the value of education directed at a social purpose and the importance of the woman's role beyond that of wife and mother (Blumberg, 1966; Conway, 1969; Goldmark, 1953; Huggins, 1971; Levine, 1971; Linn, 1935; Wise, 1935). In addition, these families tended to be more strongly influenced by religious values, particularly those associated with British Christian Socialism and the Social Gospel movement in the United States. Women in the COS, therefore, embraced both the "mission" aspect of social work and its growing emphasis on scientific philanthropy and innovation. For them, social work was simultaneously cause and career (Becker, 1968; Clark, 1970).

Most women, however, were not drawn to charitable activities by radical social impulses. They were motivated more by a desire to protect families, children, and themselves from the hazards of industrial society than by a wish to carve out a new role for women in that society. Many agreed with Jane Addams that women possessed a unique combination of rationality and intuition which made them especially suited for what she termed a "civilizing mission" (Hymowitz and Weissman, 1978). Even awareness of their own exploitation within organizations like the COS did not "radicalize" such women.

Consequently, the COS reinforced prevailing sexual stereotypes by recruiting men for executive positions, paying them far higher salaries than women in comparable roles, and firing married women as bad examples to their peers (Archives of NY COS; Archives, Philadelphia Society for Organizing Charity). Only after considerable struggle within the COS and other social work agencies did women begin to occupy a larger share of administrative and supervisory jobs (C. Chambers, 1986; Rauch, 1976; Archives of the National Federation of Settlements; Kessler-Harris, 1982; Hymowitz & Weissman, 1978; Becker, 1968). In order to do so, women had to break the pattern of traditional role behavior and imitate the practices of men, including their social prejudices. At least one woman leader in the COS movement, Zilpha Smith, joined male colleagues like Joseph Lee and Jeffrey Brackett in supporting the openly anti-Semitic work of the Immigrant Restriction League (Becker, 1968; Leiby, 1962).

Early social work leaders retained such views because they seldom consulted with representatives of the populations for whom services were created, and because their professional lives were every bit as insulated as their personal lives. Their ranks were largely homogeneous, with few non-Protestants and virtually no members of racial minority groups admitted. The few outsiders admitted to leadership circles tended to represent sectarian agencies which attempted to apply COS principles and philosophy in their own communities.

It is not surprising, therefore, that many poor Jews, Catholics, and blacks regarded the services which these agencies developed as alien and threatening and turned instead to self-help organizations such as the Irish Emigrant Society, *Die Deutsche Gesellschaft*, the Hebrew Benevolent Society, and the White Rose Home for Girls (Handlin, 1959; Becker, 1968; Boroff, 1975; O'Grady, 1931; Karp, 1976; Hymowitz & Weissman, 1978). Through the 1870s, in fact, most of the social services provided to new immigrants were delivered by voluntary sectarian and self-help organizations, serving as many as 50% of new immigrants immediately upon their arrival (Riis, 1890). Their provision, unfortunately, was hampered by the limited resources available even to the well-off members of ethnic communities and by the distrust, fear, and mutual strangeness which existed between "old" and "new" immigrant groups. This problem was especially pronounced among the small, urban black elite who founded organizations like the Urban League early in the twentieth century (Carlton, 1982).

Unlike the COS, self-help organizations provided concrete services such as employment counseling, material relief (especially to newcomers, widows, and orphans), education, social supports, and burial funds. They also served as institutional means to resist the explicit and subtle attacks on immigrant culture and tradition by the public schools and organized churches. Many immigrants soon recognized that the price of "Americanization" was the loss of their unique heritage, their language and customs (Letters to *New York Jewish World,* 1901–12). Self-help organizations strengthened ethnic cohesion through recreational, educational, and social activities. They provided a foundation for the development of ethnically based trade unions, business associations, and political parties. In short, they served as an anchor, providing a modicum of material and psychological security in the dangerous and unpredictable environment in which the immigrants were attempting to survive and prosper. Their presence made the creation of a cohesive social work enterprise more difficult for the COS.

PROFESSIONAL VERSUS VOLUNTARY WORK

Another persistent problem in the field of organized charities was the role differentiation between paid staff and volunteers. A continuing tension existed between the ideology of charitable agencies, which exalted volunteer status, and the reality of service delivery, which required education and expertise particularly in the areas of administration and supervision. Shortly after the Civil War, as paid workers became more conscious of their own professional aspirations, such tensions heightened, and the boards of charitable agencies reacted defensively to the demands of paid workers for salary increases and sanction of their superiority over volunteer staff (AICP, Minutes, Board of Managers, June 9, 1866). Nevertheless, the increase in social distress in the 1870s compelled charitable organizations to rehire paid workers, who soon reestablished their dominance of the agencies' relief distribution activities (deForest, 1904; Becker, 1961; Schuyler, 1915).

As the COS replaced "old-style" charitable agencies, paid staff—usually the district agents—were restricted to administrative functions, fundraising, and recruitment, and were regarded as the "handmaidens" of the friendly visitors who made the final decisions about cases. The primary standard by which paid staff were measured was "whether [they] increase[ed] or diminish[ed] the amount of fruitful volunteer work in the community" (Devine, 1898; Rauch, 1975.) In the aftermath of the depression of the 1890s, however, COS leaders realized that volunteer friendly visitors could not adequately cope with the extensive intellectual demands of their work or the charitable organizations' growing need for efficiency in operation, and they increased their professional staff by as much as one-third (Kusmer, 1973; Levin, 1969). At the same time, other socioeconomic and cultural changes further diminished the pool of potential volunteers. This strengthened the position of paid workers within the COS, weakened the position of other organizations in the charitable field, especially those which were church-sponsored and relied exclusively on volunteers, and enhanced the attractiveness of public welfare activities in which all staff were salaried (Richmond, 1896e; C. J. Davis, 1901b).

Within a few years, the importance of volunteers in social work, especially friendly visitors, rapidly declined (Gutridge, 1903; Folks, 1893a; Richmond, Davis, op.cit.). By 1907, more than 50% of the major COS had abandoned the use of friendly visitors entirely (Jones and Herrick, 1976). Soon volunteers were restricted to carefully defined and supervised activities and, in many cities, did little more than routine office work. By 1917, their number declined to 25% of that of the peak years of voluntary activity (Kusmer, 1973; Becker, 1964).

Once the dominant position of paid workers was secured, the issue of wages became a real concern. Data on social workers' salaries at this time are sparse and widely varied due to the indistinct definition of the boundaries of the social work enterprise and, perhaps above all, because social-work wage scales reflected the disparity in wages which existed throughout the U.S. As the COS and other large social service organizations spread to small and midsize cities and into rural areas, workers were paid according to prevailing rates for the region. These rates were uniformly lower for women. Many workers had caseloads of unmanageable size; virtually all were terribly underpaid, starting as low as $6−8/week. A part-time paid visitor, for example, earned as little as $180/year in some communities, while the annual salary for the (male) Superintendent of Inspection of the New York State Board of Charities ranged from $1,800 to $2,500 (NY Civil Service Records, 1899; letter of Charles S. Fowler, Chief Civil Service Examiner, to Homer Folks, November 25, 1899; unsigned article in *Charities*, April 20, 1901; Robert Treat Paine, 1901; letter of John S. Newbold to H. LaBarre Jayne, July 8, 1902). An inspector for the New York State Board received a starting salary of $1,200/year for men and $900/year for women. This compared favorably to similar posts in other states and to the salaries of paid workers in COS at the time (letter of Meigs V. Crouse, Supt. of Children's Home in Cincinnati, to Folks, July 30, 1903).

The transition of social work from a largely volunteer enterprise to one dominated by paid staff with specialized expertise was by no means smooth. Paid social workers bemoaned the lack of well-trained colleagues and began to push hard for programs which would swell their ranks with better-educated and more-skilled staff. Yet, they recognized the difficulty of recruiting young people because of the low salaries, lack of clear lines of authority within social agencies, and the absence of a clear definition of the purpose and methods of social work (Folks Archives, letters, November 1895—May 1896).

Ironically, many potential sponsors of social work resisted efforts to make charity work more scientific and financially rewarding out of concern that a transformed charitable enterprise would lose the moral attributes of the old charity. In a sense, these tensions indicate the transitional nature of the environment in which social work emerged as a professional enterprise. The efforts social work leaders made in the generation before World War I to define the social work commodity and to recruit new producers and sponsors embody, to a significant degree, an attempt to reconcile these tensions in a manner satisfactory to all parties concerned, just as the social reforms of the Progressive Era "first emerged as a more-or-less conscious effort . . . to stabilize American society" (Ehrenreich, 1985:19).

THE SETTLEMENTS

The other major branch of the social work enterprise in the late nineteenth century was the settlement house movement and its affiliates in such social service agencies as the YMCA and the Salvation Army. Settlement houses practiced a more democratic conception of social work, emphasizing community participation and the link between social services and broader social themes like democracy, equality, and social justice. Settlement work had the quality of a social movement, which was its greatest attraction, especially to young people and social reformers. It was also the source of the settlements' difficulty in establishing credentials as a legitimate branch of professional social work.

Settlement "residences" opened in the late 1880s and early 1890s in urban slums like New York's lower East Side and Chicago's South Side, exhibiting many of the characteristics of secular missions. Early settlements were staffed largely by women from the same class background as their COS counterparts, with similar personal needs, social biases, moral codes, and social goals. Settlement women, however, tended to be better educated than their COS counterparts and less likely to be married (C. Chambers, 1986). To some observers, like Josephine Shaw Lowell, settlement house residents and friendly visitors differed only in the settings in which they labored. Mary Richmond argued, however, that the daily contact of settlement workers with the poor, labor unions, and a broad assortment of domestic radicals, along with their greater receptivity to some of the newer currents in social thought (particularly those which looked to environmental conditions as the source of social problems), transformed their orientation into one with dangerous implications for the field of social work (Boyer, 1978; C. Chambers, 1963).

Influenced by the women who provided the movement's early leadership, particularly Jane Addams, the founder of Hull House in Chicago, settlements created an institutionalized form of self-help for the new urban poor, attempting to meet concrete needs and to socialize the poor into the new industrial order. At the same time, other influential leaders like Florence Kelley, a close friend of Addams, director of the National Consumers League, and the first translator of Friedrich Engels into English, pushed the movement strongly in the direction of institutional change. Kelley recognized that concrete assistance to the immigrant poor needed to be augmented by efforts to alter the physical and social environment which produced so many of their problems (Blumberg, 1966; Conway, 1969; Goldmark, 1953; Levine, 1971; Linn, 1935; Lynd, 1961; Wise, 1935).

Although women like Addams were involved in both aspects of settlement work—for example, she and Lillian Wald, director of the Henry Street Settlement in New York City, were instrumental in creating the Women's Trade Union League in 1903—their conception of the role of settlements as agents for social change was limited by their desire to reduce the level of social conflict and to seek solutions satisfactory to all classes (Addams, 1895; Wald, 1915). Thus, both contemporary and modern commentators have criticized settlements as simplistic undertakings which reflected many of the prejudices of their age (Riis, 1890; Woods & Kennedy, 1910: 430–31; Kessner, 1977: 135–39; Gans, 1964). Nevertheless, the settlements' recognition of the interconnection between the well-being of individuals and the betterment of society, coupled with their advocacy of programs to serve poor and working-class women and children, laid the foundations for the policies of the New Deal and the Great Society (National Association of Social Workers, 1977; Skocpol and Ikenberry, 1982).

In addition, despite Victorian attitudes about sexuality (Addams, 1912a: 22), many settlement leaders shared a deep commitment to feminist causes, such as the promotion of women's suffrage, a viewpoint radical for its day which set them apart from the political mainstream and their more conservative counterparts in social work. This "social feminism" (O'Neill, 1971) provided the basis for cooperation between "liberal" and "radical" settlement workers on such women-centered issues as public health, temperance, pornography, prostitution, and white slavery. Through social feminism, settlement workers became involved in the wider cause of social justice. In fact, for some, "social justice activities became the principal justification for feminism" (O'Neill, 1971: 135).

These cooperative efforts also facilitated the growth of female support networks linking settlement leaders like Addams, Kelley, and Wald to each other and to radicals outside of social work such as Crystal Eastman and Emma Goldman (Cook, 1979). Such networks enabled settlement workers to strengthen their ties with working-class women and to overcome, in part, the social distance created by their disparate class and educational backgrounds (cf. Addams,

1893b). In New York, for example, working-class women enlisted the help and support of Lillian Wald in their union-building drives in order to "lend respectability to a venture otherwise viewed as disreputable" (Banner, 1979).

The feminist orientation of many early social workers strengthened the public's perception of the field as a "women's profession," yet one dominated by women who defied traditional social and cultural norms. This negative impression surfaced during World War I when reform efforts sponsored by women social workers came to national attention and approached enactment into law.[2] To a considerable extent, the conscious professionalizing efforts of social work, especially in its early years, included an attempt to correct this impression in the public mind.

By the early twentieth century, over 100 settlement houses had been established throughout the East and Midwest, 32 in New York State alone. Their work and philosophy challenged many of the basic assumptions of the COS about the political economy and the social environment it had created. The research of Robert Hunter (1904) and Edith Abbott, for example, questioned the prevailing view of poverty as linked to individual behavior and morality and developed the concept of the "public economy" in which government intervention was the ultimate solution to people's social and economic distress (Weisz-Buck, 1982: 5–6, 12).

Few members of the settlement movement, however, had consciously radical or revolutionary intent in their work. Most viewed the consequences of monopoly as *administrative* problems which could be resolved without drastic institutional change. Nevertheless, their work went counter to the complacent view of the United States as a land of boundless opportunity. Old-style charities, in their view, further divided society into classes, increased the number of poor, and made their condition more static (Tucker, 1903). The goals of the new movement would be, instead, "justice, not charity" (deForest, 1901). It was in the potential implications of that quest for justice, if not in its actual achievements, that the settlement house movement represented a threat to the established order.

Settlement Methods

Although settlements borrowed as much as the COS from emerging corporate techniques, fundamental distinctions in focus and methodology appeared early in their development. Mary Richmond noted that settlement workers were more receptive to the progressive social currents of the era, such as the work of Lester Ward and John Dewey in sociology and education, which provided the basis for a synthesis of religious and secular thought (Hofstadter, 1955). Ward's assertions that "class distinctions depend entirely upon environmental conditions and are in no sense due to differences in native capacity" provided a guide for both the service and reform aspects of settlement work (Ward, 1974). Dewey's emphasis on the ability of applied intelligence to transform society and on the social responsibility of intellectuals to apply themselves to that transformation served as an intellectual justification for the moral compulsion many settlement residents felt to do good works (Dewey, 1916; Hofstadter, 1959; J. Chambers, 1980).

By combining the scientific method's emphasis on explanation and prediction with the corporate enterprise's focus on efficiency, settlements "launched a search for systems through which to manage change in an orderly manner" (C. Chambers, 1963; A. Davis, 1967; J. Chambers, 1980: 110–12). This aspect of settlement work was the clearest in its goals and its implementation. What proved far more difficult was the translation of these goals into a comprehensive, unified *method of practice* which would legitimate settlement work as a sphere of activity within the U.S. political economy and enable settlement workers to attract the resources and sponsorship they needed to sustain themselves as a professional enterprise (Powers, 1895: 591).

At first, the eclectic methods of the settlements were a definite asset. By adopting the roles of good neighbor and good citizen (rather than those of philanthropist and reformer), and by promoting these roles in others, settlements exercised considerable influence on the communities in which they were established. This influence ranged from electing good government candidates, to forging ties with organized labor, to educating the middle and upper classes about the nature of urban social problems (Woods, 1901).

Yet the settlements also experienced a variety of early problems, such as a shortage of qualified residents (and concomitant morale difficulties), instability caused by frequent leadership changes, and conflicts with local authorities over issues such as housing codes (Addams, 1910; Wald, 1915). Moreover, the dual role which settlements professed—to broaden the educational and cultural opportunities of the poor and to promote a broader conception of democracy throughout society—did not lend itself easily to a distinct, unique service commodity or a distinct organizational form. In fact, settlement workers viewed "social work"—one of four aspects of their work along with reform efforts, work in rural communities, and visiting nursing—largely in terms of organized clubs and classes offered to the immigrant populations of the neighborhoods in which they were located (Wallach, 1903).

Another major barrier to professional influence was the lack of clarity as to what constituted a "settlement." The term was applied to a range of diverse organizations—university settlements, college settlements, church settlements, and social settlements (Hoy, 1904)—whose objectives ranged from the training of college graduates for social service work, to the delivery of specific services, to attempts "to bring men and women of education into closer relations with the laboring classes in [the] city for their mutual benefit" (Wallach, 1903: 10). In addition, some churches appropriated settlement names to their missions, thereby adding to the confusion (letter of Henry Moskowitz of Downtown Ethical Society in New York *Evening Post*, September 23, 1908).

Shortly after its emergence, therefore, the settlement movement abounded in contradictions. It attempted to provide service *and* to reform existing institutions, to respond to the peculiar cultural currents of a community *and* to promote its own nonsectarian gospel. The movement tried to overcome ethnic and class barriers while holding onto class-based ideals and prejudices. Finally, it strove to establish an alternative sense of justice and democracy through the acquisition of support and sponsorship from the very classes who benefited most from retaining a foothold in the status quo. The consequences of this latter contradiction were, perhaps, the most profound for the movement's future.

Settlement workers even disagreed over what their clarion for justice signified. Robert deForest argued that justice involved some redistribution of resources to combat inequality (1901: 431), with the specific goal of expanding the opportunities of the poor, while Robert Woods stated rather vaguely that settlement work attempted "to get suggestions to bear on procuring a better life in the nation" (quoted in *New York Times*, 1916 n.d.). Although some settlement workers professed socialist sympathies, most favored redistributive efforts which would be made possible by increasing the overall wealth of the country (Tucker), prefiguring modern Keynesian policies.

Nor was there consensus as to what should constitute the practical program and methods of settlement work. Some people defined the settlements' function in terms of "social uplift," including such specific reforms as improved housing, coordination of social service efforts between public and private agencies, expansion of public welfare services, especially in areas of prevention, and the establishment of a broad range of educational, cultural, and recreational activities (Hoy, 1904). Others believed that settlements should focus on shaping public opinion, developing a better general understanding of the social environment, and promoting cooperation between social classes. George Herbert Mead (1907: 110) considered the primary purpose of the settlements not to "fight . . . evils, but [to] determine . . . what evils [exist]; not [to] enforce preferred moral judgments, but [to] form . . . new moral judgments."

Implicit in both views of settlement work was the belief that the implementation of settlement goals would serve the interests of all classes in American society and would create Whitman's "city of friends" (Barnett, 1906: 186–89). In other words, a "community of interest" would exist in which all classes would benefit from the achievement of social justice. Not surprisingly, this community of interest contained many of the major ingredients of the prevailing social philosophy of the age: the importance of education as the basis for expanding economic opportunity, the focus on individual achievement and the role of self-help, and even the identification of social uplift in terms of the Americanization of immigrant groups (Tucker, 1903; Wallach, 1903; deForest, 1901). The latter was precisely how William Alexander Hoy (1904: 4) proposed settlements should "sell" their goals to the general public: "[The Settlement] is the work of America for all who long to become Americans. It is the work of Americans for America. It is an affair of high sentiment. It is equally an affair of conservative, matter-of-fact business."

Thus three approaches appeared within the settlements. One emphasized the delivery of concrete services as a temporary solution to social problems that economic growth would eventually correct (Ward, 1974; Commager, 1967). A second approach expanded the notion of concrete services to include advocacy on behalf of poor women, children, and their families (Addams, 1902; 1908). And a third and most radical approach viewed the social settlement as a vehicle for radical reform of U.S. society and, in some instances, the implementation of revolutionary social goals (Kelley).

By the second decade of the twentieth century, settlement houses also began to move into the cultural arena and to focus increased attention on the development of recreational alternatives to popular attractions of mass culture like the movies and vaudeville (Addams, 1910). This development, which soon transformed the character of settlement work, emerged out of three conflicting motivations. One was a moral reaction, rooted in the values of the Protestant middle and upper classes, to both the substance and form of popular culture. Rather than propose censorship, the Progressive strain within the settlements favored the promotion of more suitable activities for the physical and intellectual betterment of the working classes (whose available leisure hours had increased by 25% between 1900 and 1920) (Addams, 1912b).

A second, contradictory motive was the encouragement of "cultural pluralism" as an alternative to the cultural homogeneity being stressed in public schools and the popular press. The influence of John Dewey and progressive education on the settlements, particularly on Jane Addams, was decisive in this area, especially in the settlements' emphasis on workshops and other "learning by doing" experiences (which also were adopted by social work educators with their early and continuing emphasis on field work).

A final motive stemmed from the efforts of the broad-ranging settlement movement to define a distinct service commodity which it delivered and for which it could obtain the support of economic and political sponsors. As described above, the early years of the settlement movement produced a plethora of activities, ranging from hands-on services to public education to aggressive social reform efforts. None of these activities was distinct enough or attractive enough to powerful sponsors to emerge as a clearly defined area of expertise for settlement workers and, thereby, give them a foothold on the ladder of occupational specialization and control. The growth of organized recreation offered settlements the opportunity to "sell" their services in the marketplace in a manner which was politically acceptable and consistent with the established interest of the settlements in the promotion of education and culture.

By the outbreak of World War I, as Mary Simkhovitch (1926) later noted, settlements were well on their way to entering the social work mainstream by becoming involved in the larger task of social education—a task which was not only popular but also far more conducive to the overall professionalizing efforts of social work (Boyer, 1978: 160ff.).

CHAPTER FOUR

Fashioning Social Work into Casework

INTRODUCTION

Most interpretations of social work's professional development tie it closely to the creation of a *method* to guide its practice and research efforts. The establishment of a certified *technique* enabled social workers to assert "some rational control over the drift of life" in late-nineteenth-century America and to convince the general public "that social work consisted of more than benevolence and well-wishing, [and] that it had a scientific and ethical component" in which qualified individuals could be instructed (Trattner, 1979: 194). In turn, the need for such skills led to a preference for paid workers with the requisite education, experience, and ethos, over volunteers.

This interpretation, however, leaves several crucial questions unanswered: (1) Since self-help was the ideological cornerstone of both COS and settlement activities, why weren't resources channeled directly to those groups to be used for such ends instead of through the auspices of a specially trained core of charity agents and settlement workers? (2) If self-help implied the inculcation of a sense of autonomy and capacity, why did the methodology which emerged in the COS rely so heavily on the worker to define the clients' needs and develop a plan to solve them? And, (3) how can the precipitous decline in the use of volunteers within social work be explained in an era in which people had significantly more leisure time and in which a role for women outside the home and family was increasingly acceptable?

The answers lie in the connection between the transformation of the U.S. political economy and the eventual purpose of professionalized and rationalized social service in the emerging system. As long as the scientific basis of social work did not conflict with broader political-economic needs, its practitioners gained in their pursuit of professional recognition. As long as their practice supported the values of the dominant culture toward those in need and conformed to prevailing attitudes about organization and control, social workers retained the sponsorship they so avidly sought. It is entirely possible that the aim of professionalization itself encouraged social workers to conform to the goals and forms of relationships preferred by the sponsors upon whom they relied for support.

The transformation of casework into the primary social work commodity began in the 1890s and early 1900s when both the COS and the settlements started to imitate many of the features of corporate management, particularly its emphasis on *organization*, in the fight against poverty and urban blight. At first, this strengthened social work's professionalizing impulse without appearing to sabotage the pursuit of social reform. The utilization of scientific methods, in fact, appeared to complement the broader social goal of exploring the underlying causes of poverty (Bolin, 1973) by providing new insights into the nature of urban poverty, the class character of urban ethnic groups, the family structure and values of recent immigrants, and the limitations of existing social service programs in improving the lives of the poor (Wald, 1904; Warner, 1894; Kessner, 1977; COS Archives; Watson, 1922). COS workers, however, had difficulty in applying this knowledge to direct service delivery and in translating the results of field research into practice because of their reliance on part-time, untrained, unscientific friendly visitors as staff. Their highly personal approach, paternalistic in tone and morally laden, conflicted with the secular and scientific intentions of the COS by hearkening back to the evangelical practices of an earlier era (Boyer, 1978; Thompson, 1843). Until this conflict between intention and methodology could be reconciled, social work's aspirations for professional status would be frustrated.

THE RATIONALIZATION OF CHARITY WORK

During the 1890s, more and more charity workers demanded a clearer definition of their job responsibilities. Troubled by the lack of specificity in their work, and concerned that the careless and ill-defined methods of their organizations were creating an unfavorable impression in the eyes of potential supporters, they called for "radical measures" to make social work more appealing to its practitioners and more consistent with the emerging view of professional work in the society at large (Folks Papers, letters of Charles Fenn to Folks, November 25, 1895, February 18, 1896, July 15, 1896, August 6, 1896; Richmond Papers, letters to Richmond; Vaile Papers, letters to Vaile).

Social work leaders also bemoaned the absence of clear methodological definitions to guide workers in their agencies. Edward Devine of the New York COS stressed the need to support those agencies which "are solidly based on personal acquaintance and real knowledge" (Devine, December 29, 1897). Homer Folks, the Executive Secretary of the NY State Charities Aid Association (SCAA), argued that the basic principles of the COS—investigation, registration, cooperation, and friendly visiting—were necessary but insufficient conditions for the development of clear goals and methods for the friendly visitors. He felt that a clear definition of the methods of friendly visiting "would add such momentum to the Charities Organization movement that it would become an irresistible force, *a controlling factor in the administration of all private societies for assisting the poor, and of all public aid*" (emphasis added) (Folks, 1901: 4; Devine, 1901; Richmond, "What Is Charity Organization?," and "The Work of a District Agent," 1896).

Yet existing charitable agencies like the SCAA and those in the U.S. child-saving movement had failed to make a serious attempt to articulate the nature of the services which their workers performed (see Folks, 1898, 1901; Archives of New York SCAA, 1917). Nor were U.S. social workers able to emulate models of practice developed by their European counterparts (O. Hill, 1900–1901). This absence of a clearly defined social work commodity contributed to "a certain . . . arrogance [among COS workers] about being workers" and a growing sense of alienation in the Settlement movement (Richmond, 1899a: 3; Addams, 1910; Simkhovitch, 1917; Gilbert, 1977: 57).

Jane Addams argued (1902: 4) that these tendencies might be reversed by bringing "ethical coherence to the workplace" and by drawing clearer distinctions between so-called "ordinary work" and professional activities, as expanding occupational enterprises like medicine, engineering, law, architecture, and business had already done to justify greater material and status rewards (Gilbert: 1977:

44, 58). The notion of professions as "callings," however, was not a sufficient condition to achieve occupational dominion, which rested instead on the demonstration that such work was based on reason, objectivity, and empirical research, and thus consistent with the overall rationalization of the political economy and the increasing use of scientific principles to solve persistent problems of public policy.

Social workers soon recognized that techniques of intra-agency coordination and the incorporation of ideas from business management such as standardized forms, regular reports to "stockholders," and the use of "cost/benefit analysis" to determine the allocation of agency resources would give existing social service agencies greater control over the social welfare market (letters of Fenn, January 7, 1896, January 13, 1896; C. Davis, March 1901). Although many workers contributed to this development, Mary Richmond of the Baltimore, Philadelphia, and New York COS, and Amos Warner, a professor of economics at Stanford University, played the most influential roles.

Warner's book, *American Charities* (1894), attempted to distinguish charity work from philanthropic benevolence and mark its practitioners as educated, knowledgeable men and women. He assumed, to the pleasure of the COS leaders, that private charities dominated the social service arena and that the social work commodity was delivered *by* individuals *to* individuals, through the auspices of private agencies, especially the COS (Powers, 1895; Folks, 1898b; Richmond, 1901c: 113–14). Richmond's work went further and identified two distinct problems for social work in defining its unique "product": (1) the need to specify the knowledge base and techniques which distinguished trained social workers from mere dabblers in benevolent activities and which could be transmitted to new workers through formal educational mechanisms like training schools; and (2) the danger that social work, as it grew, would become fragmented between generalist and specialist. "At what point," she asked, "is specialization liable to retard social advance?" (Richmond, 1903: 3).

Richmond's initial presentation (1896e) of the COS definition of the social work commodity emphasized the ongoing importance of investigation and registration. She argued that their promotion had two major goals: to disseminate the methods of the COS to other service agencies and to maintain COS control over access to services, especially by limiting applications for relief to those made by the friendly visitor herself (pp. 7, 47–59). Within this definition of social work, the worker was the indispensable element in the helping process and the instrument of COS philosophy by deciding which clients would be served (and how) and by determining the degree of cooperation which the COS would establish with other organizations (Richmond, 1899b).[3]

While Richmond received high praise from COS officials and reviewers for her work (*American Journal of Sociology* and *The Dial*; Henderson, letter of April 26, 1899), many social workers outside the COS field were extremely critical of the methods she proposed. The Reverend James Huntington, for example, objected to the application of business principles to the field of charity and argued that Richmond had sanctioned the existence of a double standard of behavior, one for the rich and the other for the poor.

The harshest criticism of Richmond's ideas came from Jane Addams in a widely read essay, "The Subtle Problems of Charity" (1899), and in her book *Democracy and Social Ethics* (1902). Addams rejected the methods Richmond espoused because of their excessive rationality and their assumptions about the social relationship between worker and client, which, she argued, forced the worker upon the needy in the role of a moral guardian. This role widened the social gap between workers and clients and made it impossible to establish the friendship and engage in the "moral uplift" Richmond proposed. Addams also attacked the "negative, pseudo-scientific spirit" which underlay Richmond's work, its "cold and unemotional" tone (Addams, 1899: 6–7).

Richmond responded to Addams's criticisms shortly after the publication of *Democracy and Social Ethics* in a handwritten letter of several pages (Richmond Archives, Columbia University). Acutely sensitive to Addams's harsh characterization of charity workers, Richmond defended her efforts to provide friendly visiting with greater structure. Her rebuttal of Addams, never before published, is worth quoting at length.

> . . . Organized charity is a painfully imperfect thing, but it is a great advance on the disorganization which it replaces, . . . not a thing to deplore at all but a thing to spend ourselves lavishly upon until we make it better and best. . . . It seems to me that organized charity . . . represents a finer social quality and

greater social value than their natural promptings . . . could ever have represented. . . . The only cure for the pseudo-science of much of our present investigation is more investigation. . . .

Richmond also criticized Addams for the divisive impact her writings had on the field of social work as a whole:

> . . . Anything that discourages people from acting together in charity is a harmful thing to say just at present. . . . To say that the juxtaposition of the words "organized" and "charity" is distasteful to you is to discourage and delay improvement in associated charities effort. To say that we are trying to substitute a theory of social conduct for the natural promptings of the heart is also most distinctly discouraging especially when you make it very clear in [your] book that you are opposed to leaving the industrial situation to any such uncertain arbiter. Leaving things to the natural promptings of the human heart never passed a child labor bill or a good school bill, but organized charity and organized labor combined [to accomplish that] in Maryland the other day. (Letter, Richmond to Addams, n.d., 1902)

Richmond's promotion of standardization and efficiency in charity work was not a novel idea at the turn of the century. In the early 1890s, as an executive in both public and voluntary social service agencies, Homer Folks had repeatedly stressed the importance of sound administration, careful investigation, control, cost efficiency, and cooperation with local schools and churches in the field of family and child welfare (Folks, 1897a; 1893b). What was different about the call for standardized practices in the early 1900s was the connection between the proponents of standardization and the self-interest of a well-organized faction within social work, the COS.

Such standardization required a model for social workers, a guide to how future workers should be selected and trained. To fill this need some leaders looked to the social scientist, stressing the importance of applied sociology and applied psychology (Lies, 1901). Most, however, preferred the model of the physician. They argued that the function of the caseworker was rehabilitation, and that since diagnosis and treatment went hand-in-hand with rehabilitation, a good caseworker should emulate the skills of a good doctor (Ufford, 1901).

The emerging terminology of casework illustrates this reliance upon the medical model. Robert Treat Paine stated that the word "case" was chosen "because we get into using it as a physician does" (Paine, 1901: 332). Edward Devine added that the concept of investigation was "precisely analogous to the diagnosis of the physician" (Devine, 1901: 322). Although Richmond also based her service model on the role of the physician, she argued repeatedly for a more egalitarian relationship between workers and needy individuals (Richmond, 1905). In language strikingly similar to that used by Jane Addams, Richmond advised those under her supervision that "a knowledge of these larger matters will not save you unless, as time goes on, you become deeply impressed by the essential likeness between yourself and the visited. The differences, though they impress us most at first, are superficial. The likenesses are fundamental" (Richmond, 1896a: 4; Addams, 1910).

Practitioners all across the country became the "lab assistants" who experimented with these new ideas as they were suggested. Gertrude Vaile's memoirs ("Memories of the Old West Side," Archives) recollect this trial-and-error approach to model building: "The conception of casework, as more fully developed by Mary Richmond, was not new when *Social Diagnosis* was published [in 1917]. In a sense [our office] became, to a modest degree, a sort of experimental station or clinic for testing out some of Miss Richmond's ideas and theories . . . because of the relationship between . . . Richmond and Amelia Sears [Vaile's supervisor]."

As Richmond (1901) expanded her schematic conceptualization of social service work, she began to stress the creation of working conditions conducive to a more professional type of practice, the establishment of formal workload guidelines and greater emphasis on recordkeeping procedures.[4] She also emphasized the themes of improved organization of both paid and volunteer workers and the need for *full-time* employees (Richmond, 1902).

CONTROL OF THE PROFESSION

Richmond's early writings and speeches frequently referred to cooperation between charitable agencies as the "keystone of the arch of charity." The basis of this cooperation, however, appears to have been the development and acceptance of "thoroughly efficient case work [as the] best stepping-stone" toward the attainment of common goals (Richmond, 1901a; Richmond, review in *International Journal of Ethics*, 1905: 505).

To help develop and promote the casework method, in 1904 Richmond began to draft what became her classic, *Social Diagnosis* (1917). Based on an analysis of COS case records, and designed especially for newer workers, Richmond's outline strove to integrate the old and new views of charity in a method which conformed to prevailing attitudes about the importance of science, efficiency, and, above all, systematic technique (letter of March 9, 1904; Philadelphia SOC, 29th report, 1908).

One problem for Richmond concerned the issue of professional autonomy—that is, how to develop a methodological formulation which recognized that charitable work was practiced through agencies, while professional status was distributed on the basis of individual credentials and accomplishments. Her model sought to blend these countervailing tendencies by establishing the principle of associated charitable work in which "individual citizens who want to be charitable shall band together in voluntary associations" (Devine, 1901). A related problem was how to join the old and new views of charity without losing the balance between individual charitable impulse and collective organizational effort. While the old view of charity started with the simple assumption that distress should be relieved, the COS transformed this moral imperative into a structured technique by applying the principles of investigation, cooperation, and personal service (letter of Lydia Burkin to Richmond, May 1, 1907).

The new view of charity, however, looked beyond individual causes of misery to the social environment. There was growing recognition among some friendly visitors that their work placed too much emphasis on moralism and benevolence and needed to be directed more toward the good of the whole community (letters to Richmond from friendly visitors, Spring 1907). The application of this perspective transformed charitable societies into agencies for the improvement of social conditions. It was also attractive to sponsors because it appeared to offer a viable alternative to socialism (Devine, 1908). Yet it was fraught with pitfalls for social work in its aspirations for professional status.

One peril was social workers' difficulty in demonstrating both specific knowledge of social conditions and the skills required to remediate them in order to justify their requests for resources and support. A second resulted from the problem of reconciling social work's historic emphasis on individual betterment with the growing sentiment that social work's purpose was to promote the common good (Devine, 1908). Friendly visitors feared that the application of the "new view" might eliminate much of the personal satisfaction they derived from their work. "Do not let your philanthropy drown your charity," they implored (letters of various social workers to Richmond, Spring 1907). Ten years before the publication of *Social Diagnosis*, Edward Devine suggested a possible solution to this dilemma: "Has the time already come for psychological diagnosis, for the study and treatment of character in adversity?" (Devine, 1908).[5]

Despite these trends, Richmond's influential views did not pass without criticism in the still-nascent field of social work. Some saw them as rather narrow and self-serving, "a form of self-righteousness which inspires us to give to others a part of what already belongs to them" (Anonymous, October 26, 1907: 701, 705). Although the COS strove to sculpt the emerging profession in its own image, the diverse experiences of social workers and the increasingly diverse backgrounds from which they came produced different interpretations of the plight of their clients and different solutions to this plight (Frankel, 1901: 314–21). Eastern agencies, for example, were less likely than their Midwestern counterparts to set aside general funds for relief and tended to rely more upon churches, other private charities, and benevolent individuals to assist families in need. Such differences influenced the way in which agencies from different regions defined social work practice and even the social work profession (Vaile, 1915b: 256–62).

Because of the COS's emphasis on efficiency, many people continued to believe that their major purpose was the elimination of waste and fraud in the relief practices of public and private agencies. This perception alienated many young people from all charitable interests to the point where donations and participation on agency boards declined. At the same time, the view of the COS as "charity police" encouraged an increase in manipulative behavior among some clients and a growing ignorance among others as to the actual functions of the agencies. Each of these developments, in turn, became obstacles to better cooperation between charitable organizations (Richmond, 1901a).

Other frequently cited obstacles included rivalries between sectarian and nonsectarian charities and the inevitable duplication of effort which ensued, widespread ignorance of social problems among church leaders and COS volunteer staff, and the separation of relief-giving from treatment. To resolve these dilemmas, Samuel H. Bishop of the Brooklyn, New York, COS suggested "the necessity for considering the possibilities of a new and better adjustment of our societies to one another and to their common work and some effective economy both of money and energy" (Bishop, 1901; C. Davis, 1901b; Richmond, 1901a; 1901b; 1901c).

One available institutional model which offered the prospect of solving such problems was the corporate trust. But despite its obvious attraction, COS leaders continued to oppose the tendency toward consolidation. Richmond maintained that "even in its own field charity organization claims no monopoly, for a number of other agencies, such as the SCAA's and the more progressive state boards of charities [share this] . . . difficult task." She preferred to encourage cooperation through the introduction of the "District Plan," by which the COS could coordinate all services provided by schools, police, public health officials, church charities, and influential members of the community (Richmond, "What is Charity Organization?," n.d., Archives).

Yet, in spite of Richmond's disavowal of monopolistic control of the charitable field, such ideas assumed the dominance of the COS because of their superior organization and resources. Consequently, during the first decade of the twentieth century, through their growing ties to thrift agencies (to encourage savings), industrial training schools, tenement and sanitary reform commissions, anti–child labor committees, and the public schools, and through their introduction of standardized service practices such as investigation and registration, the COS began to establish control over the emerging social work enterprise and to make the definition of their work identical to that of social work as a whole.

THE ROLE OF THE RUSSELL SAGE FOUNDATION

Despite their successes, COS leaders interested in professionalization faced a formidable internal task: the transformation of a relatively new occupation with a limited number of practitioners and many diffuse service functions into a unified body. Its accomplishment required a secure source of financial support under COS control as well as the legitimation of their views as the social work center. In the decade before World War I, COS leaders found the sanction and resources they were seeking in the Russell Sage Foundation (RSF), which together with the New York School of Social Philanthropy (later the New York School of Social Work) and the New York COS became the center of gravity of the emerging profession.

Created during the Progressive Era, the RSF viewed the promotion and professionalization of social work as one of its chief "progressive" projects. Through this and other endeavors, the foundation, like the Community Chest movement later, helped to rationalize social reform and channel it into the development of social welfare services rather than a more fundamental redistribution of wealth or power.[6] In fact "no other institution has ever had a comparable influence in the creation of a new profession" (Coon, 1938: 76, 77).

Between 1907 and 1931, the foundation distributed nearly $5.8 million in grants to social work organizations, professional social work associations and studies, social work publications, social planning organizations and projects, and social welfare causes, such as the prevention of tuberculosis, health care, housing reform, and criminal justice. It funded such projects as the American Association for Organizing Family Social Work, the National Social Workers Exchange and its successor, the American Association of Social Workers, the American Association of Hospital Social Workers, the Child Welfare League of America, the National Social Work Council, and the journal *Survey* (Glenn, Brandt, & Andrews, 1947).[7] Yet, it is significant that virtually no Sage Foundation dollars went to settlement houses or to the organized settlement movement, which, significantly, had no other comparable foundations to draw upon.[8]

Robert deForest, New York counsel for the Central Railroad of New Jersey, director of several banks and large corporations, and president of the New York COS from 1888 to 1931 and of the RSF for 25 years, served as the catalyst who brought together the professional aspirations of social workers and the RSF's financial resources and legitimacy. In the same year that deForest launched the Russell

Sage Foundation, he hired John M. Glenn, who had chaired the executive committee of the Baltimore COS, to serve as RSF director, a position he held for 25 years.

It is not surprising, therefore, that the New York COS received almost a third of the $1.8 million in grant monies allocated by the RSF between 1907 and 1917, years when the RSF also shared physical facilities with the New York School of Social Philanthropy (Glenn, Brandt, & Andrews, 1947: 223–24).[9] By 1909, when Glenn hired Mary Richmond to direct the RSF's new Charity Organization Department (she was replaced at the Philadelphia SOC by Porter Lee), both Mary Richmond and the RSF had been working on a national COS organization for several years.

A significant aspect of this work involved the merger of the journals *Charities* and *The Commons* in 1905. With Richmond playing a major role, the new journal, *Charities and the Commons*, rapidly became an instrument for organizing the COS field through its Publications Committee and its Exchange Branch. In 1907, Richmond hired Francis McLean, superintendent of the Brooklyn Bureau of Charities, as a paid field secretary with money from the new Sage Foundation. This grant opened the door to RSF development and control of the national COS movement.

McLean was really the organizing genius of the COS movement. As field secretary, he traveled around the country setting up local organizations, building relationships, and later developing councils of social agencies. Yet McLean envisioned a much more democratically run organization than he was allowed to create by deForest, Richmond, and Devine. To McLean's suggestion for creation of a centrally located headquarters in the Midwest and a five-to-seven-member elected board with one Sage representative, deForest replied,

> . . . To secure centralization of effort, let there be an executive committee of this general committee, of which Miss Richmond should be chairman, composed of a few members who can readily meet and have represented on that executive committee both Sage Foundation and "Charities." I note what Mr. McLean says about Chicago headquarters, and if Chicago were the city that contributed most brains and most money, or an equal amount of brains and money, to the movement there would be

geographical reason for the choice. Inasmuch, however, as the movement both in initiative, effort, and money support is an eastern one I should think New York would be the most effective headquarters. (Ormsby, 1969: 40, 41)

The executive committee proposed by deForest was, in fact, subsequently organized as the Departmental Committee of the Field Department of *Charities and the Commons,* chaired by Richmond. Its composition reflected deForest's concern for RSF/Eastern leadership control.[10]

By 1909, the 23 member societies in the Exchange Branch were ready to begin planning for a national association for organizing charities. This was the point at which the Sage Foundation, which had been financing the Field Department of *Charities,* decided it should be reorganized as the Charity Organization Department of the foundation under Richmond's direction. In this way, the foundation could retain firmer control over the movement and, presumably, over McLean's organizing activities as well.[11]

As planned, the Charity Organization Department began on October 1, 1909, and directly supervised the Charity Organization movement until June 1911, when McLean was finally able to found an autonomous membership organization, the National Association of Societies for Organizing Charity (NASOC). Yet this development did not signify the end of RSF involvement in charity organization. In fact, their relationship continued to be almost as close as before the separation (Glenn, Brandt, & Andrews, 1947: 127). Responsibilities in the COS area were soon divided between the NASOC board and the department.

Under McLean's direction, the NASOC increased its membership from 62 societies in 1911, to 143 in 1914, to 220 in 1925. More significant, it branched off in two directions, on one hand emphasizing social planning through the organization of local councils of social agencies, and on the other, stressing family casework. The association also changed its name from the American Association for Organizing Charity, adopted in 1917, to the American Association for Organizing Family Social Work (AAOFSW) in 1919. The changes in name and emphases by the association represented important events in the fashioning of a professional commodity.[12]

CONCLUSION: TOWARDS *SOCIAL DIAGNOSIS*

By 1912, professional caseworkers had virtually replaced friendly visitors in the COS, and casework, now focused on families rather than individuals, had become "an integral part of [the] charity organization program" (Richmond, 1912: 174). Although the COS had taken considerable strides toward establishing political control of the social work profession, the question of intellectual control over the field persisted. Richmond suggested that the COS establish its monopoly in the family casework field by having its definition of casework be accepted as the standard "and then what happens to ourselves, to our separate societies, and to our movement will in no wise [sic] matter" (Ibid.). To achieve this end, professional education would have to be improved and the task of the caseworker "dignified" (Ibid.: 177–78).

Although Richmond continued to stress the separation of relief-giving from treatment, she proposed a definition of casework sufficiently broad to encompass both the private and public welfare functions which she foresaw the COS fulfilling in greater volume in the years ahead. Other social work leaders in the voluntary and public sectors shared this perception. Some, like Homer Folks, however, preferred that the state, rather than private agencies, expand its role in the delivery of casework services to families, particularly in the area of prevention, since it possessed resources lacking in the private sector, and "is the natural guardian in common law of the child and the insane" (Folks, 1912a).

Richmond's turn toward the psychological aspects of individuals offered charity workers the opportunity to synthesize old and new charitable views and to retain the emphasis on one-to-one relationships within an agency context. It also afforded them the chance to advance their professional aspirations by formulating a unique emphasis for their work which moved beyond benevolence and morality into the sanctified realm of scientific expertise. In other words, COS leaders recognized that the problem in establishing satisfactory personal relationships between friendly visitors and clients could be overcome by substituting the goal of *professional* service for that of *personal* service, which, in turn, required a highly organized, scientifically based technique as a framework for its practice. In 1911,

Richmond finished the first draft of *Social Diagnosis,* her effort to spell out this technique.

Drawing upon sources as diverse as the *COS Bulletin,* the *Survey,* and the works of Adolph Meyer, W. E. B. DuBois, and others, Richmond appears to have intended to develop a method which integrated material from a broad range of social and behavioral science and to appeal thereby to disparate elements within social work. Yet, her outline focused only on how these different components could be applied to the relief of *individual* distress through the establishment of a relationship between worker and client. By emphasizing the personal influence of the worker and the importance of interviewing techniques (Richmond draft, Archives), Richmond seemed to have accomplished little more than apply a scientific veneer to the long-standing COS methods of investigation and personal service.

Both John Glenn and Edward Devine criticized Richmond's proposed practice model. Glenn noted that the prescribed relationship appeared to stress the dominance of the worker and the antagonism between worker and client, and to encourage the worker to stray from the purposes of the COS. He also questioned the use of the word "clinical" to describe the method Richmond detailed and asked her for a more specific definition of casework.

Finally, Glenn commented that Richmond's desire to improve the "mental equipment" of COS workers was unclear. Did she mean this should occur through formal education or through personal development? The former would imply the need for the expansion of existing training programs, while the latter would suggest the need for more in-service professional development (Glenn to Richmond, September 1911; Devine to Richmond, n.d. [1911]). This was the very issue with which schools of social work were grappling in the first two decades of their existence. By no mere coincidence, Richmond, Devine, and Glenn were critical actors in the resolution of this issue and in the determination of the future direction of social work education.

CHAPTER FIVE

Training the Commodity Producers

INTRODUCTION

Educational institutions played a critical role in determining control of the social work profession. Training schools reproduced prevailing definitions of the service commodity, ideas about the goals of social service, and patterns of leadership within the profession. Through their relationships with universities, public and private funding sources, and credential-granting bodies, they shaped the public's perception of the social work enterprise and influenced social work's ability to achieve its professional goals. By 1917, such schools had established fairly uniform admission standards and curricula, and had attached themselves to powerful elements within academia, the corporate elite, and the professional practice community (Queen, 1922; Tufts, 1923). These patterns began to emerge in the wake of the Depression of 1893.

FROM TRAINING SCHOOLS TO SCHOOLS OF SOCIAL WORK

The failure of charitable organizations to respond adequately to the economic and social crisis of the 1890s resulted in large part from a shortage of resources and trained staff (Grinker et al., 1961). Recognition of these deficiencies inspired several papers at national congresses calling for the establishment of training schools in philanthropy (NCCC *Proceedings*, 1891; C. Kellogg, 1893; Brooks, 1894; Dawes, 1893; Richmond, 1896). Such schools would instruct new workers in the latest techniques, enhance the status of charity work, and, through their recruitment of well-educated and wellborn young people, strengthen the reputation of charitable agencies among the urban middle and upper classes (Folks, 1893a). As Richmond (1896b: 8–13) saw it, this development would also assure the success of the COS approach by producing qualified staff whose work would be "steady and continuous," thereby both "creat[ing] in our charitable communities a demand for trained charitable service [and] supply[ing] this demand."

The impetus to establish training schools, therefore, "did not originate with educational authorities who had seen a need and were moved to meet it" (Tufts, 1923: 111), but rather was created by marketplace forces of supply, demand, and control of production—all critical for profession building. The expansion of the social work enterprise could not proceed unless potential sponsors were convinced of the quality of the product they were being asked to support. To assure this result, control of the product was to remain with the "active centers of social work"—that is, the COS—rather than under the auspices of external bodies such as university faculties.

Within a few years, the COS (and some settlement houses) had established informal apprenticeships and more formal two-to-four-week "workers-in-training" programs, which, however, attracted few workers. Gradually, some agencies, such as the Boston Associated Charities, introduced more sophisticated training for friendly visitors which emphasized techniques of investigation and registration, and the development of a cooperative spirit.

Richmond favored an apprenticeship type of program which combined elements of existing programs in the Baltimore COS, child-saving agencies in Pennsylvania, and the YMCA School at Springfield, Massachusetts. Her model followed a middle course between university-based programs of study which tended to stress philanthropic theory and the administration of charities (such as later developed at the University of Chicago) and existing COS training programs which were too expensive and specialized. The COS supported such programs in Philadelphia, Boston, and other large cities through funds for training new workers, weekly training classes and training stipends (*Bulletin* of SOC, 1901).

The New York School of Philanthropy

In the summer of 1898, 27 friendly visitors enrolled in the first Summer School in Applied Philanthropy, established by the New

York COS under the leadership of Robert deForest. The school soon succeeded admirably in its two basic goals: to demonstrate the scientific basis of philanthropy and thereby give social work a stronger claim to scientific and professional status, and to provide a forum for social work leaders, particularly from the COS, to recruit and train workers in their philosophy and methods. Books by Amos Warner and Edward Devine were required reading before entering, lectures by COS leaders like Zilpha Drew Smith and Mary Richmond dominated the curriculum, and graduates were more likely to find jobs in COS-type agencies than in any other service organization (Ayres, 1901; *Charities*, July 13, 1901, and August 3, 1901). In its first three years, the school trained 70 students from 17 states, half of whom were college graduates. (This was three times the number of charity workers who held college degrees.)

At the same time, social work programs which focused largely on theory and research emerged as offshoots of departments of sociology in large universities like Harvard and through the Institute of Social Science at the University of Chicago. Some of these programs were short-lived; others, like that at Simmons College, soon switched to or merged with the practice orientation of their COS-created counterparts.

By 1904, with the help of powerful board members like J. Pierpont Morgan, the New York program expanded from six weeks to a full year and developed as a quasi-independent entity, the New York School of Philanthropy, associated with the New York COS—a structural model soon duplicated in most major Eastern and Midwestern cities. The school's existence thus strengthened the relationship of the COS with powerful political sponsors, including Abraham Hewitt, the mayor of New York; Seth Low, the president of Columbia University and a former mayor; Bishop Henry Potter; Daniel Coit Gilman, president of both the Baltimore COS and Johns Hopkins University; and Joseph Choate, the United States Ambassador to Great Britain (cf. letters published in *Charities* during the summer 1901).

Despite this support, serious problems remained to be resolved. First, the distinction between training, which stressed technique, and instruction, which was university-based and emphasized theory, was unclear. While COS programs in large cities had concentrated on the former, the absence of a unified body of knowledge weakened the claim of social work to scientific status and produced paid workers of uneven quality (Brackett, 1901).

Another problem was that the generally low caliber of charity workers reinforced the prevailing myth that anyone willing was capable of doing charity work. This problem was exacerbated by the improper utilization of volunteers by the COS. Such volunteers were no longer the critical staff of agencies, but were still viewed as the symbol and spirit of charity organization (Gutridge, 1903; Brooks, 1901).

A third difficulty lay in the fact that the settlement movement had a head start in the area of worker and community education. Before the turn of the century, settlement houses in Detroit, Chicago, and Boston had set up fellowship programs in cooperation with such distinguished schools as the University of Michigan (Brackett, 1901). These programs emphasized the mutuality of interest and purpose of the agency, worker, and service recipient, stressed the unique attributes of each worker and client, and promoted the view that these qualities could best be expressed through the vehicle of the group. Settlement leaders regarded such education as "prophetic of a new democracy which will have a deeper understanding of the problems of the different elements in society" (Morgenthau, 1913).

Differences arose as to the source of attraction of new workers to the social work enterprise. COS leaders believed that improved training itself would create a more skilled and, hence, more professional workforce (Philadelphia SOC, 24th Annual Report; Philadelphia SOC, 23rd Annual Report). They strove consciously to impose a particular view of charitable work on all those who desired to practice it. Although COS leaders disavowed any intentions to forge a "monopoly of charity workers," they agreed that "people should recognize there is one right way and a number of wrong ways of . . . helping a family or an individual" (Richmond, "The Importance of Training," pp. 3–4).

Homer Folks argued, however, that the subjective perception of being professionals, of having a *career* in charity work, would stimulate workers to improve their knowledge and skills (Folks, 1893a: 2). He maintained that young people would be attracted to philanthropic work when the field improved its self-image and raised its salaries to a level comparable with other professions. This would require stronger ties to powerful political elites (an area in which men like Folks excelled) and the instillation of a corporate esprit among charity workers.

Another area of disagreement was the relative weight to be given in training programs to theory/knowledge and methods/techniques. On this issue, the lines of difference were particularly sharp. Public welfare and settlement leaders argued for a strong link between the professionalization of social work and a concern with a broad and complex range of social and economic issues (Cf. brochures for University of Pennsylvania preliminary course, 1906; New York School Catalogues 1908–12; pamphlet from Boston School of Social Work, 1909–10; letters of Richmond to Devine & reply, March 19, 1912, March 20, 1912, as well as New York School report, 1911–12).

By contrast, COS training programs focused increasingly on *techniques* of working with families, COS methods, the analysis of individual problems, and the role of the friendly visitor. (See, for example, lecture series by Buffalo COS, 1908, in which Assistant Director Porter Lee played a key role.) These training programs, funded largely by the agencies themselves, initially through special funds and later with the considerable assistance of the Russell Sage Foundation, emphasized the education of previously untrained, often new, personnel; socialization into COS values and methods; screening of applicants before admission; the distinctions between paid and volunteer workers as to their functions and educational needs; and the clear relationship between training and the professionalization of charity work in order to influence public opinion among the business class (Phila. SOC reports; Richmond, "The Importance of Training"). The emphasis of COS training on rules and the passive role of clients in the casework process symbolized their concern with businesslike efficiency and social control over the poor (Grinker et al., 1961).

Still another dispute concerned the target of the schools' recruitment efforts; that is, who should be attracted to and benefit from the training programs? This issue was connected to the vital question of auspices: Who would provide the resources to run the programs?

Other programs—in Philadelphia and especially in the Midwest—were less concerned about the type of work for which their students were being trained and strove to recruit liberal arts graduates and those already employed in such diverse fields as the ministry, education, probation, child welfare, criminal justice, charity organization, medicine, and nursing (U. of Pa. brochure, 1906). Operating under the assumption that "for those who have had specialized training there is a steady demand," university-affiliated programs did *not* distinguish between paid workers and volunteers, or between field agents and potential executives. Homer Folks claimed "the antithesis is not between those who are paid and those who are not . . . , but between those who give to such work all their time . . . and those . . . whose main business is something else" (Folks, 1893a: 10; Folks's remarks at commencement exercises of the New York City Training School for Nurses, May 16, 1903). These broad goals required the advantages and resources which only a well-financed university could provide.

Students' reactions to the two different educational approaches were mixed. Most social work educators reported a desire on the part of students and among their supervisors—including those in COS programs—to acquire a broader view of society and an in-depth understanding of philanthropic principles (Smith et al., 1899; letters of Devine to Richmond and Glenn, March 20, 23, 1912). At the same time, enrollment in technique-focused courses soared. When Mary Richmond delivered the 1914 Kennedy Lectures at the New York School, entitled "First Steps in Social Case Work," in which she spelled out the "art" of individualizing social problems, over 1,100 tickets were sold, compelling the school to take the unprecedented step of repeating the series (press release of New York School, March 1, 1914).

THE RSF INFLUENCE IN SOCIAL WORK EDUCATION

COS-backed educational programs received an enormous boost through the subsidization of the Russell Sage Foundation (RSF) and the close, supportive relationships between the RSF and the New York School (Sage Foundation Archives) which vaulted them into the emerging leadership of social work education. Mary Richmond's appointment to the faculty of the prestigious New York School in 1910 provided a powerful means to shape the direction of social work education throughout the U.S. in its formative years, permanently stamping the profession with the COS imprint of an emphasis on practice techniques and practice-based research.[13]

The RSF provided fellowships and paid fieldwork placements to approximately one-third of the New York School's students; enabled schools to hire new staff, pay fieldwork instructors and expand their enrollments; strengthened the role of research in the schools' curricula; and, through the establishment of courses open to the public and the publication of a wide range of research projects with general social utility, helped "awaken the intelligent interest and cooperation [of the community] in the promotion of [its] welfare" (letter of Graham Taylor to RSF, October 24, 1911; 1911–12 Budget of New York School; letter from Brackett to RSF, October 17, 1911; letter from Carroll M. Davis and Samuel Sale to RSF, October 30, 1911; letter of Thomas J. Riley to RSF, November 16, 1911).

The financial dependence of the schools on the RSF, however, made them strongly susceptible to the views of its leaders, especially Richmond, whose work *First Steps in Social Service Treatment: A Textbook for Caseworkers* was published in September 1911 by Sage. Under her influence, fieldwork curricula were revised to reflect a more technique-oriented approach, one which emphasized COS philosophy, goals, and methods. COS and other casework-dominated agencies became the major sources for student placements. While school policies acknowledged the experience of settlement workers, nearly all students were required to complete a placement at a COS-type agency (New York School *Field Work Guide; Catalog* of New York School; letters of Brackett and Taylor). The influence of the COS was further strengthened by its close relationship with the schools in the employment of graduates in executive and supervisory positions (correspondance between Adah Hopkins, Registrar of New York School, and Richmond, December 12, 1911; January 19, 31, 1912; Brackett letter to Richmond, 1911).

By contrast, the earliest schools of social work were not designed to prepare graduates for careers in settlement-type agencies. For example, in the first three years of the New York Summer School, only 10% of those who completed the course of study entered settlement work, while over half went to work for COS or related organizations (Ayres, 1901: 186–89). Ten years later, the situation for settlements in the four leading schools of social work had worsened considerably, due largely to the influence wielded by the RSF in its distribution of fellowships.

In 1911, the Sage fellowship program purposefully moved into the gap created when the College Settlements Association stopped providing research fellowships and redirected its limited resources to scholarships designed to recruit and train students for settlement work (*Survey*, November 19, 1910). In addition to promoting research through the Bureaus established at each school, the RSF recruited the "best college material" to the social work profession and subsidized their training in COS work, hospital social services, and child welfare agencies (Richmond letters to Glenn, December 22, 1911, and December 27, 1911). This support helped to disseminate COS standards and techniques into new and reorganized social service agencies by COS-trained graduates. The establishment of COS scholarships "in selected departments of social work" and the exchange of training services for staff in return for paid fieldwork placements further aided this dissemination (Richmond, ibid., and letter of Glenn, December 22, 1911), thereby enabling the RSF to have a considerable impact on the development of social work and social work education outside of the realm of family casework in such fields as medical social work (cf. correspondence between Richmond and Devine May 27, June 2, 1914).[14]

School Curricula

With the support of the RSF, schools of social work raised their admission standards and made their courses of study more rigorous (letters of Breckinridge to Richmond, February 6, 1911; Richmond to Cannon, April 22, 1911; Z. Smith to Richmond, April 30, 1912). The growing emphasis on field instruction—"analogous to the clinical experience given to the student of medicine"—was the most significant of these developments, especially since it coincided with the orientation of the COS (letter of Richmond to Brackett, September 9, 1911; New York School *Field Work Guide*; letter to Cannon, April 22, 1911).

These changes required an expansion of staff and, more important, greater coordination between the School, the COS, and the Sage Foundation, for which Richmond took personal responsibility (letter of Mary Grace Worthington to Richmond, April 16, 1912; Richmond to Brackett, September 9, 1911). The changes strengthened the influence of the COS by providing the apparatus through which schools of social work could exercise greater control over their fieldwork supervisors, the nature of field instruction placements, and the professional behavior of students (letters in Richmond's RSF files, Richmond Archives).

Richmond also pushed for a revision of the schools' curricula, de-emphasizing "the economic basis of social work," and stressing, instead, "the painstaking working out of the techniques of each of the more important social work processes" (Richmond to Devine, March 19, 1912; Goucher College brochure, Archives; Memo of New York School, January 15, 1915; Richmond letter, March 19, 1912). Devine, the director of the New York School, strongly opposed Richmond's proposal (letters of March 20, 23, 1912), and, in a confidential letter, appealed successfully for RSF director John Glenn's support (letter, March 23, 1912).

Nevertheless, the trend toward more practice-focused, particularly casework-focused, education proved inexorable. Richmond's influence, and the indispensable financial support of the RSF, were decisive, as was the profession's reading of market trends for the future.[15] The publication of *Social Diagnosis* in 1917 and its promotion by the sympathetic new director of the New York School, Porter Lee, symbolized the transition "from Darwin to Freud, from environmentalism to the psyche [which] had startling consequences" for social work education and the profession as a whole (Lindeman, 1952: 7; Queen, 1922: 23–24; Warner et al., 1929: 37–38).

CHAPTER SIX

Neither Charity nor Enterprise: The State of Social Work at the End of the Progressive Era

PUBLIC/PRIVATE DIFFERENCES

By the outbreak of World War I, the Eastern COS began to dominate the social work enterprise and, hence, to define the social work commodity, by virtue of their control of national social work organizations, major social work publications, and training schools for social workers—all goals outlined by Francis McLean at a 1909 meeting of major COS leaders in Buffalo (minutes of Exchange Branch luncheon at Buffalo Club, June 14, 1909, Richmond Archives). COS influence continued to grow in the period that followed because, even in public welfare practice, the application of "thoughtful, sympathetic case work" seemed to represent the "only possible way . . . to safeguard either the public fund or the people who must turn to it for help" (Vaile, 1915a; 1915b; 1915c). Conversely, private charity could only "remain strong and well-supported" if it could demonstrate that it was providing "a needed service that is different from anything done by public funds and authority" (Ibid.).

While public welfare advocates suggested that public and private social services be distinguished by the types of clients with whom they worked (Folks, c.1909–12; 1911, 1913; Folks & Elwood, 1915), the COS favored the "extension and reorganization of public outdoor relief as a fund to be drawn upon by qualified agencies in connection with their treatment of their own clients" (Lee, 1915a). Within this framework, the function of the COS was "the organization of family resources and their correlation with various community resources in a plan that makes possible . . . normal life." In other words, the COS were to have complete control over the definition of the service commodity, who delivered it, to whom it would be delivered, and in what context. The state would serve solely as a resource depository from which the COS could draw funds in order to perform its self-appointed role (Vaile, letter to Lee, 1915).

Thus, representatives of the voluntary and private casework agencies, led by the COS, promoted a view of social work which stressed private and increasingly professionalized control of the service function, which they defined largely in terms of family casework (i.e., counseling). Public welfare advocates in a variety of fields shared the belief in professionalization and the definition of social work in casework terms, but felt that a true social service could best be delivered via a public agency. Such an agency, once divested of its destructive "political nature," could best combine the goal of personal service with the satisfaction of "sheer material needs" (Vaile, letter to Lee, 1915).

DECLINE OF THE SETTLEMENTS

In the debate about the future of social work practice, what had become of the settlement movement? Despite the breadth and apparent strength of the settlements—the National Federation of Settlements had over 650 participants at its sixth annual conference in New York in 1917 (Archives, National Federation of Settlements)—by the outbreak of World War I, settlements were on the verge of being relegated to marginal status in the burgeoning social work enterprise.

How did this occur? The core of the problem for settlements appears to rest in their lack of a clear definition of the social work commodity (Editorial in the *Survey*, "A Program for Social Work," October 3, 1908: 2). The broad scope of the settlements' vision and their wide range of activities made it difficult to interpret settlement work to potential sponsors and the general public by establishing a link between a scientific method and their daily practice. Their soaring rhetoric produced different interpretations even within settlement ranks.

While some considered the settlements an integral part of social movements aimed at broad social change, others interpreted their role more narrowly. Settlement houses were to be places of companionship (alternatives to the saloon), personal development, and civic education. Settlement work was, in this view, merely friendly visiting on a group scale and "the proper handmaiden of charity organization" (Warner, 1903: 308–15). From this conception of settlement work flowed an enormous variety of educational, recreational, and cultural programs, concrete social services, and community-based associations in which neighborhood residents, existing community institutions, and settlement workers cooperated (White, April 2, 1915; cf. Simkhovitch, 1917, 1926).

As the number of sociocultural programs swelled, the focus of settlement work moved away from social reform, although settlement leaders continued to be closely identified with social justice causes. Yet, the settlements did not become the keystone for a permanent coalition of reformers and radicals with branches in the labor movement, ethnic communities, and college campuses. Nor did they create lasting institutions which worked toward social justice. In the process of disseminating their ideals among the middle and upper classes, the initial thrust for social justice had largely been forgotten (Taylor, 1906; Kelly, 1906; Barnett, 1906; Mead, 1907).

This transformation had two consequences for settlement workers. They experienced even greater difficulty in defining their unique knowledge and skills, while their actual and perceived connection to reformist and radical causes became a liability as the country's political mood shifted to the right in the waning years of the Progressive Era. The antiwar activities of Jane Addams and Lillian Wald (see Wald letter to *New York Times*, 1916, n.d., Wald Archives) and the settlements' defense of prosecuted labor leaders increased the antagonism of powerful elites toward the settlements and swung the tide of public opinion against them (cf. Addams, 1910; Wald, 1915; Blumberg, 1966; C. Chambers, 1963; A. Davis, 1967; Duffus, 1938; Epstein, 1948; Goldmark, 1953; Levine, 1971; Lynd, 1961; Trolander, 1975; Weinstein, 1969).

A second explanation for the diminished role of settlements within social work lies in their failure to pursue the tasks required of an occupation striving for professional status. Although settlement leaders cultivated and established close ties with powerful sponsors in politics and industry, they tended to use these ties to promote social legislation rather than to strengthen their hold on the social service marketplace (Folks, 1916; Warner, 1894; 1929; Hoy, 1904). Unlike the COS, they adopted an inclusive attitude toward other service providers and cooperated closely with schools, trade unions, churches, and public social welfare agencies (Folks, 1911; 1913; c. 1909–12; Lodge, 1901; Keller, 1901). The programs they helped establish were placed under the control of existing authorities from other professions, thereby replicating the prevailing hierarchy of occupations throughout the health and mental-health care fields.

The settlement movement, therefore, lacked access to outlets other than settlement houses in which its particular service commodity could be distributed. This failure was particularly significant since organizations such as hospitals and public schools were expanding dramatically in the decades prior to World War I (C. Chambers, 1963; J. Chambers, 1980; Folks, 1911; Folks & Elwood, 1911). Meanwhile, with the support of the RSF, the COS expanded opportunities for their practitioners in a variety of social service and non–social service agencies (Richmond, 1912; 1896d).

Moreover, the settlements' philosophy of training and service was not conducive to the establishment of a unique occupational domain. Whatever their class biases and their often awkward attempts to bridge class and cultural barriers, the settlements strove to create a more egalitarian relationship between providers and recipients of services. This approach was diametrically opposed to the prevailing conception of professionalism in the U.S., which stressed the expertise of the professional and a service ideal which underscored the unequal relationship between the parties to the service transaction.

A final explanation for the settlements' demise may lie in the demographic composition of the settlement movement's membership and leadership. While the COS and the settlements initially drew recruits from the same socioeconomic strata, there is evidence that the class and cultural characteristics of settlement workers began to change in the two decades prior to World War I to a far greater extent than among their COS counterparts. With their close ties to ethnic associations, labor unions, and immigrant churches, the ranks of settlements swelled with working-class young men and women, particularly Jews and Catholics (Cook, 1979; Wald, 1915; C. Chambers, 1963, 1971; A. Davis, 1967; Trolander, 1975). Although the settlement leadership continued to be dominated by upper-income WASPs, the infusion of new workers from different backgrounds produced three significant results.

The growing class and ethnic diversity strengthened the tendency toward a heterogeneous vision of settlement work which made the definition of the settlements' service commodity that much more difficult to express. Simultaneously, the material aspirations of many of the new recruits strengthened the drive to carve out a unique occupational enterprise which settlement workers could control. These aspirations made the trend toward recreational and educational activities which could serve a broader clientele more attractive. Finally, a sizable and vocal minority of these new recruits seized upon the settlements' call for social justice and interpreted this rhetoric in more radical ways than did their upper-class predecessors. This heightened tension within settlement ranks and between the settlement movement and an increasingly conservative public.

Nevertheless, the influence of the settlements continued to be felt in the symbols and rhetoric of the social work profession through national social work organizations and publications, if not in the focus of social work practice (cf. McLean study in RSF Archives, 1918). The reformist thrust of the settlements had imprinted its values on the social work enterprise, and the dominant forces within that enterprise could not ignore those values without risking the diminution of the profession's status in the eyes of the public. Social workers in the family casework movement understood the importance of this symbolism best of all (Almy, 1912). Their awareness reflected the precarious position that even the dominant social work faction held within the U.S. political economy and portended far more serious consequences for the social work profession when the next great wave of social reform broke in the 1930s.

PART III

The Growth and Consolidation of the Social Work Enterprise: 1916–29

As a general proposition it seems clear that many of the perplexing dislocations of present society are traceable to a faulty distribution of wealth and income.

Eduard Lindeman, 1936

CHAPTER SEVEN

Historical Context

LEGACY FROM THE PROGRESSIVE YEARS

By 1916, the United States was well on its way to becoming an urban, mass society. About 50% of its approximately 100 million people lived in cities and towns of 8,000 or more, compared to about 28% in 1870. Industrial entrepreneurs had linked disparate communities through an extensive railroad, riverway, and telephone communication system; improvements in printing machinery had made a popular press feasible; and mass production and marketing technologies began to introduce standardized consumer durables into homes everywhere. National and regional markets replaced local markets, stimulated and managed by organizations of like size. Materialism and the drive for wealth had become the pervasive values of American culture. The transformations wrought by industrialization, immigration, and urbanization penetrated every aspect of American life in an interdependent, self-generating cycle of development and change.

The particular legacy of the previous 40 years of industrialization and progressive reform provided social work leaders in 1916 with a strong base from which to mount their drive for occupational control. A consensus had developed among business and professional elites and a growing middle class that U.S. society needed an enlightened response to the widespread social disruptions caused by industrial growth. Church-sponsored benevolence was no longer viewed as adequate to deal with these problems. The belief was strong to the point of ideology that science and technology—efficiency and expertise—could and should be applied broadly in government, the economy, and social welfare to solve problems and advance the public good.

To meet the needs of the new industrial society, secondary education was revamped and became almost universal. At the same time, the modern university, infused with the spirit of the scientific method and sizable injections of public and private support, expanded enrollments dramatically, and emerged as the major credentialing institution for the country's skilled personnel. Private industry provided the organizational model for wielding political influence, creating and controlling new markets, and scientific management. As product and service markets widened geographically, local and regional political structures became strategically less appropriate. Consequently, "interest groups increasingly needed to petition the government not as representatives of localities but as spokesmen for wider, more inclusive, national constituencies" (Berkowitz & McQuaid, 1980: xii).

The disruptive costs of industrialization that helped to create a need for a more scientific social work also produced unprecedented economic growth. Although the fruits of this growth were distributed unevenly, a middle class of educated and trained white-collar and service workers, professionals, skilled laborers, and technicians had begun to develop. This group became the labor pool and the consumer market for social work services, and formed a broadened financial base to support private philanthropy.

Simultaneously, the growth of the philanthropic foundation in pre–World War I America provided a socially respectable outlet for vast accumulations of surplus wealth. Their timely allocations often made a critical difference in the success or failure of countless social and cultural endeavors, the social work enterprise no less than others. These resources, however, did not come free of cost.

> . . . [F]oundations do not represent a "conspiracy" on the part of the guardians of vested wealth designed to influence culture in one direction. More accurate would be the statement that these vested funds represent a consistently conservative element in our civilization, and that wherever their appropriations are accepted there enters at the same time this subtle influence in the direction of protecting the value system in existence, that is, of conserving the status quo. (Lindeman, 1936: 11–12)

THE NEW ERA: 1916–29

In the New Era between 1916 and the Great Depression, Americans struggled to cope with relentless industrial change in all its manifestations—a process substantially intensified by the impact of World War I. On the whole, U.S. society experienced enormous economic growth and a significant rise in the standard of living. From 1922 to 1928 the gross national product, measured in constant dollars, rose by almost 40% while per capita income rose by 30%. With continued improvements in technology, the output per factory work-hour increased by nearly 75%, while the average 60-hour work week in 1900 dropped to close to 48 hours by 1928. The real earnings of employed wage earners increased approximately 22%. These gains, together with improvements in public health and medicine, the smaller size of families, compulsory education, and the arrival of the cheap automobile, gave many Americans a taste of the well-being previously reserved for the most wealthy.

Despite these aggregate gains, U.S. prosperity and social and economic development were distributed extremely unevenly. One study in 1924 estimated that 85% of the population received 60% of the total income, or approximately $430 per capita, as compared to 6.4% of the population who received 25.6% of the total income, or approximately $3,000 per capita; 1.7% of the population received 14.8% of the total money income, with a per capita income of $5,000 or more. Or, put in terms of wealth, 1% of the people, in 1928, owned 59% of the wealth; 13% of the people owned 90% of the wealth; 87% of the people owned 10% of the wealth; and 75% of the people owned practically nothing (Lindeman, 1936: 3).

Thus, amidst growing affluence in the United States, the incidence of poverty in the 1920s remained high. Unemployment averaged almost 5% (accurate statistics were not really kept), and without unemployment insurance many became destitute. Agricultural workers as well as workers in the older industries, such as soft-coal mining, railroads, shipping, and textiles, which were less able to control their markets, were particularly vulnerable. So also were rural dwellers, Southerners, blacks, and new immigrants, 4.1 million of whom came to the United States between 1920 and 1930 despite the restrictive Immigration Act of 1924.

These conditions signaled the need for a stronger federal role in planning and controlling an increasingly national political economy. During his first term, President Woodrow Wilson acted like a strong executive who was aware of this need. Wilson attempted to weaken business's monopolistic control of the economy through the Clayton Anti-Trust Act and the creation of the Federal Trade Commission, which was to prohibit "illicit competition." In a departure from an earlier antipathy, Wilson also gave presidential support to organized labor through recognition of unionization and collective bargaining, through his use of the Division of Conciliation within the Department of Labor to deal with labor disputes, and through provisions in the Clayton Act that exempted labor from antitrust prosecution. But by 1916 both Wilson's and the Democratic party's congressional power had eroded to a slim majority. With U.S. entry into World War I, the liberal reform agenda, with its thrust toward an increasingly active role for federal government, was severely frustrated.

World War I and the events surrounding it defined the character of the New Era. Four major and interrelated themes in this period were significant for the professionalization of social work. These were: (1) a climate of cultural and political repression; (2) the legitimation of business/government partnerships to mobilize for war and manage peacetime problems; (3) welfare capitalism and the enshrinement of managerial and technical expertise as the means for its achievement; and, (4) the uninhibited construction of a consumer society.

With the entry of the United States into the war in April 1917, labor unrest which had been prevalent during the economic slump of 1913–14 began to subside. Partly this was a function of the end of unemployment and the advent of labor shortages as men were drafted into the armed forces and immigration all but stopped. But also industrial disquiet and political dissent were curbed under the time-honored banner of patriotism and the need for unity in a national crisis.

The outbreak of war became an excuse to pass repressive legislation, such as the Espionage Act of 1917 and the Sedition Act of 1918. Now with the law on their side, conservatives "enforced" such legislation in the streets and the courts. The Department of Justice sponsored an American Protective League which recruited over 100,000 members to ferret out dissidents. Vigilante groups were organized with the support of state law and the press. In the summer of 1917 a *New York Times* editorial said: "It is the duty of every good citizen to communicate to proper authorities any evidence of sedition that comes to his notice" (Zinn, 1980: 360). Socialists and the militant Industrial Workers of the World (IWW) became ready objects of harrassment and violence. For opposing the war, Eugene

Debs, the 64-year-old leader of the Socialist Party, was convicted of violating the Espionage Act and sentenced to 10 years in prison. In 1919, after the war was over, the Supreme Court, led by Oliver Wendell Holmes, unanimously affirmed Debs's guilt. He spent 32 months in jail before President Harding finally released him in 1921, during which time he received about one million votes in the 1920 presidential election. For taking a similar position, Jane Addams, an "American heroine" prior to the war's outbreak, also fell from public grace in the popular press.

The racism, bigotry, and intolerance awakened by the war did not subside after the armistice of November 1919. Conservatives associated racial and ethnic minorities with radicalism and labor strife. During the inevitable postwar inflation of 1919, more than 4 million workers were involved in labor shortages or strikes. Strike-breaking efforts by business and the Department of Justice deliberately fomented ethnic and racial divisiveness, deported aliens, used red-baiting, and resorted to violence to restore order. In the name of internal security, in 1919 Attorney General A. Mitchell Palmer illegally used "John Doe" warrants in mass raids to arrest some 6,000 suspected "traitors," most later found to be innocent, and to deport some 550 "radical" aliens to the Soviet Union. All of this occurred with the sanction of veterans' organizations, business groups who hoped to destroy the labor movement, and, with few exceptions, the popular press.

By the 1920s, the IWW had been destroyed and the Socialist Party was in disarray from attacks and internal dissension. Still the refrain of "100 percent American" echoed throughout the country. In 1924 Congress set quotas on the flood of "dangerous" immigrants who were not of Anglo-Saxon racial, ethnic, or national origin. Between 1917 and 1925 some 600,000 blacks moved north, threatening earlier patterns of racial segregation. The Ku Klux Klan followed to enforce its version of white supremacy, and by 1924 it had 4.5 million members. In the face of the violence and widespread racial hatred of the 1920s, many blacks turned to Marcus Garvey's black nationalist movement for survival. As for unions, in the face of antilabor attacks and the challenge of welfare capitalism, by the end of the decade organized labor declined from a 1920 peak of 5 million members to about 3.5 million, roughly its size when the war began.

National unity to fight World War I could not be created by overt political and cultural repression alone. To forge a national consensus the government also undertook an active propaganda campaign in which thousands of speakers working for the Committee on Public Information rallied support across the country for the President's noble promises of "a war to end all wars" and "making the world safe for democracy." Domestically, Wilson's version of democracy in action was embodied in his approach to national mobilization for this first "modern" war.

The mobilization and coordination of the war effort potentially afforded Wilson the opportunity to centralize responsibility for economic and social welfare policies in agencies within the federal government. Out of necessity, Congress gave the President extensive powers to commandeer essential industries and mines, control prices and supplies, and operate the transportation and communication systems. Instead Wilson was receptive to arguments that voluntary cooperation between public and enlightened private organizations was a more realistic and preferable alternative. Accordingly, Wilson delegated the powers of mobilization and coordination to a multiplicity of boards organized under the supervision of the Council for National Defense and administered by top leaders from private finance, industry, and the railroads. They included financier Bernard Baruch, head of the War Industries Board which had the primary responsibility for industrial mobilization; Edwin F. Gay of the Harvard Business School; Gerald Swope of the General Electric Company (a former resident of Hull House); Walter Gifford of American Telegraph and Telephone; and numerous other top-level corporate administrators. Eventually, as the government sought to ensure industrial peace and maximize industrial output, unions were recognized and cooperative labor leaders were also brought into the partnership. They served most notably on the National War Labor Board which attempted to prevent strikes and ensure steady production schedules in return for the guaranteed right to organize workers.

With these arrangements, "the heart of the new order was a network of cooperating industrial committees that linked the war agencies to private organizations and drew upon both public and private power to enforce agreements reached by consultation and bargaining" (Hawley, 1979: 23). The larger significance of the arrangement was the power that private enterprise gained to define the public interest as synonymous with corporate welfare. The belief that the enlightened corporation could harness the expertise of science, management, and technology, and, in concert with government, could promote order and progress for all Americans became the mainstream liberal ideology. Widespread acceptance of this "new liberalism" put big business back in charge of the economy.

The consolidation of the private sector's control of the political economy during and after the war was abetted by the official neglect of antitrust laws and the positive encouragement of business combinations deemed to be in the public interest during the national emergency. In the 1920s Warren Harding's "return to normalcy" expanded on this encouragement by repealing progressive taxes on income, inheritance, and profits, raising tariffs, subsidizing various industries, and not meddling with business combinations. While normalcy was not defined as pure laissez-faire, it was, in the words of Nevins and Commager (1976: 461), "a felicitous combination of two policies—one, freedom of private enterprise from government restraint, and the other, generous subsidies to private enterprise. Government withdrew from business, but business moved in and shaped most government policies."

Nowhere was this more true than in the influential Department of Commerce run by Herbert Hoover during the terms of both Harding and Calvin Coolidge. Through his interventions with antitrust and regulatory agencies, Hoover turned the Department of Commerce into virtually a cooperative arm of the business and trade association community. By 1929 some 2,000 national trade associations had been formed to run conventions, publish trade journals, lobby, collect and disseminate statistics and information, pool resources, arbitrate industrial disputes, and formulate codes of fair trade practice. Favorable Supreme Court rulings in this pro-business climate, unchallenged by Congress, furthered the process of association building, corporate merger, and consolidation.

The impact of this associational and pro-trust activity changed the face of the political economy by centralizing the industrial, transportation, and finance sectors under the dominance of a small number of giant corporations, and by accelerating mass production and consumption. Between 1919 and 1929 literally thousands of small firms disappeared or were swallowed up by combines. As corporations grew, many like General Motors also organized vertically to combine production of raw materials, manufacture, and distribution outlets under one company. By 1933 some 600 corporations owned 53% of all the wealth in the country, while the remaining 388,000 firms owned the balance. The corporations channeled much of their surplus wealth into private foundations and community trusts. About half of the 359 community trusts and foundations in existence were formed in the postwar decade. During that period they contributed between 5% and 10% of the total charitable budget of $20.751 billion for all private educational, religious, and charitable enterprises in the country.

The New Era inaugurated John Kenneth Galbraith's "new industrial state," whose two-part economy consisted of "the world of the few hundred technically dynamic, massively capitalized and highly organized corporations on the one hand and of the thousands of small and traditional proprietors on the other" (Galbraith, 1971: 28). Monopoly capitalism in the 1920s came out of the transition from a war production/consumption to a peace economy. Its emergence solidified America's movement toward an economy planned not by the public sector, but by the giant corporations whose continued growth and security required the creation and control of the production process and mass consumer markets.

While organized labor gained acceptability during the war, as soon as the war ended, private enterprise reverted to its stance of bitter resistance to the closed shop and union contracts. Consistent with their new image, enlightened corporate leaders in the 1920s looked for alternatives to the rigid principles of scientific management to maintain control over production and ensure a stable, pliant workforce suitable for the modern production system. They turned to the developing field of personnel management, which was greatly influenced by the human relations work of Elton Mayo at the Western Electric Company beginning in 1924. Personnel relations became a specialized department in the larger firms. They concentrated on employee welfare programs as well as activities to encourage voluntary conformity with company needs, such as more selective hiring, incentive programs, educational activities, and various participatory structures. By 1929 it was estimated that half of the companies with 5,000 or more employees had such specialized departments.

The appearance of "welfare capitalism" in the form of company unions and other employee benefit packages posed a strong challenge to organized labor and proponents of governmental welfare structures. It effectively promoted the image of the socially responsible corporation whose profits were linked to American progress and well-being. Company unions tended to occur in the largest and wealthiest national corporations, such as General Electric, Goodyear Tire and Rubber, International Harvester, Inland Steel, and the Pennsylvania Railroad. The number of employees working under company union plans grew from 400,000 in 1919 to more than 1,400,000 in 1926, and 70% worked for companies with more than 10,000 employees (Berkowitz & McQuaid, 1980: 55). Other corporate welfare benefits were even more widespread by the end of the postwar decade. They included safety programs, group insurance plans, mutual aid associations, and retirement pension programs. Despite these activities, the majority of industrial workers were not covered by voluntarily instituted corporate welfare programs of any kind by the end of the decade. Nevertheless, their existence began to fill a vacuum in state and federal welfare planning, and lent credibility to the assertions of leaders in private enterprise that both organized labor and a system of federal social protections were unnecessary.

Private enterprise needed more than new technologies and a stable labor force to sustain its immense productive capacities. It also required the sustained demand for its products by a large supply of able and willing consumers. The structuring of mass markets was accomplished through new techniques of product distribution, advertising, and consumer financing. Chain stores in retailing, food, and drugs provided advantages in economies of scale, stock volume, and display possibilities over smaller proprietors. Advertising tripled its expenditures in the 1920s, developing as a major industry in its own right with Madison Avenue at its center. Aided by the power of the new mass communication technologies of radio and film, national advertisers whetted the public's appetites for consumer durables and created new desires, redefined its criteria for success, and helped to overcome its traditional concern for thrift. Relatively rare before the war, consumer credit through installment buying became the new mechanism to underpin mass purchasing power, especially for automobiles, appliances, and furniture. By 1929 total consumer debt had reached about $7 billion dollars.

Structural changes in the economy conditioned social development in the New Era. The acceleration of technological innovation and the rise of new industries after the war, with the concomitant decline of agriculture and older extractive industries, textiles, railroads, and shipping, precipitated the growth of urban centers. Cities became the centers of business, government, entertainment, education, literature, and the arts. The urban mind and way of life diffused throughout the society. The automobile, the radio, and motion pictures, along with advertising and the popular press became the major forces for standardization in the creation of a mass society. Changes in the labor market generated new employment sectors and left more time for leisure and consumption. With more time available through labor-saving devices and the socialization of children at an earlier age outside the home in schools, women moved increasingly out of the home as well and into the labor force as white-collar workers and quasi-professional employees. By 1920 over 900,000 women were employed as telephone operators, stenographers, retail clerks, and trained nurses, positions that did not exist 50 years earlier (Maher, 1931). Under the influence of a powerful capitalistic economy, the family became less of a cohesive unit of social support for its members. It was more subject to break-up, as indicated by a rising divorce rate in the 1920s; and it served more as a consumer of goods and services and a means of reproducing the producers and consumers of the new industrial state.

SUMMARY

The political-economic context of the New Era established a powerful set of conditions under which professionalization could take place and provided a model for its accomplishment. In the management of World War I and the transition to a peacetime economy a new industrial state began to take shape controlled by giant corporations. An "enlightened" private enterprise dominated the machinery of politics and governmental administration casting progressive thought into its own version of social progress through voluntary-government partnership and corporate social responsibility. At the same time throughout the period intolerance was tolerated and even promoted as a means of imposing tighter social control over political dissidents, labor organizers, and ethnic and racial minorities.

These methods assured the development of a wedge between aspiring professionals and poor and working-class groups. Class conflict would force sides and could not serve as a means for professional aggrandizement. Furthermore, the separation of politics from administration in government at all levels made it difficult for professionalizing groups to ally with their potential constituencies—labor and the poor—as equals in a struggle for political power. Professionalism had become identified with the alleged political neutrality, scientific objectivity, and expertise of management and science.

In an expanding economy, the claims of the new liberalism carried a certain degree of credibility. *Noblesse oblige* passed from individual philanthropists to enlightened corporations whose productive capacities had vastly expanded due to technological innovation and increased control over newly created national markets. Surplus wealth, channeled into the resources of foundations and community trusts, produced a kind of corporate feudalism for educational, religious, and charitable endeavors. Corporate methods and values also influenced the technology and spread of charitable fund-raising through the Community Chests and various national agencies, although private philanthropy still remained a major source of funds for charitable endeavors in many communities.

The mass production/consumption society clarified the need for production and control of national markets for professional services. Advancements in mass communication and transportation made this possible. The application of industrial mass production technologies when transferred to the production of professionals implied the disutility of apprenticeship training as a viable approach for building a unified professional enterprise. With universities accepted as the new centers for the acquisition of scientific knowledge and certification, and corporate enterprise providing an organizational model for market control, by the end of the postwar decade professionalizing occupations gained a clear image for achieving their ends.

OVERVIEW: SOCIAL WORK IN THE NEW ERA

It is significant that when social workers began to look for a means to control their occupation, they turned to professionalization rather than unionization as their avenue for collective mobility. For the charity organization workers and caseworkers in other settings who were removed from the labor movement in their daily work this was not surprising. But even settlement workers who had strongly supported the labor movement in their public statements and neighborhood work did not pursue unionization.

This choice reflected the social class of most social workers and an acceptance of the dominant ideology of U.S. capitalism embodied therein. Social workers were either not from working-class backgrounds or, in the case of newer workers, were striving for a higher social status than their forbears had attained. Their leaders, persons such as Jane Addams, Graham Taylor, Grace and Edith Abbott, Julia Lathrop, Edward Devine, and Porter Lee, were deeply committed to improving social conditions and the quality of life. At the same time, having advanced university educations, they had internalized a belief in scientific expertise, education, and efficiency as neutral forces which could be harnessed in the service of creating a society free of class conflict.

While some social workers held more radical ideas about revamping structural inequalities, the majority believed their service work would improve society by promoting social harmony and understanding. This mission was in keeping with the needs of an aspiring occupational group. In order for professionalization to succeed, occupational entrepreneurs had to appeal to a broad cross section of the American middle class for sponsorship and sanction. One disillusioned social worker and critic, Roger Baldwin, founder of the American Civil Liberties Union, and a person out of the settlements, express his dismay this way (Baldwin, 1922):

> Social work's difficulty as a solvent of anything is its utter dependence on moneyed interests for its very existence. If it is not the charity of the rich that sustains it, it is the taxpayers who represent property per se. Social work is hamstrung in achieving any thorough-going social reform by the very nature of its livelihood and its class character. It is in essence a class institution. It is work done by one class for another—the propertied for the propertyless. There is no social work for the rich or well-to-do, much as it is needed.

The routes that social workers took toward erecting a professional enterprise were the traditional ones taken by other professions—

especially medicine, the model of the Flexner Report—namely, forging ties to societal elites who could provide support and legitimation, a movement toward university-based education with increasingly selective entry to the field, active professional associations to promote social work standards and to gain exclusive control over the right to practice, and development of an individualistic, technological, "scientific" methodology that would be consistent with dominant societal values.

The period between World War I and the onset of the Great Depression was one of great growth and consolidation for the professional social work enterprise. Opportunities for social work existed in a wide variety of fields including: public recreation; public and private child welfare agencies; institutions for delinquent children; juvenile and adult probation; prison reform and administration; housing; treatment of tuberculosis; public health and sanitation; immigrant aid; social legislation; and investigation of industrial conditions, child labor, municipal research, and commercial organizations (Davis, 1915). This was also the period when professional social work became irrevocably defined in terms of social casework. During these years social workers established legitimacy and a national presence through the formation of influential national organizations such as the American Association for Organizing Family Social Work (1919), Community Chests and Councils of America (1919), the Child Welfare League of America (1920), and the National Social Work Council (1921). In 1917 the National Conference of Charities and Correction changed its name to the National Conference of Social Work; and by the end of World War I, the Home Service chapters of the American Red Cross had touched nearly every county in the United States. (These agencies, however, could not be sustained in rural areas during the 1920s. In 1928, only about one-third of the rural counties in the country had one or more forms of organized rural social work [SWYB, 1929: 393], and the paucity of services and relief available through both public and private sources contributed strongly to the urgent need for federal assistance during the 1930s.)

Social work's major professional associations were also organized in the post–World War I era: the American Association of Medical Social Workers (AAMSW, 1918); the National Association of School Social Workers (NASSW, 1919); the American Association of Social Workers (AASW, 1921), and the American Association of Psychiatric

Social Workers (AAPSW, 1926). The AASW was by far the most influential of these associations by virtue of its membership, its nationwide chapter structure, and its activities. In 1930, for example, the AASW had a paid membership of 5,310, as compared to the AAMSW with 1,700, the AAPSW with 364, and the NASSW with 275 (Cohen, 1958).

A further mark of social work's growing legitimation was the AASW's ability to get social workers included in the federal census of 1930 as a distinct occupational group, "social and welfare workers." This effort revealed a body of some 31,241 paid workers, exclusive of some additional occupations commonly regarded as part of the social work domain, such as "keepers of charitable and penal institutions" (15,020).

On the education front, between 1915 and 1930 the number of social work schools grew from 15 to more than 40. Twenty-eight of these were affiliated with the American Association of Schools of Social Work, which was formed in 1919 with 17 charter members. Perhaps more significant, the majority of these AASSW members had become affiliated with universities. Closely related to all of the above developments was the establishment of several major social work journals during these years: *Social Casework* (originally *The Family*) in 1920; *Child Welfare*, 1922; the *Survey Midmonthly*, 1912, which aimed at social work practitioners, and its counterpart, the *Survey Graphic*, 1923, which aimed at mobilizing lay leaders and public opinion in welfare matters; and the *Social Service Review*, 1927.

In all of this, a confluence of societal forces provided opportunities and constraints that allowed one segment of the charity workers' community—namely social caseworkers—to become dominant and to define the character of the emerging profession. The previously influential reformist segment lost influence. This is not to say that a deliberate contest was waged between these segments, leading to winners and losers. Rather it is to suggest that one group was better able to assert its interests aided by developments in the larger political economy of industrial capitalism and the culture of American society that was fashioned around it. If the previous 30 years had stimulated awareness among charity workers and social reformers that they shared a common background and progressive outlook which merited vocational status in the division of labor, the New

Era years, 1916–29, produced the defining character of this new vocation and the consciousness that professional status was the desired end of collective action. It also produced a set of fundamental issues and the definitional contours of professional debates that have preoccupied social workers since that time.

In general, these issues and problems have concerned the questions of how to define the domain and boundaries of the enterprise and its commodity; how to assert control over the production and distribution of social workers; and how to assure consumption of their work. The form these issues took then has also persisted, defining and working out a balance between reform and service delivery, between control by social agencies and training institutions, between specialized and generic practice, and between volunteer and professional roles.

In the following four chapters we shall explore the questions how, in the context of larger societal forces, social workers erected the structure of a professional enterprise, and how that enterprise came to be defined largely in terms of the delivery of social casework services. This analysis will reveal the political-economic basis underlying many of the issues that have plagued social work over the years.

CHAPTER EIGHT

Fashioning the Social Work Commodity

INTRODUCTION

For social work, as for other occupations, the process of professionalization followed a pattern responsive to market opportunities. Between 1900 and World War I, "the welfare field was moving from a highly undifferentiated stage toward the establishment of agencies with special areas of function" (Cohen, 1958: 108). In response to market demands, a division of services and related agencies had begun to appear, fueling them at the same time, along the lines of: "family; child care; health and medical; mental hygiene; courts, probation, and parole; leisure time; civil rights; aid to migrants, transients, and travelers; help for immigrants, aliens, and foreign born; assistance for specific racial groups" (Cohen, 1958: 109). These and other fields of practice for social workers covered a broad range of organizational settings, public and private, and encompassed many kinds of roles. Outside of the better-known family welfare associations, settlements, mental hospitals, and child guidance clinics, there were new specialties that gave social work a distinctive character in the first two decades of the twentieth century. Social workers could be employed as administrators of municipal recreation activities, recreation supervisors, and playground leaders. In the field of child care, they could become directors of institutions for dependent children or children's aid societies; they could run a state child welfare bureau or supervise child welfare agents; they could place homeless children in foster homes or work directly with children as cottage parents, educators, and recreation specialists; or they could work with the families of abused and neglected children, to "rescue children from vicious or immoral surroundings" (Davis, 1915: 335). Another related service field involved administrative or direct work in institutions for delinquent children or in juvenile probation. Work with immigrants might be as immigration secretary of the YMCA and involve organizing citizenship classes, clubs, socials, meetings, or helping with job development and integration in industrial plants (Davis, 1915).

As specialized services and their corresponding agencies grew, social work leaders saw the opportunities for expansion, but also the need for consolidation and centralization in order to build an enterprise capable of taking advantage of the new service market and to clarify the distinctive competence of the professional social worker. The stage was thus set for the period of growth and consolidation that followed during the New Era years. Specific periods of differentiation/specialization and centralization/consolidation are fashioned from the resources available at the time and shaped by an era's political economy. The time periods are not uniform in length or character. The dialectical pattern of alternating periods of differentiation and centralization is discernible over the course of social work's evolution. Other aspiring occupations have followed a similar path, for it represents the outcome of the contradictions inherent in a competitive, market economy.

By the time the United States entered World War I, medical, psychiatric, child welfare, and family casework had already taken root as social work specializations. The needs created by the war gave social caseworkers an unparalleled opportunity to promote their special interests and redefine their functions. The most important outcome of the war for social work was the birth of an extensive new market for "casework above the poverty line" (Watts, 1964). This development accelerated the infusion of psychiatric knowledge and ideology into casework and solidified the inchoate separation of casework specializations. It also hardened an incipient dichotomy between casework and social reform. With the rapid expansion of the social work employment market and a new definition of need, social workers moved quickly, through professional associations and schools, to extend their means for product and market control. In the late 1920s caseworkers unified around a common core, consolidating their hold over the pubescent professional enterprise. Finally, professional aspirations coupled with a reactionary political-economic climate diverted the social work mainstream away from its long-standing concern with poor relief and social reconstruction, until the Great Depression generated a new set of political-economic realities.

SOCIAL DIAGNOSIS

The publication of Mary Richmond's *Social Diagnosis* in May 1917 occurred just after U.S. entry into World War I. It was not written, as popularly believed today, in direct response to Dr. Abraham Flexner's denial of the professional status of social work at the 1915 National Conference of Charities and Correction. Richmond had been formulating her ideas about social casework for two decades and had been working specifically on *Social Diagnosis* for about ten years. Based on research in a variety of agency settings, reviews of case records, and direct interviews with caseworkers, the book represented a sophisticated formulation of the social work commodity by one of the profession's chief theoreticians.

The printing of *Social Diagnosis* was also an event of great political import for the emerging profession. The leaders of the profession's dominant faction—the Eastern and Midwestern family casework agencies—consciously sought to promote the book widely and to ensure favorable reception by prestigious reviewers in national journals. In this way, COS leaders hoped to gain the acceptance of their definition of the social work commodity by influential sponsors in the academic and professional strata of society, and through them acquire the backing of corporate and political elites and the general public for the professionalizing efforts of social work.

Throughout 1917, Richmond successfully solicited distinguished reviewers like John Dewey, Roscoe Pound of Harvard Law School, Dr. Richard Cabot of Massachusetts General Hospital, and Dr. Adolph Meyer of Johns Hopkins University (Richmond Collection, letters between Richmond and Richard Cabot, May 10, 1917, May 21, 1917; letter of Arthur Kellogg to Richmond, September 6, 1917). As a result, highly favorable reviews appeared in such diverse and prestigious journals as the *American Economic Review*, the *Journal of Political-Economy*, the *Political Science Quarterly*, *The Dial*, the *American Journal of Sociology*, the *Journal of Criminal Law and Criminology*, the *National Municipal Review*, and *The Nation*. A

positive response from economics journals was particularly important as economists were widely regarded as the leading social scientists of their day and recognized as "pioneers in the process of academic professionalization" (Skocpol and Ikenberry, 1982: 20). The
diversity of the journals which reviewed *Social Diagnosis* symbol-
izes both the interconnectedness of the various fields within U.S.
social science and the breadth of the social work enterprise at the
end of the Progressive Era. The reaction of critics to the book reflects
also, in some way, the public's perception of social work's progress
toward professional status.

Most reviewers agreed with Meyer that the book was an "invalu-
able" addition to the literature, or, in the words of Robert Gault of
Northwestern University, a "milestone." Others stressed the work's
scientific spirit, its lack of dogmatism, and its emphasis on the integration of casework and social reform (reviews by Gault, *Journal
of Criminal Law and Criminology*, November, 1917; Meyer letter,
May 19, 1917; review by W. H. Hick, *American Economic Review*;
review by Helen Bosanquet, *Charities Organization Review*, June 2,
1917; *Catholic Charities Review*, April 1918; letter of John Dewey,
December 1917, *American Economic Review*).

While well-orchestrated reviews enhanced the status of social
work nationally, well-organized marketing efforts by Richmond allies in schools and agencies solidified the hold of the casework faction on the aspiring enterprise. The Sage Foundation enabled Richmond to publish the book cheaply so that "social workers with
small incomes [could afford to] own it and get familiar with it"
(Richmond Collection, letter to Dr. Richard Cabot, March 18, 1918).
Porter Lee, Richmond's protégé at the COS of New York, who was
to play a critical role in the internal struggles of the social work
profession in the 1920s, required students to buy Richmond's book,
shaped his practice course at the New York School to the book's
outline, and circulated a leaflet to colleagues urging them to do likewise (Richmond Collection, letter to Richmond, May 17, 1917).

The genius of *Social Diagnosis* was that it codified the activities
of social caseworkers previously interpreted as "investigation" and
redefined them as "diagnosis," which signified to many a strengthening of social work's professional attitude. Through its style and
content *Social Diagnosis* transformed subjective casework behavior
into an objective collection and assessment of evidence and persua-

sively linked it with processes managed by scientists, attorneys, and physicians. The negative connotations associated with social work investigations were deftly erased, replaced by a rational-scientific framework applicable to all social work practice. Eventually this new framework was captured in the still popular "study-diagnosis-treatment" trilogy.

The successful marketing of *Social Diagnosis* helped to forge a unified view of the social work profession based upon the conception of social work being promoted and practiced in the Eastern family casework agencies; it also helped to advocate the necessity of technical training for all social workers within the framework it proposed (Gault review and *Catholic Charities Review*). *The Nation* (June 14, 1917) went so far as to exclaim, "No social worker who hopes to rise in the profession ought to be without this book; and no student of applied sociology should fail to pore over it." Amelia Sears in the *American Journal of Sociology* (1917) called *Social Diagnosis* "the only comprehensive text book on social work [practice] ever written . . . [which] when accepted and acted upon will revolutionize the methods and organization of public and private charitable and correctional agencies. . . . The book dignifies all social work and marks its first steps on the road to becoming a profession."

Social Diagnosis remained a bible for social work education and internal agency training throughout the 1920s and 1930s, a status that may have prompted Porter Lee, director of the New York School of Philanthropy, to comment, "This book closes one epoch entirely and carries us a long way into the next one" (RSF, 1918, Richmond files). However, it was probably Mary Richmond's connection to the Sage Foundation and her national presence, along with other COS leaders, in training Red Cross caseworkers during World War I that sustained its popularity more than the durability of the text itself. Although the conception of practice in *Social Diagnosis* opened a window to the importance of individual character, therapeutic relationship, and treatment, it did not advance the insights which had already begun to surface from psychology and psychiatry. Virginia Robinson (1930: 67), a proponent of a more psychodynamically oriented practice, looking back a little more than a decade later, saw *Social Diagnosis* as "rather an analysis and summary of the bases upon which social casework was operating up to that time," but for the 1920s there was "no doubt that the interest in the individual and his psychological problems has revolutionized the case work movement of the country." Mary Richmond's 1922 defeat as a candidate for the presidency of the National Conference of Social Work may have symbolized the beginning of this shift in focus.

ADAPTING THE SOCIAL WORK COMMODITY
TO A NEW MARKET

The literature on casework developments during World War I is divided over whether family casework or psychiatric social work with individuals flourished more as a result of the war (see, for example, Robinson, 1930, and Watts, 1964). But this issue pales in significance beside the much larger accomplishment of the war for social work, namely, the creation of the market itself for "casework above the poverty line" (Watts, 1964). The American Red Cross (ARC) was the chief instrument for this market growth through its assistance to servicemen and their families via the Home Service and in U.S. Public Health hospitals. The services provided by the Red Cross during and after the war, however, were defined and controlled largely by social casework leaders whose allegiance was to the Charity Organization and psychiatric social work movements rather than the Red Cross organization per se. (Homer Folks was an exception.) Their concern, usually stated as a desire to maintain "professional standards" for social work services, could be better translated as a desire to maintain control over the new markets.

Until World War I the Red Cross had mainly served as a disaster relief organization. Charity Organization workers had been involved with the Red Cross in these efforts from time to time. Active in humanitarian relief work in Europe since 1914, the ARC enjoyed almost overnight popularity when the United States entered the war in April 1917. Membership rose phenomenally, from 22,000 in 1915 to nearly 21 million in September 1918. During the war the ARC collected some $400 million with the help of the high-level businessmen's War Council. With the blessing of the American public, nothing was too good for American servicemen and their families, including a wartime program, irrespective of social class, which was needed to determine Red Cross supplements to the family budget and to help with other family arrangements or disruptions, to manage communication between war front and home front, and to deal with problems of physical and mental disability and death. Social work professionalization and its definition as casework advanced on the coattails of this widespread public support for the Red Cross.

Upon the request of the War Department, social workers became involved in setting up and administering the new wartime program. Once involved, they actively took it over and shaped it to their ends. Since the Red Cross itself was not equipped to set up and administer a full-scale wartime service program rapidly, "in March, 1917, W. Frank Persons, of the New York City COS, was appointed head of the department of civilian relief (which would include the new wartime program). He had influential contacts in social work by virtue of the association of his agency, the New York School of Philanthropy, and the Russell Sage Foundation" (Watts, 1964: 305; Watts's account is followed here). Persons and the other social workers he unofficially involved, especially Mary Richmond, attracted hundreds of social workers to the ARC. Richmond actually named the program Home Service. As large numbers of untrained volunteers were required to fill out the corps of service delivery personnel, social workers were deployed strategically in training and supervisory roles to defend against any loss of professional status through lowered standards of service.

Implementation of this strategy was supported through a nationwide training program jointly directed by Porter Lee, head of the New York School, and T. J. Reilly, head of the Brooklyn Institute. They organized a condensed, but comprehensive, casework course, packaged as an Institute and taught in colleges and social work schools across the country. Lee wrote the *Syllabus of Instruction*, based on *Social Diagnosis*; Mary Richmond prepared the initial manuals of instruction for Home Service workers and frequently planned, lectured, and prepared annotated case records for student use.

Information about the Home Service appeared often in the popular press and the *Survey*, stressing the themes of "the importance of Institute training for Home Service workers, the importance of interagency cooperation, and ARC intent to avoid competition with existing social agencies" (Ibid.: 307). Home Service chapters "spread the gospel of social casework" throughout the nation, with 3,700 chapters reaching into 15,000 communities, of which only some 300 were large enough to have had social agencies before the war.

The extraordinary success of this "casework above the poverty line," which depended on relationship rather than relief to hold its clients, naturally raised the question in social work circles about continuation after the war. The Home Service network had the potential for expansion into a family service system under the auspices of the ARC. But the notion of a postwar Home Service for civilians, which would mean extending the Red Cross charter beyond veterans services, encountered stiff resistance from the family welfare field, and particularly from Mary Richmond. In order to keep the support it would need in peacetime, the ARC avoided confrontations on the issue. Instead, it directed its programs to rural communities and small towns which had not had services before the war. Without the support, financial and otherwise, generated by the war, Rural Home Services failed and slowly faded away.

Meanwhile, after the war, family casework services under the control of social workers had begun to grow. Undoubtedly influenced by the success of the Home Service experience, and bolstered by Mary Richmond's support at the Sage Foundation, the American Association for Organizing Charity (formerly the National Association of Societies for Organizing Charity) made a fundamental policy shift at its annual meeting on May 31, 1919. It established family treatment rather than relief giving as its primary function. The fifteen resolutions of the Committee on Future Scope and Policy accepted at the meeting were remarkably consistent with the substance and philosophy of *Social Diagnosis*. They included expressions of responsibility for improving unhealthy social conditions and for social planning through central councils of agencies. But the centerpiece was the sixth resolution on family casework, which read:

> Be it resolved that Charity Organization casework in the future be limited to *Family* (emphasis in original) casework, which is, of course, understood to include the single man and woman. This does not necessarily mean assuming all the family work of any community. In many places the family field is already wisely divided with other agencies, such as so-called relief societies, the Society for the Prevention of Cruelty to

Children, and Widow's Pension funds; but it should be clearly understood that the need for family casework is the primary factor in determining our casework function. This would mean that relief giving in itself would no longer be considered a function, and that Charity Organization societies would assume responsibility for relief only in those families where they were doing the family casework. (Ormsby, 1969: 118–19)

The upshot of the recommendations was to refocus the work of the Association's 200 member agencies "on what Porter Lee termed 'disorganized families' rather than on 'destitute families,'" opening the way "to serve other than poor families and to make family casework treatment available to all families in the community who needed it" (Ibid.: 81). The final recommendation of the committee reflected the association's new direction by once again changing its name, this time to the American Association for Organizing Family Social Work. The social work commodity was slowly and subtly being fashioned to a new service market.

THE PSYCHIATRIC CHALLENGE

The flowering of psychiatric social work in the 1920s was also a product of the war and the initial work of the Red Cross in the Home Service and particularly in the public health hospitals. The power of medical/psychiatric knowledge and ideology to pervade other casework specializations, and ultimately to redirect the entire field, lay in its capacity to provide entree to and control over the rich new market for social work among the growing middle class. (Its power still derives from this capacity.) An association with medicine and psychiatry also helped. A set of potent concepts for understanding and treating deviant behavior and character formation expanded on principles opened up in *Social Diagnosis*. Individual and family problems could now be interpreted in psychological and psychodynamic terms befitting a "more worthy" clientele, rather than in terms of moral and economic deficiencies. This is not to imply that either social work theory or practice in the 1920s were "deluged" by a wave of psychoanalytic theory, as several revisionist studies have pointed out (Alexander, 1972; Field, 1980). Rather, there is evidence of wide discrepancies between the psychodynamic ideas espoused by a small number of social work leaders and the actual practice of social caseworkers, and a slow, uneven dissemination of information and technologies, even in the more receptive child welfare field (Field, 1980).

Even so, the new-found potency bound up with the psychiatric perspective enabled the psychiatric social workers to mount an effective challenge to the preeminent position of the family caseworkers. In this light, the move of the AAOC to give up relief and emphasize family treatment could be considered more than a response to new opportunity. It was also a recognition that family caseworkers had to extend and modify Mary Richmond's synthesis to preempt the momentum of the psychiatric segment.

As stated in Part 1, social work control of a market means that social workers must regulate the distribution outlets where services are exchanged, namely, the agencies. In the agencies social workers must be willing and able by virtue of their positions to insist that only persons who meet qualifications established by social workers should be hired to fill staff vacancies. This, in turn, requires the presence of training institutions and associations that produce the social workers who can set the standards and fill the vacancies. In other words, a group of social workers has to recognize a market opportunity and be able to organize itself enough politically to take advantage of it; these are the political-economic functions of professional schools and associations.

Leading psychiatric social workers recognized that meeting the service needs associated with World War 1 represented a promising marketing opportunity. The challenge was how to effectively take advantage of it. The stresses of the war experience for very large numbers of military personnel and their families had precipitated a host of problems that fell into the purview of psychiatrists and social workers. Psychiatrists held commanding positions in the public health hospitals where war-caused neurological disabilities and "neuroses" were treated. In medicine the psychiatric segment was winning new respect through these circumstances and the influx of Freudian ideas from Europe. Social workers were involved from the beginning in the necessary accompanying services to families through their Red Cross "franchise" in the Home Service and public health hospitals. But unlike the central prewar position of the COS movement, the psychiatric movement, headed by Mary Jarrett at the Boston Psychopathic Hospital, was still fairly limited. An insufficient number of social workers had experience in psychiatric work in 1917–18 for the psychiatric social work "wing" to gain a firm foothold in the new market.[16]

The immediate solution to this problem of market control was to increase the production of suitably trained psychiatric social workers. This was accomplished by the establishment of a school for psychiatric social workers at Smith College in 1918 under the joint auspices of the college, the National Committee for Mental Hygiene, and the Boston Psychopathic Hospital. At the same time, the New York School of Social Work developed a department of mental hygiene, and the Pennsylvania School of Social and Health Work offered courses in social psychiatry which were reorganized on a departmental basis in 1919. For impressionable young social workers who entered these programs the new psychiatric content was heady stuff and its intrapsychic focus was clear. Bertha Reynolds's description of that first summer at Smith captures this aura:

> The revolutionary content of what we learned in that summer at Smith stayed with us, if the classifications did not. We thought in terms of patients as individuals. We social workers were most concerned, as the psychiatrists were, with what went on inside the patient. It was also our job to know what, in his family, community life, and war service, had contributed to his illness. We were eager to help get the patient back to normal living, but to do so mainly by restoring him to himself, when, as a whole person, we liked to believe that he could cope with his life conditions in his own way.
>
> Our concentration on therapy, rather than on the social accompaniments of the patient's illness, was brought out when the class was eagerly awaiting the assignments for six months of field practice. When the announcement was finally made in August, those who could not be accommodated in army hospitals or Red Cross units, but were sent to the New York Charity Organization Society, were highly disappointed. "We did not come here to learn social work but psychotherapy," they said. (1963: 61)

The high status of psychiatry and the potential of the market rapidly attracted recruits to the new casework specialization. At the National Conference of Social Work in Atlanta in 1919 social workers crammed into a hall to hear Mary Jarrett (Smith College), Dr. Jessie Taft (Philadelphia), Dr. Bernard Glueck (NY School), and Dr. Edith Spaulding (Smith College) talk about the preparation for the new field of psychiatric social work. Prophetically, the chief issue raised at this meeting was whether the knowledge base of psychiatric social work should be fundamental for all casework training or reserved only for specialized training (Jarrett, 1919). According to Virginia Robinson (1930: 54), "The swing of opinion then, as later, seemed to be in favor of accepting the psychiatric point of view as the basis of all social casework." The challenge of cornering the market was well on its way to being overcome.

Psychiatric social workers solidified their position in the early and mid-1920s when the freshly minted graduates of the new training schools organized and took over the social service departments of veterans hospitals, state mental hospitals, mental hygiene clinics in general hospitals, and child guidance clinics. Philosophically the climate was right for the ascendancy of psychiatric casework and other aspiring service occupations. It was congruent with the "return to normalcy" engineered by successive Republican administrations, which meant adjusting individual and family behavior to the corporate-inspired norms of mass materialism. More broadly, individual rehabilitation was also congruent with the increasing secular rationalization of American society and its notion that through science, environmental mastery was possible, including the restoration of deviant individuals to economically contributing roles.

In "Re-Thinking Social Case Work" (Apr. 1938: 8) Bertha Reynolds later offered a more cynical interpretation. She suggested that the "extraordinary vigor" with which psychiatry and psychiatric social work "took hold" in the 1920s was related to the fear of mass rebellion should the illusion of prosperity be punctured.

Was it because of an unacknowledged fear that people who had begun to move and think in masses would not be easily silenced if they began to speak of very real wrongs? The ruthless suppression of strikes and denial of civil liberties suggests this.

In a period of general disillusionment, reforms seem futile. Studies of individual behavior may well have seemed safer than a search for the causes of sickness in society. Perhaps, after all, it was better to assume that those who agitated for reforms could best be explained, and thus silenced, by one of the new terms for describing a psychopathic personality.

More mundane explanations for the rise of psychiatric social work also apply. In the public health hospitals, psychiatric social workers gained a foothold when the Red Cross was asked in 1919 to organize social services for treating mental diseases like those in civilian hospitals. By 1920, 42 hospitals had such services, and 15 of these psychiatric social work departments were headed by graduates of the first training class at the Smith College School. Psychiatric social workers were solidly entrenched and Red Cross scholarships had made some of this training possible. Their control was demonstrated in 1927, when the Veterans Bureau (1921) took over the operation of social services from the Red Cross. Before the transfer, the bureau established a social work section as part of its medical service, which drew up Civil Service requirements and job functions for the psychiatric social workers throughout the veterans hospital system. Psychiatric social workers shaped these bureau standards through the organized efforts of the Psychiatric Section of the American Association of Hospital Social Workers, later the American Association for Psychiatric Social Work (1926). At the annual meeting of the Psychiatric Section in May 1926, President Maida H. Solomon reported:

> Another interest of the Executive Committee has been its effort to cooperate with the Veteran's Bureau in raising the standards for psychiatric social work. For the first time this year examinations for field positions were rated by a psychiatric social worker. The matter of the possibilities for reclassification of psychiatric social workers in the government service is now being studied by a member of the Executive Committee. (SWHA, Annual Address, unpublished, 1926)

In the mental hygiene field, state mental hospitals and general hospitals with psychiatric clinics burgeoned, and both included psychiatric social workers on the staff teams. In 1920 there were about

100 such clinics for adults or combined adult/children's services; by 1930 the number had risen to 372 (French, 1940: 60). Psychiatric social workers also wrote regularly for *Mental Hygiene* (1917), the journal of the National Committee for Mental Hygiene, which provided an additional independent forum for their ideas outside of social work proper.

Psychiatric social workers gained an especially strong base of power in the child guidance movement where the special contribution of social workers to the treatment team was recognized from the outset. Private foundations undergirded this base through their financial and philosophical support for the movement within social work and nationally. The critical breakthrough came in 1922, after two years of preparatory work. The Commonwealth Fund granted $527,200 to a proposal for a five-year delinquency prevention project from the medical committee of the National Committee for Mental Hygiene (NCMH), headed by Dr. Thomas Salmon. The project set up four divisions: a Bureau of Children's Guidance under the auspices of the New York School of Social Work; a Division on the Prevention of Delinquency of the NCMH to set up and operate experimental child guidance clinics in eight cities; a National Committee on Visiting Teachers; and a Joint Committee on Methods of Preventing Delinquency, to coordinate and interpret the program. The Commonwealth Fund's entrance into this field actively stimulated the organization of child guidance clinics, and by the mid-1920s many local foundations all over the country had jumped on the child guidance/delinquency prevention bandwagon.[17]

The Commonwealth Fund project profoundly affected social work's acceptance of a psychiatric world view. It helped to attract students to this specialization, supported their training, established curricula, and publicized and legitimated the field generally. Furthermore, its close association with visiting teacher work diffused the psychiatric model into school social work.[18]

The close relationship between the Commonwealth Fund and the New York School of Social Work also secured the prominence of psychiatric social work as well as the school's leading position in the field. The association was no accident, as the director of the Commonwealth Fund, Barry C. Smith, had graduated from the New York School in 1914. The fund financed the Bureau of Children's Guidance, first under Dr. Bernard Glueck, who was succeeded by

Dr. Marion E. Kenworthy in 1924. But the fund also financed the school's Mental Hygiene Department which spread psychiatric courses throughout the curriculum. Just within the New York School, over the five years of the bureau's life, 944 different students passed through these courses, 203 students gained field work opportunities, 44 of whom graduated in mental hygiene; and 70 students received Commonwealth Fund fellowships. The fellowships also continued after the five-year project had ended (Meier, 1954: 62–63).

CHAPTER NINE

Funding and Elite Support for Social Work

INTRODUCTION

Two forces stand out politically in the professionalization of social work during the New Era: the Russell Sage Foundation (RSF) and the financial federation movement. The RSF provided critical financial support for the promotion and expansion of family casework and the growth of social work's professional associations and schools. But since the singular influence of the RSF in shaping the character of professional social work has already been reviewed in Part 2, here the RSF's continued influence will be integrated into the discussion and analysis of the developments it helped to shape. The particular impact of financial federations, however, deserves special emphasis. In their crucial role of financial supporters of voluntary social services and as legitimators of a particular definition of charity, financial federations also significantly influenced the nature of social work practice.

FINANCIAL FEDERATIONS

One aim of professionalization is to maximize occupational control over its economic markets. This aim is easier to achieve when the occupation has a sizable body of consumers who want its products and can afford to buy them. Law and medicine each had a middle- and upper-class clientele with the necessary financial resources and desire for their services. Hence these occupations could organize on a fee-for-service basis and protect themselves from control by outsiders. Their success is apparent. Social work did not benefit from any such market advantage. From its inception, its market had been primarily low-income and low-status populations that often could not and/or did not seek social work services and certainly could not afford to pay for them. Consequently, social workers could not market their services in the form of solo or group practices based on fee-for-service, and they could not therefore establish decisive control over their occupation. The development of the public and voluntary social service agency as an organizational type is a unique function of this market situation. Until the mid-1930s, when the public sector hugely expanded its financing for social services, social work's only option for financial support was private philanthropy. In either case social work has struggled continuously with the inability to maximize control over its occupation and consequently has been saddled with an ambiguous professional status.

Without control of a clearly desirable commodity that could be sold in an open consumer market, social work's need for legitimacy and financial resources before the New Deal made it largely dependent upon voluntary charitable contributions and the sanction of societal elites. In the beginning years of social work, these were intimately related in the form of a relatively small population of philanthropic individuals and families who provided the bulk of the support for charitable work. This was an insufficient financial base for social welfare provisions in a rapidly expanding industrial society. Nor was individual philanthropy sufficient financially or extensive enough socially to support social workers' aspirations for professional status. The burgeoning of financial federations in the World War I era solved some of these problems, albeit with some cost. In this respect, financial federations played a special and critical role in social work's professional evolution.

Financial federations as a form of organization were clearly creatures of their times. They began as an organizational innovation before World War I in several large cities, such as Denver (1887), Boston (1895), Cleveland (1913), and Cincinnati (1915). But they could not really flourish until the demands of the war, the postwar "return to normalcy," and the cultural and technological features of a new mass society had established a set of nurturant conditions. In 1918 there were 26 financial federations of Community Chests; by 1929 there were 330, which meant that virtually every city with a population of 100,000 and many smaller centers had some sort of financial federation for purposes of charitable fund-raising.

Like the Charity Organization Societies and the Councils of Social Agencies which the COS movement sponsored, financial federations were expressions of an effort to rationalize the machinery of social welfare. The financial federation brought representatives of the business sector and the social agencies together in a joint organization to raise money for private, agency-based, social welfare services and plan for their development and coordination. The motivations for federation and the fund-raising practices which evolved in the 1920s have not changed significantly today. "It was argued that a financial federation provided for more efficient collection, less annoyance to those solicited, more givers, larger contributions, social education, and greater cooperation in social work" (Dillick, 1953: 91).

The principles of federated fund-raising were essentially: (a) the organization of an emotional, mass appeal for funds, (b) carried out by an army of volunteers, (c) through a single, unified community-wide campaign, (d) with differential solicitation for various segments of the donor population, and especially reaching into the workplace and the corporation. This approach relied heavily on business leadership and new developments in mass communication and public relations technologies to attract contributions. It featured the application of business methods and ethics to philanthropy under the rubric of community cooperation and managerial efficiency.

The major attraction of the financial federation to social work agencies was that it supplied a steady source of financial support for their work. For its adherents, "the financial federation was 'an effort to widen the channel for a greater flow of voluntary contributions from the economic surplus by means of modern efficiency and modern organization, in order that we may purchase more quickly better social conditions and a better social order'" (Lubove, 1965: 189). Between 1916 and 1929 federations provided the financial underpinings for the voluntary social agencies where social work was widely practiced. In 1929 the "economic surplus" tapped by the Community Chests for their constituent agencies was approximately $71,500,000. An equivalent amount of goods and services would cost approximately $479,000,000 in 1987 dollars, using the Consumer Price Index adjustments for inflation (U.S. Dept. of Labor, 1987).

Equally as important, financial federations served as the primary vehicles for selling social work and legitimating it throughout the country. For all intents and purposes federations became "a public relations arm of professional social work, seeking to convince the average citizen that support of welfare was a fundamental civic obligation" (Lubove, 1965: 202). The model for an effective campaign came from business advertising in which social welfare was now a new product to be marketed. "If merchants and manufacturers could 'get returns on thousands of millions of dollars expended each year in practical publicity,' so could social work. The returns to the community would not be measured in dollars and dividends, but in health, happiness, and better lives. . . . The challenge was to adapt techniques developed by business in order to compete with business for the consumer's dollar'" (Lubove, 1965: 203). In 1924 the assessment of the success of the Community Chest movement by one of its major social work spokesmen was that . . . "No movement in the long history of social work has so quickly caught the popular fancy. Through Community Chest methods practically the entire populations of many cities have become interested in social work. Social problems and ways of solving them have become popular topics of conversations. Social work in these cities is recognized as one of the vital forces in the life of the people" (United Way of America, 1977: 52).

Without any other viable alternatives social work leaders were in no position to refuse the kind of political and economic support offered by the financial federation, though many were initially wary of it. Resistance to financial federations developed in 1917, for example, when the American Association for Organizing Charity, the national organization of the COS movement, went on record as being opposed to integrating the councils of social agencies that they were developing alongside the financial federations. Its special committee on financial federations felt that the campaigns did not build up a stable constituency; the committee also feared loss of contact and interest between givers and agencies, expressed doubts about their system for allocating funds, and argued that social work was too easily subordinated to the imperatives of raising funds. Resistance also came from many national organizations, like the Red Cross and the YM-YWCAs, who feared the centralized control of their local community branches would hamper their own considerable fund-raising abilities.

World War I overcame the opposition. In the mobilization of community support for the war, government and business joined hands to reach into the local communities and form hundreds of defense councils and war chests. School centers conveniently became the base for these operations, usurping the growing neighborhood organization movement in the process. The slogans of the Council of National Defense and the United States Bureau of Education were respectively: "Every school district a community council for national service", and "Every schoolhouse a community capital and every community a little democracy" (Dillick, 1953: 71). The American Red Cross and the YMCA raised unprecedented sums of money through their business-directed campaigns conducted in conjunction with the local chests. By the end of the war in 1918, some 400 war chests had raised more than $100,000,000. At the same time, the approach of the financial federation was deeply etched into the community mind. By establishing a pattern of concerted, community-wide campaigns, with centralized budget allocations, the business sector also gained an avenue for controlling voluntary social welfare. Congress further assisted the growth of the Community Chest movement by making charitable contributions legally deductible from taxable income to promote the war chests.

Before World War 1, community organization in social work encompassed a wide range of activities (Fisher, 1984). The conservative tendencies of the charity organization and settlement movements for rationalization of social services and social integration competed with more liberal and radical tendencies toward social and economic reform movements of every kind, e.g., industrial safety, labor organization, women's suffrage, civil rights, public health, social insurance, recreation, and peace. Community organization had also included a bottom-up, political reform component, aimed at developing local participatory structures and citizenship training. Examples of such efforts were the previously mentioned school/community center movement which peaked in 1919 with 667 centers in 107 cities, and the Cincinnati Social Unit Experiment from 1917 to 1920. For some leaders, such as Mary Parker Follett, neighborhood organization represented the very foundation of industrial democracy, the basis of a "new state." Its ambitious aims were:

> to give a knock-out blow to party organization, to make a direct
> and continuous connection between our daily lives and needs

and our government, to diminish race and class prejudices, to create a responsible citizenship, and to train and discipline the new democracy; or to sum up all these things, to break down party organization and to make a creative citizenship the force of American political life. (Follett, 1918: 217)

While reform activities did not end after the war, as financial federation leaders became the chief legitimators of social work, they were able to impose their narrower, more conservative views of community organization. Thus the prevailing definition of the community organization function in social work became agency service coordination, administration, community fund raising, and community integration. Community organization as social and political reform was de-legitimated. This direction was presaged by the formation in 1918 of a national organization of financial federations, with the presumptuous name of American Association for Community Organization (AACO). Its organizers included: Charles R. Cooper, head resident of Kingsley House in Pittsburgh; Sherman C. Kingsley, executive director of the Cleveland Welfare Federation; William J. Norton, former director of the Cincinnati Federation; C. M. Bookman, executive director of the Cincinnati Council of Social Agencies; and Elwood Street, executive director of the Louisville Federation of Social Agencies. The AACO's purpose was "to encourage and stimulate collective community planning, and the development of better standards in the work of community organization for social work" (United Way, 1977: 38). This community planning function increasingly included partnership with the previously independent councils of social agencies, a fact officially recognized in 1927 in a change of name from the AACO to the Association of Community Chests and Councils (ACCC).

The imposition of a conservative definition of community organization by federation leaders in the 1920s was not an idle abstraction. It meant the imposition of community integration by the business sector through the exclusion from the Community Chest, hence from financial support, of controversial organizations or groups that challenged the existing social order. C. M. Bookman articulated this perspective at an AACO national conference in 1924 when he warned that:

Community Chests, in order to be successful, must develop public opinion favorable to their work. There are, however, many social movements instigated by minorities which, though sound in their social point of view, are nevertheless militantly opposed. In their own interest, as well as in the interest of the Community Chest, these minorities should not trust their programs to public opinion. Such agencies should not be members of the Community Chest. (United Way, 1977: 54)

The full import of conservative business control of the social welfare apparatus was captured by Jesse Steiner in 1925 (pp. 81-82) in one of the earliest textbooks on community organization, a text which generally viewed community organization as a force for community integration. Steiner observed that "capitalistic industry" had a vested interest in "scrutiniz[ing] proposed social changes to see if they in any way endanger the existing economic system." Thus industrial leaders opposed the restriction of immigration, social insurance, workman's compensation laws, parcel post, and "any other social changes that were clearly in the interests of the mass of people."

Social work and social workers were valued in this struggle so long as they conformed to these conservative interests and indeed were sometimes used to advance them. This was as true in Southern mill villages where mill employers controlled the direction of community work to prevent discussion of wages and working conditions, as it was in the steel industry where "the social worker is welcomed and cordially supported when he comes along to pick up the wreckage, but he must not question economic policies if he turns his attention to preventive work." And, still more to the point, it was true also of the corporate controlled financial federations (Trolander, 1975).

A case in point is the difficulty of including the budget of an organization like the Consumers' League in a joint financial campaign of a welfare federation. The fact that the success of a financial drive for the support of social agencies would seem to be imperilled by the inclusion of an organization that is frankly concerned with industrial policies and problems throws light on industry's conception of the proper sphere of social work. (Steiner, 1925: 81–82)

In terms of the professionalization of social work, then, the financial federation movement financed social work and diffused it throughout the nation, while also fashioning social work into a service commodity compatible with the corporate values of industrial capitalism (Leiby, 1978).

CHAPTER TEN

Consolidating the Social Work Enterprise

SOCIAL WORK'S LABOR MARKET

After World War I social work's occupational sphere included a sufficiently large group of practitioners from which to build a profession, but occupational control was problematic. Above all, occupational control requires the capacity to regulate commodity production. If the commodity is a human service, this means regulating the people who provide it in terms of who the providers will be, the kind and quality of the service, and the auspices or conditions under which it will be offered. Social workers were not unified as a vocational group. They did not agree among themselves about social work's knowledge base, practice boundaries, or the qualifications necessary for practice. Nor were qualifications controlled by any central body which held their allegiance or the allegiance of their employers. Therefore, qualifications were neither uniform, stringent, nor binding. Unification was a central task for building the profession; and, in fact, unification (in the sense we are discussing it) is still a greater or lesser concern for all professions as any prior basis for unification is always subject to negotiation and change due to changing political, economic, and social conditions.

To correct this situation, social work leaders recognized the need for coalitions of practitioners and training schools on a national scale. These organizations would perform such regulatory functions as promotion, gate keeping, and socialization through activities like standard setting, licensing, lobbying, and educational accreditation. They would be the true foundation of a professional enterprise for social work. Like other industrial corporations, the new enterprise would slowly replace a diffuse, idiosyncratic response to market opportunities for social work with a centralized, better-coordinated, and more standardized system for market control and mass production. These activities were the essence of professionalization. Due to aspirations to higher social class and status, this was the route that occupations based on abstract knowledge and service chose to follow to gain security and power in a corporate capitalist society.

Specific statistics on the number of social workers in the United States before 1930 do not exist, as the federal census used the classification "religious, charity and welfare workers" prior to that time. In 1920, the number of persons so occupied was 46,000 (compared to some 19,000 in this category in 1910) (U.S. Bureau of the Census, 1975). This bit of information offers some insight into the task which faced social workers aspiring to professional status after World War I. First, the classification suggests the extensive growth but undefined limits of social work activity at that time. Second, the classification also indicates the fuzzy image of social work held by the public. Both the image and the reality would need to be altered. Third, the numbers show the pool of workers from which the profession had to be constructed. To gain market control the profession would have to include a significant number of these workers and win their allegiance to a common vision. At the same time, it would have to exclude some equally significant, if not much greater, portion in order to carve out a unique sphere of occupational control.

No single organization entirely monitored the expansion of the social work labor market during World War I, and none controlled it. In the final analysis, though, a profession is a vocation, a means of earning a livelihood. Without market control, social workers could not establish "careers" with decent salaries. This concern was very much in the minds of the social workers who organized the National Social Worker's Exchange (NSWE) as an independent agency in 1917. The NSWE succeeded the Social Work Division of the Intercollegiate Bureau of Occupations (1913), whose purpose was to find social work jobs for college women. More than a vocational bureau, the NSWE also dealt with recruitment, salary levels, working conditions, standard setting, and job analysis.

In 1918, the manager of the NSWE, Edith Shatto King, found herself swamped by requests for hundreds of social workers from a variety of voluntary and public social agencies (*Survey*, 1918). She had a sufficient supply of applicants to refer to these positions, but many were deemed unsatisfactory due to their lack of training. A number of these "unqualified" applicants included "women of education and refinement, for the first time in their lives forced to earn a livelihood through war necessity," but inadequately prepared for social work positions and often "not adaptable or able to benefit by training, as is the young college girl." Could these have been women who might have volunteered their services in better times?

Even after the war ended, the demand for social workers continued in all areas but industrial social work. In 1921 the Vocational Bureau of a reorganized NSWE reported that it had handled 1,522 positions representing every field of social work, of which 643 were filled by social workers recommended by the bureau. The breakdown by field was: casework (all facets), 537; group activity, 252; social reform, 233; institutions, 208; industry, 51; miscellaneous, 241 (*The Compass*, May 1921, September 1921, March 1922).

The oversupply of untrained social workers faced by the NSWE in 1918 also had not abated by 1921. At the end of that year, the Vocational Bureau had registered 3,596 individual social workers for specific positions, vocational information, or general reference services; 923 of these were registered for the first time, raising the total number of "case records" in the Bureau to over 6,000, a figure far in excess of the numbers receiving any sort of university training in social work. In addition, 3,334 persons came to the bureau "for more casual information or personal services," making a total of nearly 7,000 individuals who had received some assistance from the bureau that year (*The Compass*, March 1922).

With an inadequate supply of trained social workers and a ready supply of the untrained, in a high-demand market context, many social agencies continued to hire and train workers on the job. Furthermore, the demonstrated superiority of trained workers was by no means publicly accepted yet, though headway had been made in some quarters. This state of affairs made for low social work salaries and benefits. Salary scales were also kept down by the independent incomes which "[made] it possible for some would-be case workers to follow an unprofitable profession" (*The Family*, March 1920: 7). While wages were going up in other fields, in 1918 "visitors and case workers in charity organizations receive[d] less than competent stenographers, while settlement and civic workers in many instances [were] earning less than men and women in trades" (King, 1918). In 1920 the Committee on Salary Schedules of the American Association for Organizing Family Social Work (AAOFSW) reported that casework salaries were inadequate to cover living costs (*The Family*, April 1920). In 1921 and 1922 social workers in all areas did not fare much better, most earning less than $1,800 annually (*The Compass*, March 1922, Wilder, March 1922). Social workers in the public sector were both underpaid and lacked civil service protections and career advancement opportunities. A study of social work salaries in public welfare departments, which by 1924 existed in all but six states, found "on the whole a rather low scale for executive officers, a fair rate for typical field workers, low maxima for social work staff, and a lack of salary ranges of the kind that would promise advancement" (Klein, 1924: 6).

With the law of supply and demand working as well in social work as it was in other industries, social work leaders faced an anomaly. The NSWE wanted to recruit and train new and different types of workers, but the salary standards were too low to attract them. In order to raise salaries, they had to assert stronger control over the employment market. At this juncture it became apparent that a long-range strategy was necessary, and there were really only two alternatives, unionization or professionalization. The momentum was clearly toward the latter. The views of influential leaders in family casework were shared by many. They believed that to raise salaries, the "moving impulse [would] have to come from the workers themselves, rather than from the boards of the supporting charitable public; for the public will accept underpaid service as long as it can get it" (*The Family*, April 1920). But unionization was not genteel enough to be a suitable option.

Nor will the workers unionize and make demands—they are too devoted to embarrass their employers in this way, and too much wrapped up in the fortunes of the families under their care to dream of using the strike method of enforcing attention to the justice of their cause. . . . Moreover, there is something about a union, and all things associated with the idea of a union, which is obnoxious; the press of the country has put unions in ill odor, and social workers, like school teachers, are too respectable to try to attain their ends in this way. (*The Family*, April 1920: 8)

The time was ripe for an encompassing professional organization which would have the support of social work practitioners as well as the larger social agencies where they could be employed. The lead for higher salaries and qualifications would have to come from "the great societies, with general secretaries who are strong enough to stand up against and educate their boards, and well enough paid to insist on higher pay for themselves" (Ibid.). By 1920 two attempts to form an inclusive professional association had aborted. The first was organized informally by Mary Richmond and Ida Cannon in 1918–19 as a "Committee on Professional Organization"; the second, parallel to this, came from the "Conference on Demobilization" after the war. The conference consisted of a body of some forty agency executives and leading social workers who actually drafted a tentative constitution for a National Association of Social Workers in 1919. Neither group had a sufficient network of contacts to build a national association. The National Social Worker's Exchange proved a willing and more apt vehicle.

THE PROFESSIONAL ENTERPRISE TAKES HOLD

The Professional Association

The functions of a professional association must be broader than an employment agency's. It must develop a coherent ideology and engender normative cohesion among the members of the occupational sphere it seeks to control. It must also recruit enough members to be politically able to convince the public of its right to a special occupational status. In its original form, the National Social Worker's Exchange did not provide these broader functions. However, it did have the advantage of being a membership agency with a central membership list in 1920 of some 1,700 members and 83 institutions (Buell, 1923). These members could be said to share a collective consciousness about social work, which was helped along by a monthly newsletter, *The Compass*.

The NSWE also had other critical advantages. Its involvement in the social work labor market had opened channels of communication with potential social workers and social agencies, public and private, around the country. This network extended well beyond its paid membership. Structurally, its board of directors contained representation from the major clusters of social work activity and from major cities. It included reformers and settlement leaders such as Dr. Charles Beard, Robert Woods, and Sophonisba Breckinridge, as well as family caseworkers like Gertrude Vaile and Frank Bruno.[19] As representatives of cities, board members were expected to be concerned with local needs and conditions in addition to the national picture. All of these features gave NSWE the potential for bringing in the new blood and energy it would need to build a vital enterprise.

At the same time, the NSWE was also controlled by the "Eastern social work establishment" without whose sanction it could not hope to flourish. Its evolution from the Intercollegiate Bureau of Occupations had entailed financial help from the New York School and the Russell Sage Foundation and rent-free offices in the RSF building. Its board included John M. Glenn, director, RSF; Mary van Kleeck, head of the Division of Industrial Studies, RSF; C. C. Carstens, director of the RSF-funded Child Welfare League; and, Porter Lee, Director of New York School. In the transition from the Exchange to the American Association of Social Workers (AASW), this "Eastern social work establishment" also managed to gain control over the emerging professional enterprise.

In 1919, Josiah Bradley Buell, a 26-year-old protege of Mary van Kleeck, was one of the young leaders who contributed to fashioning the early professional enterprise. While working on a study of the U.S. Employment Service in conjunction with the Sage Foundation, Buell was approached by Edith Shatto King, manager of NSWE, for advice on NSWE's problems. With the approval of the Exchange board, Buell chaired a committee to study the possibilities for further professional development;[20] it recommended formation of a national-level professional association. Discussion and wide circulation of the report for several months sparked the interest of social workers across the country.

In the spring of 1920 the NSWE formed a steering committee to follow up on the association idea. Its members were Brad Buell, Mary van Kleeck, Clare Tousley, Veronica Wilder, and Philip Jacobs, publicity director of the National TB Association. By the next winter, the Exchange board had appointed a large Central Council with wide geographical representation. It then turned over authority for the NSWE to the Central Council and its Executive Committee. C. C. Carstens was president. Buell chaired a committee of the new Central Council on Publicity and Education, whose job "was to get a new agency promoted, floated, and organized" (Buell, 1967: 17). After a year of planning and organizing, the membership of the NSWE (and anyone else who could attend) voted the American Association of Social Workers into existence at its annual meeting, held on June 27, 1921, during the National Conference of Social Work in Milwaukee (Buell, 1967; *The Compass*, February-June 1921).[21]

During the period of preparation for the Milwaukee meeting the "Eastern social work establishment" set the machinery in motion to dominate the AASW. One avenue of control was the preselection of an executive of "national reputation" for the association, who was hired as the National Director of the Exchange in June 1921, three weeks before the switch-over. Mary van Kleeck led a search, which, after several rejections, selected Graham Romeyn Taylor. Taylor was an associate editor of the *Survey* and well known as an author and researcher with an interest in civic affairs and various reform activities. Nevertheless, he was not a leading social work leader of his day. Nor was he a principal figure in the settlement movement despite the fact that, as the son of Graham Taylor, founder of the Chicago Commons, he had literally grown up in it. His hiring came about more prosaically. Barry Smith, director of the Commonwealth Fund which also had granted funds to the Exchange along with RSF, exerted influence on Taylor's behalf, as a way of fulfilling an obligation to the elder Taylor (Beissel correspondence, 1967).

Graham Romeyn Taylor apparently did not express strong convictions about the nature of the social work enterprise during his year-and-a-half stint as AASW's director. Or, if he did, these did not revolve around past associations with the social reform/settlement wing of social work. At the Milwaukee meeting, the founders of AASW established the governance structure for the association, a 9-member Executive Committee and a 58-member Central Council, and elected a proposed slate to fill the positions. Unlike the membership of the old Exchange Board, not one of these Central Council members was a social reformer or settlement leader of the stature of a Robert Woods or Lillian Wald.[22] No one from the "Chicago School" was represented, not the Abbotts, Sophonisba Breckinridge, or even Lea Taylor, Graham R. Taylor's sister (SWHA, NSWE minutes, June 1921).[23]

The composition of the executive committee consolidated the "Eastern establishment's" position. Its officers were: Owen Lovejoy, NYC, National Child Labor Committee, president; Clare M. Tousley, NY COS, 1st vice-president; Bradley Buell, NSWE, secretary; W. W. Norton, New School of Social Research, NYC (not to be confused with W. J. Norton of the Community Chest movement), treasurer. The remaining members elected by the central council were: Harriet Anderson, American Red Cross, Washington D.C.; Grace H. Childs, member of a distinguished New York family; David Holbrook, director, AAOFSW, NYC; Philip Jacobs, National TB Association, NYC; and Mary van Kleeck, RSF, NYC. The 2nd and 3rd vice-presidents—respectively, Gertrude Vaile, AAOFSE, Denver, and Rose J. McHugh, National Catholic Welfare Council, Chicago— were not members of the executive committee (SWHA, NSWE, minutes, June 1921).

After the AASW was formed, it turned to the closely related organization-building activities of determining membership qualifications, recruiting, and fostering participation. These tasks inevitably raised control issues around matters of inclusion/exclusion, ideology, and governance. Bradley Buell and Edith Shatto King, now staff members of AASW, had been heavily involved in all of these activities to date; they naturally continued this work after the Milwaukee meeting. Therefore they were also at the center of the internal conflicts that soon developed. (Taylor's role as executive is less clear.)

In 1921 the task of establishing membership qualifications was the least controversial. The association aimed to raise social work standards in the field, but few schools of social work existed, fewer still could grant two-year master's degrees, and few practicing social workers could meet stringent educational tests. It was clear that the enterprise initially had to proceed slowly and pragmatically on this front.[24] Qualifications would be continuously modified over time in response to political-economic opportunities and pressures.

The original AASW membership criteria, drafted by Buell and modified by membership input, held until 1933. Members of the

NSWE at the time of AASW's founding were "written in " as charter members of the new organization. Beyond this, the qualifications for the classification of members stressed practical experience in recognized social agencies with some substitutions allowed for approved education. Another class of junior members for persons 21 to 24 years old gave special recognition to professional education over experience.[25] A category for dues-paying organizational members was also retained.

The effect of the membership qualifications was the inclusion, by dint of experience, of almost anyone who chose to be identified with social work. A screening process was set up through membership committees of local chapters with final approval resting in the membership committee of the central council. Recruitment to the professional movement, however, progressed slowly. By July 1922 the original 1,700 members grew to 2,200, and by the following April to 2,700. In February 1930, AASW had 4,748 members; almost all belonged to one of 43 local chapters around the country (Buell, 1923; *The Compass*, March 1930: 2). These figures still represented only a small portion of the persons practicing social work in the United States.

Establishing membership control over the organization was a more controversial issue. From the perspective of the staff who were recruiting members and stimulating the development of local chapters, it was important that AASW policy not be controlled by an elitist New York group. The membership expected participatory democracy and the logic of organizational expansion demanded it. In Buell's words, "I knew also that anything that stemmed out of New York was suspect out around the country. If the idea of New York domination got around, a revolt from the provinces was sure to come. We had taken great pains to spread representation, to make people all over the country really feel that this was 'their' organization and that their voice had been important in getting it started and would continue to be in keeping it going" (Buell, 1967: 24).

Since he who pays the piper calls the tune—and this had already been demonstrated in the hiring of the AASW director—the control issue took shape around the sources for financing the organization, namely, self-support versus outside control. Buell, and a faction of the executive committee and their supporters, pushed for the principle of an AASW budget based entirely on the revenues from membership. Mary van Kleeck and Graham Taylor, whom Buell viewed as van Kleeck's pawn, and their supporters (Buell, 1967: 24), opposed this concept as unrealistic. They did not want to give up the grants from the Russell Sage Foundation and the potential for other such sources of future revenue.[26]

In a meeting preliminary to the AASW annual meeting in Providence, June 1922, the Buell faction managed to have the finance issue placed on the agenda of the annual meeting. In the interim, Harry Hopkins (later of Roosevelt Administration fame), newly arrived in New York as Assistant Director of the Association for Improving the Condition of the Poor, chaired a committee to draft a set of resolutions on this issue. The membership did approve these "Providence Resolutions" at the annual meeting, essentially putting forward the principle of a gradual increase in membership support, until full support would take effect on January 1, 1925. (The goal was actually reached in 1927.) A saving clause in the resolutions, however, also gave the association freedom to accept gifts or grants from foundations for special projects. A Joint Vocational Service was then created in 1922 as an independent entity with its own board, but closely tied to the AASW, and this was supported for several years through RSF grants.

Through the Providence resolutions and other constitutional devices that allowed for Central Council growth and representation from local chapters, the membership did retain control over the AASW. In the aftermath of the internal conflict over the resolutions, however, the AASW staff turned over completely. Graham Romeyn Taylor, never terribly convincing in this position, resigned quietly in November 1922. By July 1, 1923, Edith Shatto King, who served as an interim executive secretary, Brad Buell, and Paul Beissel had all resigned to move into other positions. Phillip Klein came on as the new executive secretary as of May 1, 1923; he was succeeded by Walter West in 1927. Harry Hopkins, whose talents had quickly become apparent through the Providence resolutions, was elected AASW president at the June 1923 annual meeting.

Throughout the 1920s the AASW worked diligently to raise social work standards and promote it as a profession. It recruited social workers to the association and college students to social work careers. It worked on defining social work and its various specializations. It developed codes for ethical practice. It encouraged other organizations and associations of social workers, such as the American Association of Hospital Social Workers, the American Association for Organizing Family Social Work, and the National Federation of Settlements, to define and upgrade their standards for practice and membership. It worked with the Association of Training Schools to develop objective standards for accreditation, basic social work curriculum requirements, and educational criteria for membership. It studied and promoted better salaries and working conditions for social workers in the voluntary sector as well as in the growing public sector. It began to consider the place of private practice in social work (*The Compass*, May 1926), and the potential for social work licensing. Above all the AASW stood for social work *autonomy*, the hallmark of any profession, and exceedingly important within social work's organizational milieu. As Porter Lee stated, "In the long run, the standards of social workers will be safer in the hands of social workers themselves than in the hands of organizations. From this point of view, the continued life of the Association as the mouth-piece of social workers themselves seems to me to be indispensable" (*The Compass*, July/August 1926: 6).

For all of this, social work professionalization proceeded slowly. The 5,000 members of AASW at the end of the decade were still too small a minority of social work practitioners to bring about any immediate and graphic rise in social work salaries and working conditions. While executive salaries rose as agency size doubled, line social workers in the 1920s still earned less than teachers. Average starting salaries, still well below $2,000, did not keep pace with rises in the standard of living (*The Compass*, February, 1926; Hurlin, 1926; November 1929; Brown, 1942: 169). When a Baltimore Chapter study in 1926 recommended $1,500 a year as the starting salary for inexperienced beginning social workers who had completed a two-year graduate training program in social work, the editor of *The Compass* replied,

Compensation of that character, after four years of college and two years of special training, would seem to be placing our profession still in the position of an apologetic seeker for a place in the sun, or in a class with those of the relative leisure class who expect from social work salaries merely some pin-money rather than a reasonable living. No profession can hope to come of age if it is not self-supporting both in respect to ideals and also in respect to economic returns (May 1926: 4).

Social work had still not solved its supply/demand dilemma. Many administrators and board members agreed on the need for trained personnel, but too few insisted on it or were willing yet to pay the higher costs (*The Compass*, February 1926: 7). One analysis suggested that,

> Social work is not essential from the public's point of view (a strike of teachers would be fatal, while a strike of social workers would be considered somewhat humorous!). . . . The law of supply and demand tends to keep down salaries, thus increasing turnover and supplying no incentive to the earnest, well-prepared caseworker to stay in that field. This will continue to be true until a professional consciousness strong enough to permeate the public becomes operative. (*The Compass*, May 1926: 1)

Nevertheless, the movement for professionalization retained a strong and committed core. Enough social workers had invested in the professional enterprise to keep it from being abandoned, and some strides toward occupational control were being made. With the help of Ralph Hurlin of the Russell Sage Foundation, the census committee of AASW succeeded in convincing the federal Census Bureau "of the practicality of recognizing social workers as a distinct occupational group" by the end of the decade (Glenn, Brandt, & Andrews, 1947: 411). This important step toward official recognition of the profession helped to set the stage for the inclusion of social work standards in public welfare in the 1930s when the public sector would overshadow the private.

As the movement for professionalization progressed, it also became more ingrown and parochial. The divisions between major segments of social work widened. The case for professionalization and technical expertise was avidly promoted in publications like *The Family, Mental Hygiene,* and *The Compass.* The *Survey Graphic/Midmonthly* (1923) and the *Social Service Review* at the University of Chicago reported on professional developments more self-critically, and emphasized much broader issues of social policy and social concern. Caseworkers did not take too well to Eduard Lindeman's criticism in the *Survey* (April 1924) that as the trained social worker becomes "the symbol of technique" rather than "the embodiment of sentiment," he would become removed from "the main currents of life," "the modern symbol of autocracy, since the expert functions by virtue of what he knows, not by virtue of what he shares in knowing." (For a response, see *The Family*, May 1924: 60.) These views represented struggles with different definitions of the meaning of community, the special community of professionals versus the shared community of all human beings.

In 1926 a study found that 60% of the 25,000 paid social workers in the United States were caseworkers, with group workers at 20%, the next highest category. More than half practiced in the nation's 33 largest cities (Lubove, 1965: 133). In Massachusetts, though their distribution was apparently atypical, with 39% concentrated in the recreation and settlement field, a 1930 study found that less than 20% of these workers had a certificate or diploma from a school of social work (*The Compass*, March 1930). In the medical and psychiatric field better than 40% had these credentials. This disparity was symptomatic of the powerful influence of the medical model and the profession's preoccupation with the development of casework technique to the neglect of social concerns.

The professional association was open to settlement workers, administrators, and researchers, but many fewer joined than did caseworkers (Brown, 1932: 122; *The Compass*, August 1929: 4). Practicality as well as ideological differences accounted for this situation and mutually reinforced it. As educational qualifications began to require training in member schools of the American Association of Schools of Social Work, the balance of membership shifted further toward caseworkers over settlement workers, reformers, and administrators. Since the curricula of schools of social work stressed casework technique, other kinds of social workers were unlikely to pursue further specialized training to meet vocational goals (Bruno, 1957: 150; Trolander, 1975: 35; Karpf, 1931). In this and other ways university-based training for social work slowly exerted a defining influence over the professional social work commodity.

The Professional Schools

Professionalizing occupations have sought university affiliation because of a long association between upper-class culture and university education. By the 1900s the university's ties to corporate wealth and the need for a skilled workforce made it the main arbiter of the professed meritocracy. Any occupation seeking professional status had to become publicly identified with the compelling values of the academy: science and dispassionate rationality. The academy, for its part, did not entirely disdain such ideological claims, even though much of professional education is highly practical. The growth of "professional" schools helped the university expand its own corporate domain.

Along with status by affiliation, the university offered unique advantages for occupational control. Specialized training programs created a professional subculture through socializing their neophytes to a consistent set of norms and values. They also provided a more efficient system than apprenticeship models for reproducing a standardized work force for regional and national labor markets. Educational qualifications could be easily used as a screen for selective entry to an occupation, and they could be defended on grounds of merit rather than privilege. In addition, as a center for certification, the university encouraged, even required, the formation of similar certification bodies for its occupational schools. Since the accrediting organization sets the parameters for the content and process of a school's educational program, in a sense it is the most basic instrument for occupational control.

Before the turn of the century, aspiring social work leaders had recognized the necessity of broader "scientific" training outside of the parochial social agencies. Since many of these leaders had been university educated in the United States and abroad, affiliation with the academy was hardly a foreign idea. The influential comments of Flexner and Frankfurter at the 1915 NCCC meetings further reinforced their beliefs.

As with other aspects of professionalization, the period after World War I was propitious for social work education in the university to take hold. Its success, worked out over several years, was a marriage of accommodation between the conflicting cultures and demands of the academy, the practice community, and political-economic realities. Some of the arrangements consummated during this period set the stage for a number of the profession's most persistent conflicts, such as whether the entry level for the profession should be an undergraduate or graduate degree, and the extent of technical versus general education in the professional curriculum.

Social work leaders needed the support of the practice community to successfully move training into the university. The agencies provided the jobs after the training, thus the incentives for students to attend the university. They provided many of the instructors for the programs; they furnished the settings for fieldwork, already the centerpiece of social work education. To a lesser degree the agencies also influenced the allocation of the financial and political resources of their philanthropic supporters. All these trump cards put the agencies into a strong position to shape the content and process of university-based training.

The advantages of university affiliation were by no means uniformly manifest to agency boards and staff. Resistance stemmed from several sources. As social work changed from an upper-class avocation to a paid vocation and as its labor market expanded, social-class divisions appeared in the work force between the social work leadership and a large proportion of its practitioners. As late as 1925 a study of a cross section of 740 social work positions found that 60.1% of the incumbents had no more than a high school education. Only about a third had had any kind of formal social work education. A high proportion of social work executives had similar educational backgrounds (Deardoff, 1925). Such administrators probably could not see the value of abstract university training and undoubtedly found the idea threatening since they could neither afford nor qualify for such education.

Ideologically and practically, the resistance partly represented a reluctance to pay a predominantly female labor force the higher salaries merited by training. As a primary vocational outlet for emancipated women (blacks were not yet in a position to compete for these jobs), social work agencies, largely controlled by the male business community on its boards and community chests, had an abundant supply of cheap labor. Also, some upper-class women with training, part of the former volunteer force, were not concerned about salaries, and thereby served as a conservatizing element in the social work labor market. In a slightly different vein, if the agencies were to give up the apprenticeship model, they would be replacing a cheap labor supply with a more expensive one. Workers would also be trained less narrowly for specific agency needs, outside of the direct control of the agencies.

By 1918, agency resistance to university-based training was already breaking down. There were some 20 "educational projects" in social work, more than twice the number a decade earlier (Bruno, 1944; Brown, 1942), concentrated in the eastern third of the country but extending as far west as Nebraska, south to Louisiana, and north to Canada. Several were undergraduate courses or programs in the departments of sociology of state universities. Several were independent schools which had evolved from agency training programs. In Frankfurter's words, most had at least a "platonic connection" to a university (Bruno, 1957: 144).

In 1919, under Porter Lee's guidance, fifteen social work schools formed an embryonic accrediting body, the Association of Training Schools for Professional Social Work.[27] This coalition marked the formal commitment by social work leaders to university-based education; it soon insisted that new schools could not be admitted without being an integral part of an accredited university. By 1923 each of the independent schools met this requirement except for the New York and Pennsylvania schools, the National Catholic School in Washington, and the National Jewish School of Social Service in New York (Bruno, 1957: 144). By 1929 the Association of Professional Schools of Social Work (its new name) had 28 members (Meier, 1954: 60). Several other institutions in the United States and Canada, unaffiliated with the association, also were offering organized social work curricula for full-time students (Hagerty, 1931; Brown, 1942: 31).[28]

The leverage for university affiliation came from the expansion of social casework during and after World War I. In particular, the Red Cross training courses in home services, offered in 15 to 20 universities across the country, demonstrated the need for training centers and the capacity to attract students and financial support.[29] There soon was sufficient market control in specialized areas of casework, first in the psychiatric and medical fields. Their lay and professional leaders were more willing and eager to hire university-trained personnel over "untrained" workers than in other social work areas (*The Compass*, March 1930). They were more able to recruit educationally qualified students, and successfully attracted elite support for scholarships and programmatic grants to the social work schools and departments. Under this stimulation, family casework also became more professionalized. Ironically, despite the concern expressed in the Milford Conference about centering social work in agencies controlled by social workers, it was the standards set by specializations located in already professionalized host settings that led the advance of social work professionalization in the 1920s.

Social work education in the university during the twenties largely reflected the composition, needs, and interests of the casework agencies and social work's market realities. Within social work, casework agencies provided the majority of social work jobs and fieldwork opportunities; caseworkers and casework agencies had organized the majority of the earlier training programs; and especially, casework agencies and sympathetic foundations rather than the universities, with a few exceptions, had provided much of their financial support. It followed that caseworkers and casework-relevant knowledge and technical skill training dominated the curricula of most social work programs, in contrast both to broader, philosophical and scientific emphases and/or to other areas of social work specialization.

The centrality of casework in social work education was also a legacy from some of the earliest and most influential social work schools. The Boston School for Social Workers (1904) was originally affiliated with Harvard and its Department of Social Ethics, as well as with Simmons College. The joint sponsorship aimed at placing a solid academic floor beneath an applied, casework program and attracting men to the new social work profession. Despite the position of Robert Woods on the Boston School's board, the training needs of the settlements were never a primary consideration in the school's program. Harvard did not actually commit any of its own funds to the maintenance of the school, only the donations solicited from personal Harvard friends by the director, Jeffrey Brackett. Since too few of its male students enrolled, Harvard was reluctant to make the effort to raise endowment money. When the Russell Sage Foundation terminated its seed grant to train COS district secretaries in 1914, Harvard soon withdrew from the partnership (1916), leaving the school to Simmons, and its narrower, casework focus (Lunt, 1974).

From 1905 to 1912, the New York School, which began as a training program for COS workers, shifted its curriculum under the directorship of Samuel McCune Lindsay heavily toward the social sciences. This led to internal conflict with the influential agency-dominated Board of Trustees and to Lindsay's resignation. When Edward Devine then resumed the directorship in 1912, under pressure from Mary Richmond at the RSF, although he did not always agree with Richmond, "social idealism gave way to 'practicality' and to emphasis upon method and technique in social work" (Meier, 1954: 42). Porter Lee succeeded Devine in 1917 and essentially maintained this direction. The New York School did not formally affiliate with Columbia until 1940.

Without the proper casework emphasis the survival of a school could be at stake, as was the case with the social activist-oriented Missouri School of Social Economy (MSSE) that began in 1901. Although it was very productive in terms of research and publication, as an urban school with a social activist philosophy and style, it rapidly became estranged from the casework practice community, the universities, and the rural-controlled legislature. Without casework agency support or an independent source of funds, MSSE went under in 1924. It was replaced by the George Warren Brown School at Washington University in 1925 with Frank Bruno as dean and strong ties to the casework community (Popple, 1978).

A few schools of social work with independent sources of financing and attachments to other segments of the social work market did manage to establish themselves and develop curriculum innovations. The Chicago School of Civics and Philanthropy (incorporated in 1908), begun in 1903 by Graham Taylor of the Chicago Commons and other social reformers and settlement leaders, offered general training as well as specialization in social investigation (Wade, 1964). Under the leadership of Julia Lathrop, Edith Abbott, and Sophonisba Breckinridge, this school seemed to maintain a balance between the narrower requirements of practical preparation for social work and a broader emphasis on social research and social legislation. Its independence and subsequent affiliation with the University of Chicago (1920) were also helped in no small measure by substantial grants for these innovations from the Laura Spelman Rockefeller Foundation, assistance from Julius Rosenwald and other foundations, and by the extraordinary efforts of Graham Taylor to raise funds to support the school as an independent venture (Wade, 1964). At Ohio State University (1906) an emphasis on community organization catered to the training needs of financial federation administrators. At Western Reserve University (1916) there was sufficient knowledge and interest from the field by 1923 to add a course in social group work to the curriculum. Three midwestern schools of social work established in state universities by 1916—Ohio State, the University of Minnesota, and the University of Indiana—were undergraduate programs designed for B.A. students and hence less specialized than the older private schools (Bruno, 1948).

Generally, these programs were exceptions, albeit extremely important ones, for as these and other institutions slowly gained strength, their leaders and professional graduates exerted a broadening influence on later developments in social work such as the inclusion of additional practice methods, social policy–relevant knowledge, and generic versus specialized training. In particular, when Breckinridge and Edith Abbott moved the School of Civics and Philanthropy into the University of Chicago, they established a beachhead of resistance to the narrowly specialized, psychiatrically oriented, and practical content of prevailing social work training in the 1920s that was so heavily tied to voluntary social agencies. Abbott emphasized the critical importance of a "solid and scientific curriculum in social welfare" (Costin, 1983), which included the study of social legislation, social research and statistics, and especially, public welfare administration (Ibid.). Yet, during the post–World War I era, few schools could escape the overriding influence of the voluntary casework agencies, which helped social work to become defined primarily as casework.

Fieldwork reinforced the hold of the casework agencies. Originally, fieldwork was incorporated into professional social work education because university-based programs developed as an extension of agency training. In the 1920s fieldwork comprised anywhere from 30% to 80% of the total time a student spent in a social work school (Karpf, 1931). A unique contribution to professional education and the linchpin of social work training, it served a number of functions. Access to the field for research purposes was of interest to university social scientists. Fieldwork also ensured that the agencies had a substitute for apprenticeship labor. Through fieldwork the agencies gained significant control over the substance and process of the training. It was the major means for socialization into the professional subculture.

As psychiatric ideas filtered into the schools during the twenties, refinements were added. Under the leadership of Porter Lee and Marion E. Kenworthy of the New York School (Lee and Kenworthy,

1929), social work education came to be defined as an avenue for personal growth; within this process fieldwork became the tool for molding the personality and attitudes of the student practitioner. The role of the field instructor also took on new significance, as an agent of socialization as well as social control, to carefully protect the portals of professional practice.

A major accommodation to the social work market and the casework agencies was the inclusion of undergraduate social work programs as an accepted part of professional education. Many social work leaders preferred graduate training to elevate social work's status, but pragmatically they were forced to compromise. Schools could not attract students with high educational qualifications when salaries after training remained as low as before it, and most social work jobs required neither university nor specialized professional education. Therefore, as with the professional association, eligibility criteria for membership in the Association of Training Schools had to be kept loose. Up until 1924 the association accepted any school, graduate or undergraduate, "having a full-time course for training social workers and covering at least one academic year, with a 'substantial amount of both classroom instruction and supervised fieldwork'" (Bruno, 1944: 154–55). More specific membership criteria were developed by 1924 for curriculum organization, content, administration, and cooperation of allied professional resources, which held until the beginning of the 1930s. In 1929 only 13 of the 28 member schools offered graduate level education, and all but 4 admitted students without a degree (Trolander, 1975: 33). The issue of the appropriate level for the professional degree did not gather force until the next two decades.

During the New Era years, casework firmly established its dominion over social work education by the weight of course offerings, philosophy, and guiding spirit. The exclusion of knowledge and skills related to social reform and social policy in the 1920s cannot be explained on grounds that they were too unscientific or unable to be codified or taught. Several studies of social work education raised the need for more broad-based, scientific education rooted in social science and social philosophy (Tufts, 1923; Hagerty, 1931). The ideology of the university espoused the ideal of science, but a careful study of social casework practice and social work's educational policies and curricula belied it. One sizable investigation (Karpf, 1931) found

> little evidence that the caseworker uses any other than the common sense concepts and judgements relating to the attitudes, emotional states, personality and personality traits of the client, or in attempting to influence his behavior, or the care of his health, the care he gives his children, his standard of living, the adequacy or inadequacy of his housing, and a host of other types of important problems and situations. The caseworkers seemingly did not resort to any definite criteria for arriving at their recorded judgements. They were, to judge from the records, largely subjective, individualistic, and unverifiable. . . . (352, 353)

> All in all, it seemed not unfair to conclude that if social workers needed a scientific background, or for that matter, any educational background for professional training, many schools of social work are sufficiently unconvinced on the matter to be willing to take in almost anyone who manifests an interest in social work and is willing to pay his tuition. . . . (354)

> We found, also, that there is apparently little agreement as to what a curriculum of social work should consist of; that there is little uniformity in the type, number, or content of courses offered or in sequences required for graduation. . . . (354)

More than anything else, the shape of social work education in the university was a product of social work's response to the nation's political economy. The unification of social casework in the 1920s through the Milford Conference and the decline of the social reform wing of social work after World War I were significant features which helped fashion the profession in a casework image.

Social Work Redefined

CONFLICT RESOLUTION AND UNIFICATION: THE MILFORD CONFERENCE

The force of the psychiatric challenge to family social work set the stage for the Milford Conference which met annually and in subcommittees between 1923 and 1928. Casework specializations organized around different settings and social agencies had existed before World War I. But in the 1920s the perspective of the psychiatric social work segment effectively pervaded the other specializations—of which family casework was the largest and most eminent—and upset the balance of power in the field. By 1926 medical, psychiatric, and school social workers all had established separate professional associations alongside the American Association of Social Workers (1921). The old social casework was encountering a new and potent core around which the professional enterprise could be organized, a core compatible with the changes in the political economy brought by World War I. Trained psychiatric social workers were moving into an ever-widening spectrum of social agencies, and the curriculum for training caseworkers in the schools of social work was in a state of flux over "the psychiatric thread running through all of casework" (Jarrett, 1919). Unless this new paradigm could be accommodated, the movement for professionalization centered in social casework might break into irreparable fragments.

The Milford Conference was the means through which this accommodation was worked out, a process begun in informal meetings as early as February 1921. The New York School, with its feet firmly planted in both family and psychiatric casework, provided the leadership and the connections. The 40 conference participants (not necessarily in all meetings) were prominent members, sometimes overlapping, of national social work organizations, social agencies, professional associations, and schools of social work. They represented different, frequently competitive segments in the casework field. There were leaders from psychiatric social work (Christine C. Robb, Mildred Scoville, and Maida H. Solomon), as well as pioneers in the medical social work area (Ida Cannon, Marie Antoinette Cannon, Janet Thurston; the family casework/COS field (Francis McLean, Porter Lee, Mrs. John M. Glenn, Margaret Rich), and child welfare and delinquency (C. C. Carstens, Henry Thurston). However, close to 50% of the members had a past or present affiliation with the New York School; almost 40% had taught courses there part time or were full-time members of its faculty.

The final report of the Milford Conference, *Social Casework: Generic and Specific,* was published by the American Association of Social Workers in 1929. It was written by a duly authorized committee of five representing the conference as a whole rather than its specialized fields. The committee was chaired by Porter R. Lee, Director of the New York School, and all of the members had a close affiliation with either the New York School or the Sage Foundation, or both.

The achievement of the Milford Conference was that it closed the ranks within the social casework field around the idea of generic casework. It recognized differences within the field, but found a politics and a language for affirming the whole:

> This report testifies to the importance of the specific fields of social casework and to the specific demands which each specific field makes upon caseworkers practicing within it. Nevertheless, the outstanding fact is that the problems of social casework and the equipment of the social caseworker are fundamentally the same for all fields. In other words, in any discussion of problems, concepts, scientific knowledge or methods, generic social casework is the common field to which the specific forms of social casework are merely incidental. (AASW, 1929:11)

In its conception of social case treatment, the committee viewed the adjustment of the individual to social living as paramount, and it recognized "the influence of one personality upon another" (Ibid., 29) as the potent factor in treatment. "The flesh and blood is in the dynamic relationship between social caseworker and the client . . . ; the interplay of personalities through which the individual is assisted to desire and achieve the fullest possible development of his personality" (Ibid.). At the same time the committee steered away from psychiatric terms in its formulation. Instead it stressed the caseworker's "use of resources—educational, medical, religious, and industrial," "assisting the client to understand his needs and possibilities," and strengthening the client's "ability to work out his own social program through the use of available resources," as the processes fundamental to achieving social case treatment goals. This approach, constructed logically on the base of *Social Diagnosis*, essentially defined generic casework in family casework terms, and therefore represented a victory for the family social work segment.

The triumph, if it can be so considered, was less a conceptual than a political tour de force. Conceptually the meaning of generic casework and the details of how the separate specializations would relate to the generic were not worked out, although it was assumed that they could be. From a political-economic perspective the triumph acknowledged a central fact of social casework reality: that only in the family and children's agencies did the social caseworkers really exercise market control, for only here "[was] the extent and form of its service determined by social casework leadership" (Ibid., 39, 40). Like it or not, all of the other specializations—social casework in hospitals, in mental hygiene agencies, in schools, in courts, in industry—operated under auspices controlled by other occupational groups. "In these fields, the extent and form of social casework services are determined by the requirements of other programs, medical, educational, legal, industrial . . ." (Ibid., 39, 40), a situation creating a risk that "this scattering of administrative control may foster a separatist tendency prejudicial to [casework's] unified development" (Ibid., 39, 40). The safeguard against this risk, concluded the committee, lay in "recognition of the paramount significance of generic social casework and its continuous contribution from all of its specific fields to its generally accepted body of knowledge and methods of work" (Ibid.).

THE WANING OF SOCIAL REFORM IN THE SETTLEMENTS

Porter Lee's commentary on the transformation of cause to function in his 1929 presidential address to the National Conference of

Social Work was an insightful observation about the institutionalization of reform in general and the more particular state of social work as the 1930s were about to begin. Said Lee,

> . . . Charity in its origin and in its finest expression represents a cause. The organized administration of relief, under whatever auspices, has become a function. The campaigns to obtain widows' pensions and workmen's compensation have many of the aspects of the cause. The administration of these benefits has become a function of organized community life in most American states. The settlement movement began as a cause, and the activities of many of its representatives still give it that character. In general, however, it has developed as a function of community life. . . . (4, 5)

Thus, concluded Lee, the social worker administering "a routine functional responsibility in the spirit of the servant in a cause" provides the greatest service of social work and represents its best hope for the future (24). Lee's observation was quite appropriate to the state of the settlement field.

Social reform in the settlement became identified with social work when social work was in transition from an avocation to a paid vocation. As the idea of professionalization took hold, the social reform segment could not sustain this definition of social work. The political economic factors that impinged upon social work, such as the repressive political climate of the New Era years, the growth of the financial federation, and the growth of casework specializations contributed much to the decline of the social reform aspect of the settlements. But also settlement reform leaders could not sustain this definition because they had failed to build an institutional base for its continuous development. They failed to bridge the social class distance that they had set out to span.

In an address to the National Federation of Settlements in 1931, Lillian Wald reflected that during the first 25 years of their history, settlements in the United States had doubled their numbers every five years; but by 1914 this period of growth had stopped and the number of houses had remained practically unchanged for the next 15 years (Wald, 1931). The decline of the settlement movement in the decade following World War I may have been even more serious than Wald indicated. In 1910, a definitive study of settlements reported that there were 413 settlement houses in the United States

(Woods & Kennedy, 1910). In the 1930s, the National Federation of Settlements estimated the number at about 230 (Trolander, 1975:27). More was at stake than a reduction in physical numbers. There was also a palpable thinning out of the voices of social reform which had been associated with the movement and their replacement by adherents of the small group social and cultural functions of settlement work.

As is often the case in historical construction, the history of the settlement movement has been largely told by, and through the deeds of, its foremost leaders and their associates, such as Lillian Wald, Jane Addams, Graham Taylor, Robert Woods, Vida Scudder, Raymond Robins, Mary McDowell, Charles Cooper. Yet they were probably involved directly in the activities of no more than 5% to 10% of the 400 settlements in existence before World War I—agencies like Hull House, Henry Street Settlement, South End House, Chicago Commons, Greenwich House, Kingsley House (Pittsburgh). Their efforts gained the settlements their reformist reputation, while the actual institution that was being built around them was underplayed. Had settlement activists shared a coherent vision of reform with each other or with their neighborhood constituents, perhaps their impact on social work might have been more potent. When the reform function could not be sustained for reasons which need to be discussed, the institutional base remained.

The leadership activities and ongoing programs of most settlement houses were much more concerned with the immediate needs and struggles of their urban neighbors than in protracted collective action. As the settlement developed into a formal organization, with facilities and regular services, an institutional identity slowly evolved (Leiby, 1978: 132–34). Typically the settlement program centered around informal education, socialization, and recreational activities for neighborhood children, youth, and adults through social clubs, classes, and other sorts of "cultural" activities. The settlement also served as a kind of nerve center of the neighborhood, a place where one could go for help of any kind, a refuge from daily frustrations, an outlet for self-expression, an interpreter of the complexities of American society. In crowded communities where physical space was hard to find, the settlement was a neutral meeting place for other social and political organizations. Many settlements also helped local residents come together to address neighborhood problems and to identify and develop needed services in and out of the settlement. This was the institution that was being created.

Was the settlement also a breeding ground for social activists? Sometimes, but not in most settlements and not for neighborhood residents. Some settlements provided a base of operation from which an articulate group of advocates could seek social reforms, armed with trenchant experiences of daily life in an urban, immigrant, or migrant slum, and the facts of urban social existence for the masses. If some settlement reformers supported the labor movement, or leftist groups, or the platforms of progressive politicians, the needs which these groups represented arose from the settlement community. But they did not constitute the organized program of the settlement house itself. Settlement leaders supported the labor movement; their neighbors comprised much of its working-class membership; but they were not union organizers. Many settlement leaders supported the socialist party, but they did not organize it as an integral part of the settlement. The drives for women's suffrage, consumer protection, workmen's compensation, unemployment insurance, mothers' pensions, child labor laws, housing reform, and peace, among others, were led by settlement workers and their associates, but not by the neighborhood people who might benefit. Even the settlement houses themselves were rarely governed by the neighborhood people who used their services (Trolander, 1975). As one observer noted, "Settlement administration, controlled as it is by the settlers and by the patrons, suffers because the neighborhood has little or no voice in the direction of the policy of the house" (Holden, 1922: 101, 102). Settlement leaders were a dedicated, generous, talented, and sincerely motivated elite. They espoused a belief in doing *with* rather than doing *for*, but in the activities they were most noted for, the latter was more true.

The use of the settlements to develop a refined class consciousness and alternative political arrangements would have meant the heightening of class conflict. This was a "foreign" idea, literally and figuratively. It was not a concept that could be entertained seriously within the framework of the settlement movement or the mind set of its leaders. Most settlement leaders were not "radicalized" by their experiences because they believed in the possibility of a reformed American democracy; they could not truly comprehend the impact of monopoly capitalism on American society. Few people could. Rather than a revolutionary political vanguard, they saw themselves as neutral mediators between the classes.

In the 1920s, for example, Robert Woods (1923) saw the settlements standing on the threshold of a "profound opportunity in the new stage of industrial history, whose dominating note must be no longer consumption but production—bringing together representatives of both sides [capital and labor] of the great issue into a new perspective determined by the general public interest, through which alone the increasing national product can be created, out of which the better standard of living for the many can be secured . . ." (164, 165). Settlement leaders did not use the powerful group technologies that were developing within their agencies and elsewhere to raise their neighbors' awareness of their political and social oppression. In the press of the immediate and profound need around them, they did not try to train a cadre of neighborhood leaders, if that were possible, to understand the significance of sustained collective action and to carry it on.

Had settlement leaders tried to extend the Progressive Movement to include the goal of building class consciousness, the legacy of World War I might well have made the task impossible. First of all, the war spurred the northern migration of blacks and Spanish-speaking minorities. During the prosperity of the 1920s, they began to replace the economically successful white ethnics who moved out of their old neighborhoods. This now familiar cycle of residential movement added racial tension and conflict to the ethnic and class conflicts that already divided working-class communities.

Second, during and after World War I, radicalism was painted with extremely broad brushstrokes. Because the settlements were inextricably bound up with immigrants, they were deviant by definition from the widely heralded norm of "100 percent Americanism." Few settlement head workers were actually members of the socialist or communist parties, but the "Red-scare" intensified the fears of conservative settlement board members and tightened their control of program activities and finances (A. Davis, 1967). Moreover, the most visible settlement leader, Jane Addams, and other settlement figures "unpatriotically" advocated pacifism. In 1919, when the New York *Tribune* and the *Times* each printed a front-page list of "A Who's Who in Pacifism and Radicalism," an attempt at public shaming by naming, it included Jane Addams, Charles Beard, and Roger Baldwin (already in jail for refusing to serve), along with a prominent list of socialist and religious leaders (Swanberg, 1976: 73). Hull House and the Henry Street Settlement were strong enough to be able to continue their reformist activities. Other settlements were more restricted and therefore stressed the less politically sensitive dimensions of their work.

Since the bulk of settlement activities required physical facilities, space, and equipment, most settlements needed substantial budgets to maintain their programs. War needs siphoned off some of their financial support, leading to programmatic retrenchments and closings. After the war, the Community Chests increasingly assumed the position of central financier and planner for social programs in most cities where settlements were operating. During the 1920s, the previously independent settlement boards lost a great deal of their autonomy to these new, centralized decision-making bodies. In Chest cities, even where settlement boards did retain some of their powers, as with hiring of headworkers, their outlook was hardly progressive. The boards, after all, were primarily composed of non-resident, politically conservative men and women listed in *Who's Who* and the *Social Register*, whose reference group was likely to be the city-wide Chest board (Trolander, 1975).

In Chicago and New York, active settlement house cities where the Community Chest did not take root until the 1930s, some reform activity was sustained (Trolander, 1975).[30] In these non-Chest cities, voluntary social agencies derived a relatively small portion of their budget dollars from a privately raised central fund. Under these circumstances, where the individual settlement board was also liberal, the progressive political activities of staff and liberal programs were more likely to receive support. Settlement federations in both of these cities also helped promote a broader vision of settlement work. Interestingly, in the most politically active settlements, Hull House, Chicago Commons, and the Henry Street Settlement, the presidents of the boards were, respectively, Jane Addams, Graham Taylor, and Lillian Wald. Because they were able to attract enough independent financing from private supporters, democracy aside, these prominent staff leaders also were able to retain board control of their agencies and use them to promote their own liberal causes.

Needless to say, neither the case of the non-Chest cities, nor that of the charismatic activist were models that could be used to institutionalize the social reform function of the settlement house.

Without an indigenous cadre of leaders to carry on the reform tradition, the settlements needed to attract a younger activist group from affluent circles. This proved difficult. Financial exigencies reduced the availability of fellowships for post-college settlement work, thereby closing off a potential source of unsocialized recruits. Perhaps because of the conservative climate, or a sense that prosperity was around the corner, or opportunities elsewhere, the number of in-house residential volunteers dwindled.

The gradual professionalization of social work in the 1920s also vitiated social activism in the settlements. Trained social workers sought paid positions. For lower-middle-class workers this was a form of upward mobility; for women it was also a form of liberation; for all, proper pay separated the professional expert from the amateur volunteer. Some caseworkers and recreation specialists accepted employment in settlements (Davis, 1967). Courses on working with groups also began to appear in social work schools in the 1920s, with philosophical support from educators like John Dewey, Eduard Lindeman, and Mary Parker Follett. However, generalist professional training for the settlement worker was not available. Narrower specialized training and socialization into the profession did not prepare the new staff for reformist roles. Thus the older reform leaders had difficulty reproducing themselves. They did not lack force of personality; they simply could not overcome the direction of the political economy.

In a way, the weakening of the reform spirit in the settlements was also a function of success. Many settlement initiatives had been incorporated by other private agencies or governmental units. These included: the nursery school and kindergarten, the public bath, visiting nurses, vocational guidance and education, playgrounds, tuberculosis screening, well-baby clinics, and labor reforms (Hart, 1931; Davis, 1967). Many reform organizations which settlements had either begun directly or encouraged during the Progressive years were well established on their own, e.g., the NAACP, the Women's Trade Union League (WTUL), the National Housing Association, and the Consumers League. Other centers for community life were also developing due in part to settlement work. Without a sufficient analysis of the political economy to guide them, and with energetic supporters hard to find, many settlement workers succumbed to the drift of the times and redirected their emphasis toward services and individual personality development through group experiences.

One direction urged by some leaders was a renewed focus on the arts. Settlements had pioneered in the development of visual arts, drama, and music programs for many years. During the 1920s, Albert J. Kennedy, Robert Woods's associate at South End House in Boston and executive of the National Federation of Settlements from 1923 to 1934, strongly advocated the idea of the settlement as a cultural arts center. Many settlements followed his lead. Recognizing the dulling impact of the new mass society, it was argued that through the arts, the settlements could combat the twin evils of standardization and materialism that stifled individuality and spirituality (Hart, 1931; C. Chambers, 1963). A qualitatively different vision of society lingered here on the edge of consciousness.[31] Its full realization in the settlement movement was lost in the hardest of American economic depressions that soon followed. (See also the discussion at the end of Part 2.)

Informal education, recreation, the arts, group work, neighborhood services, and some neighborhood planning became the stock-in-trade of the settlements, the functions that were institutionalized after World War I. But the spark of reform was also kept alive by settlement activists and others outside the settlements during this period. While prohibition proved a divisive issue for settlement (and social work) leaders,[32] other problems unified them. The most dominant, the push for governmental responsibility for housing over the private market, and the documentation of the tragic social and psychological effects of unemployment, occurred well before the Depression era. In these and other areas, settlement reformers gave witness to the continuing hardship that many Americans experienced even during "prosperity." Their studies and ideas helped to shape the public agenda. Combined with the social networks created through their action, settlement reformers provided an important thread of continuity between the Progressive Era and the New Deal (C. Chambers, 1963; A. Davis, 1967; Trolander, 1975). It is ironic that Frank Bruno (1948), looking back over the history of social work, characterized the settlement as "the conscience of America," but deemed that it had made "no direct contribution to the professional development of social work" (119).

DILEMMAS OF A PROFESSION

By the end of the 1920s a social work enterprise had been firmly established. It was controlled by caseworkers; they defined its major commodity. The political economy of the New Era had created the potential for a national market for social work and a labor pool which could be used to tap it. The market was well suited to casework, and casework leaders had risen to the opportunity. Realizing the need for market control, social casework entrepreneurs had erected the machinery to achieve it: a national association to regulate supply and demand and a set of schools with an accrediting association to standardize and reproduce the commodity and also regulate supply. The achievement was admirable, but not complete. The nature of the commodity and of the market contained contradictions that would interfere with complete control.

While social work in the 1920s was not subject to a great deal of market competition from other helping occupations, it did have internal boundary problems. Enough social workers had to be included in the profession to be able to respond to its potential market, or it might be lost, and numbers were necessary for the profession to be politically viable. This meant including practitioners whose functions were not clearly defined, but who were identified with the larger, more diffuse sphere of social work. Within the casework community, social workers differed about their roles and the knowledge and skill necessary to fulfill them. The richest markets and those most subject to control were among the middle classes whose needs demanded the specialized commodities of medical and psychiatric social workers. Within social work this was a small, but politically potent group because of its market access. The larger but less specialized group of charity organization workers had to redefine their commodity as family casework for the new market and work out enough agreement to hold the casework group together. The Milford Conference accomplished this task, but the different casework segments still retained their own professional associations alongside of the one national association. The tension in the profession between generic casework and specialized casework thus had its roots in political economic struggles for control of the enterprise and access to the social work market.

The need for inclusiveness in building the professional enterprise also meant a degree of openness to settlement workers. Numerically, settlement workers were a significant group, but their practice roles were highly generalized. During the Progressive years, the settlements had performed a critical function for the future profession. They had spearheaded a drive in American society to transform the residual function of charity to the institutional function of social welfare. Through the reform efforts of settlement leaders, the American public had begun to accept the idea that citizenship included certain communally protected rights to a standard of "welfare" and accompanying social services. World War I aborted the momentum of this drive and made it easier for private enterprise to regain control under the rubric of enlightened corporate interest. Settlement-led reform became passé. Its corpus of workers was not encouraged to join the profession, though the door was left open, until it had developed a commodity line compatible with market needs and the existing casework model. This was to develop more fully with group work in the 1930s and 1940s.

The reform spirit of the settlements also raised other complications. When private enterprise reasserted control over the political economy, it reestablished its residual view of welfare: individual responsibility for overcoming individual weakness. Through foundations, financial federations, and board positions in universities and social agencies, private enterprise controlled social work opportunities and social work purse strings—in effect, the social work market. The challenges of the settlement reformers could not be tolerated. In the short run, a social work enterprise in need of financial support and caught up in developing a specialized commodity for its new markets could accept the stifling of social reform. In the long run, the enterprise, in fact, needed the reformers because they created a climate for the growth of social services. The need for skilled advocates for social welfare and the need for resources from the upper classes exposed one of social work's most difficult contradictions, again rooted in political-economic conditions.

In American society professional status depends on the bedrock of autonomy to control one's working conditions and remuneration. Social work's origins in charity and welfare made it dependent on the financial support and approval of philanthropists, financial federations, and government for its income and settings for practice. Its middle- and upper-class direct consumer market was not large enough for solo private or group practices, and of course, once it pursued this market in a substantial manner, it would run up against competition from other professions. The professional enterprise could begin to establish the norm of professional autonomy through a code of ethics, and through standard setting. The leaders of social work's professional associations and schools began to do this, and thereby created some small realm of autonomy in practice. Still, social workers ultimately were subject to the imperatives of an organizational life not within their sphere of control. Given this situation, social work could never gain full professional status, but to the extent that was desired, it was peculiarly susceptible to the views of those who controlled its resources. In the New Era, this control was primarily in the hands of private enterprise. During the 1930s, under a different set of political-economic conditions, the weight of control shifted to government and created a new set of professional struggles.

PART IV

The Creation of a Social Welfare Industry: Social Work Between 1930 and 1950

Go talk with the unemployed, those who are on relief and those who aren't, and when you talk with them don't ever forget that but for the grace of God you, I, any of our friends might be in their shoes.

Harry Hopkins, 1933

CHAPTER TWELVE

An Overview of the Social Work Enterprise: 1930–50

INTRODUCTION

Before 1930 American society still labored in the throes of a relatively crude, industrial, laissez-faire type of capitalism with minimal social protection for its citizens. American leaders did not know how and were reluctant to use the power of the federal government to maintain social and economic good health. Abroad, isolationism and disarmament generally characterized American thinking in foreign policy, though the United States continued to play a role in the Caribbean and Central America, and its trade and investment policies in Asia were "imperialistic." Twenty years later the foundation of an American-styled welfare state had been firmly set in place, and the nation stood at the threshold of a world market receptive to its influence and about to yield up an unparalleled period of domestic prosperity.

The social transformation over the intervening years, 1930–50, was one of the most painful in American history. It took the nation's severest economic depression to generate serious welfare reform; and it took the pressure of fighting and winning a second world war to solidify it. In the process, millions of Americans suffered an indelible scarring of spirit and body; many died.

The development of modern professional social work in the United States is inextricably tied to the creation of the welfare state and the reconstruction of the American political economy. Social work and social welfare are still hard to separate. Therefore, rather than treat the sociohistorical context separately, in this section we will explore the growth of social work, weaving in as appropriate its relation to the emerging welfare state and to the larger political and economic forces that gave it form.

The Transformation of Social Work, 1930–50

On April 1, 1943, the War Manpower Commission of the Office of Defense recognized "welfare services to civilians" as an activity essential to the national defense. This action, safeguarding against raids of social agency personnel by industry (Rich, 1956: 147), also symbolized the public legitimacy that social work had achieved during the intense upheavals of the Depression and World War II. Yet much of social work's service functions in modern industrial society were not entirely of their own making nor fully consistent with their professional aspirations.

By 1945 social work had changed from a "craft" practiced across a broad spectrum of relatively small public and private social agencies into a full-fledged "mass production industry." The critical stage of this metamorphosis was brought about by the economic depression which spawned a nation-wide, tax-supported system of public welfare and social insurance. Thousands of social workers now worked in carefully classified positions within large public agencies performing increasingly standardized social service functions under a hierarchical structure of authority. (According to the U.S. Census there were 70,000 social workers in 1940.) In the voluntary sector the success of financial federations also helped to centralize the control of social work activities and working conditions in the hands of a fairly remote group of community elites (Reynolds, 1945).

These developments forced a number of social workers to question the salience of profession building. The bitter hardships of the Depression years unleashed a forceful, radical critique of American capitalism. Thousands of social workers joined together in a Rank and File Movement to protest their social and economic plight. At least for a short time social workers became conscious of their status as a working class, a class of employees who, like their sisters and brothers, had to struggle to earn a living.

For many, unionization became a serious alternative to professional association as a means to gain job protection, better salaries, reasonable working conditions and standards of practice, as well as social legislation and social and economic democracy. In 1944, the major union for public social workers, the State, County, and Municipal Workers of America (SCMWA), had an estimated social work membership of 6,500 in some 25 social work locals. Even more notable, social workers in the private sector, the main repository of practitioners with professional training and primarily caseworkers, organized and joined social work industrial unions. In 1944 the United Office and Professional Workers of America (UOPWA) had about 4,000 employees of voluntary social service agencies, organized into some 28 Social Service Employee Union (SSEU) locals. A majority of these members were social workers (Reynolds, 1945).

These flashes of radical analysis and action left only a fleeting impression on the face of social work, a tantalizing hint of the contours of a social democracy that would have to await a new set of political-economic conditions to be pursued again. *Social Work Today*, the journal of the Rank and File Movement which began in 1934, ceased publication in 1942, seldom to be cited in the chronicles of social work thereafter. The radical wing of social work gave way to the much more powerful forces of accommodation both in social work and the larger society.

Alongside the unions, the professional social work enterprise continued its assiduous preoccupation with raising the status of social work. Its activities were very different than the unions', though their interests sometimes overlapped. Through the American Association of Social Workers, the American Association of Schools of Social Work, and other kindred organizations the enterprise sought to find and regulate social work markets, "elevate" social work standards by greater exclusivity and control, and define and sell the social work commodity. Given its particular political-economic character and organizational commitments, this approach led social work along a more pragmatic course.

Among the accomplishments of organized social work in this time span were: recognition of its status as an effective national trade association; a significant role in the drafting and enactment of the Federal Emergency Relief Act of 1933, the Social Security Act of 1935, and other social legislation; passage of the 1939 amendments to the Social Security Act establishing a merit system for state and local public social service employees; the significant expansion of the social work domain in public social services; the establishment of fees for service for the first time in private social agencies; the beginnings of state certification of social workers; the acknowledgment of group work, administration, and community organization as methods of social work. By 1945 the American Association of Social Workers had doubled its 1930 membership of 5,300. By 1951 AASW membership reached 12,500 and a merger with the other professional social work associations was on its way.

Schools of social work exhibited a similar growth pattern; the number of accredited schools of social work and full-time master's degree students grew respectively from 25 schools and 1,300 students in 1929 to 42 schools and 2,280 students in 1944. Many more students were enrolled on a part-time basis and in undergraduate social work courses. The seeds were planted for the formation of a Council on Social Work Education in 1952.

Social work's accomplishments during the two decades after the market crash years did not come easily. The turbulent climate created social needs and fashioned responses more rapidly than the professional enterprise could manage. Its overriding task became securing, and working out a satisfactory accommodation to, a powerful new sponsor—the federal government and its state and local counterparts. This effort intensified many older conflicts and brought new ones to the fore, such as: the relationship between public and private social work; defining and controlling the boundaries of social work's domain; the relationship between psychological treatment and relief; whether training for professional practice should be at the undergraduate or graduate level, and technical or broad-based; the appropriate role for social work in political and social action; the degree to which a professional association could and should provide a protective function for its members. Part 4 explores the ways in which these issues emerged and were played out.

CHAPTER THIRTEEN

New Conditions, New Requirements: Misery Breeds Opportunity

THE OLD SYSTEM

The social welfare system in 1930 was an uncoordinated admixture of local and state public relief agencies, supplemented by the resources of voluntary social work organizations. By then all but a few states had established public welfare agencies of some sort. Most large cities and many counties also had public welfare departments, rather than "boards or departments of charities" or "charities and corrections." Poorhouses could still be found in smaller communities. Even in New York State the almshouse was not abolished until 1929. Forty-four of the 48 states had enacted mothers' aid legislation; in most states, children's bureaus or departments of child welfare were charged with the responsibility of protecting children against neglect or cruelty; and county or municipal boards of child welfare or boards of children's guardians were also common (Hubbard, 1929). With all of these advances wide variation existed within and between states and localities on the constellation of agencies, their administrative structures, their interrelationships, their functions, their standards of service, the quality of staff, and their provisions and coverage. Administrative appointments based on political patronage rather than competence were not unusual. State and city agencies did not necessarily provide the same services, or relate to one another administratively, or locate similar functions within the same units (Bane, 1930; J. Brown, 1940; Johnson, 1930; Lundberg, 1930; Willard, 1930).

Between 1910 and 1930 the number of public and private agencies increased steadily as did expenditures for public relief, notably in large cities. More than three-quarters of these relief expenditures came from public funds, the most rapid expansion occurring in mothers' aid. The acceleration of relief spending during the Depression was in fact only the culmination of a trend that had been going on for two decades in industrializing America (Brown, 1940).

The evolution of the public welfare system was strongly influenced by the drive of the private charity workers to build a social work profession during this same period. They succeeded in making the norms and methods of the more prestigious private agency the standard to be emulated by the public. The goal of improvement in public relief became "to substitute effective casework with more adequate relief for the inadequate system of doles which had previously obtained" (Johnson, 1930: 346). The public agency's acceptance of the casework function gradually opened it up as a market for trained social workers, though few public agencies readily passed the muster of national standard-setting groups. For example, in 1930 only 12 of the 230 members of the Family Welfare Association of America were public agencies (J. Brown, 1940; Swift, 1930). The infusion of social treatment into the public relief agency—the "socialization" of public welfare—also helped to legitimate the expansion of relief by promoting the use of behavioral rather than strictly economic criteria to determine eligibility for assistance (Lubove, 1968; J. Brown, 1940).

The social welfare system that emerged as a response to the Depression transformed social work. The public sector became the dominant force in social work rather than the private. The crisis forced the country's political, industrial, and labor leaders to realize the need for a nationwide system of social insurance and public relief. As a first step the existing public relief system was, in effect, "nationalized." The aftermath of planning and legislation created a federal old-age insurance system, a federal-state unemployment insurance system, and a federally supervised, state run, public welfare system. By the start of World War II the patchwork of public welfare arrangements had been fashioned into a much more standardized, bureaucratized, and rational social welfare industry with social work identified as its core technology. Social workers had found a vast new market for their services, but also the market came with a new set of sponsors and conditions that proved difficult to control.

The Shift to Federal Auspices

The push by organized social work for federal relief did not come immediately nor easily. In December 1930 there was no such move. Yet by the end of the summer of 1931 social work had changed its direction. The change entailed a grudging philosophical shift from local private charity as a privilege for the worthy to federal social protection as a civic right. The impetus for the change was both economic and political.

In December 1930 social work still held to the conventional American belief that economic depressions were temporary and unemployment hardships were personal. With few exceptions, social workers relied on the ideas and structures for dealing with social need that they had built around this belief system over the previous thirty years, ideas like the sanctity of well-organized private charity and its refinement through the application of professional social casework.

The growing relief burden of the family agencies forced executives and lay leaders reluctantly to recognize the need for more state and local public relief funds. This recognition was connected to an institutional concern about the anticipated demise of casework standards in the family societies if the public agencies were to close their doors. Such were the sentiments expressed at a September 1930 conference of private family society representatives to prepare for meeting the relief needs of the coming winter which was called by Joanna Colcord, director of the Charity Organization Department of the Russell Sage Foundation. If the public agencies were to limit intake, then chest and family agencies had "the moral duty . . . to besiege the city authorities for tax appropriations to meet the need," . . . and to "push for the establishment of public departments giving both service and relief" so that temporary emergency relief arrangements would not be set in place (Colcord, 1930: 206–8).

The concerns of the American Association of Social Workers were not far different from the family agency representatives. As unemployment deepened and other social science organizations focused on the unemployment problem, in December 1930 the executive committee of AASW issued a cautious public statement on the responsibility and contribution of social workers in meeting the unemployment crisis. In their view the duty of social workers was mainly "to bear witness" to the harmful effects of destitution and humiliating forms of relief; "to make clear . . . that philanthropy [could not] replace payrolls," that social agencies were not equipped to handle the volume of relief demands, that non-relief forms of social work such as health and recreation were still important, and to observe and present evidence on the problems. While preventing unemployment went beyond their "professional purview," social workers could strive to administer relief effectively using "methods which experience has proven to be more constructive to the recipient," and actively support plans for insurance and other measures to increase employment (*The Compass*, December 1930: 2).

The Community Chests, the financial underwriters of the voluntary sector, philosophically and pragmatically were strongly committed to the concept of private charity. In the early years of the Depression they could hardly afford to deviate much from President Hoover's position that the joint and voluntary efforts of government and business leaders could manage the dual problem of unemployment and relief satisfactorily. Through their mass appeals, the Community Chests were in essence administering a system of voluntary taxation to fulfill a community obligation to the needy. Their appeals were based on the rhetoric that they took responsibility for all community needs through their annual fund drive, including the provision of emergency relief. Their success was predicated on the community's acceptance of their rhetoric, and therefore they were in no position to turn away people who needed relief. At the same time, however, the Chest "had no power to enforce collection of the funds it needed to discharge its obligation. . . . Only the public agency, the legal authority, [had] such power" (J. Brown, 1940: 78–79).

Pragmatically, the chests feared they would hurt their ability to raise money if they endorsed a widespread public relief system (Borst, 1930; J. Brown, 1940). The donor community had not been educated to support a panoply of social work, administrative, and recreational "services"—the non-relief functions of the chest agencies. To get themselves off the hook, the chests hoped for some national-level declaration of support for local public relief agencies from the Hoover administration. Hoover held back, wanting to distance himself from anything that might sound like support for public relief. City officials were not pushing very hard for more relief funds either before 1931, probably because they, too, were accustomed to meeting relief needs through private charity.

By the winter of 1930–31 figures showing that public funds accounted for the lion's share of the relief dollar had already been presented at the National Conference of Social Work (McMillen, 1929) and published more extensively in the *Survey Midmonthly* (McMillen, November 1930). An Association of Community Chests and Councils investigation of local relief methods and conditions for the newly appointed President's Emergency Committee on Employment corroborated the rise in local public spending for unemployment relief. The study also found that many chests merely regarded these public dollars as a source of supplementary funds. Even confronted with data, the entrenched belief in private charity was hard to change.

By September 1930, 5 million people were estimated to be out of work; by the end of the year the figure had jumped to 7 million; by the spring of 1931, 8 million were unemployed, approximately 16% of the civilian labor force (J. Brown, 1940; Peterson, 1947; Hopkins, 1936). The massive degree of human suffering contained in these figures generated tremendous pressure on the social workers and public officials who were daily asked for relief. Finally, when private agencies were swamped and voluntary fund appeals threatened to fail, when local and state public relief agencies ran out of funds, and when the protests of the unemployed, stimulated by the organizing efforts of the Communist Party, took to the streets and relief offices and threatened the social order, the social work enterprise began to push for federal intervention. Social workers led the march to the federal doorstep somewhat ahead of much of the rest of the country for they had few alternatives.

At first most people who were unemployed suffered in quiet anguish. Because poverty was considered shameful, people tried to conceal their plight from their neighbors. As unemployment became epidemic, people grew desperate. Many vented their frustration publicly. In 1930 and 1931 protests of one form or another broke out across the country, in urban neighborhoods as well as rural towns. Some protests took the form of spontaneous outbursts of anger and looting, such as the 500 armed men in England, Arkansas, who, after a ruinous summer drought, marched on the business section of the town to demand food on January 3, 1931; or the 1,500 jobless men in Indiana Harbor, Indiana, who stormed the Fruit Growers Express Company on August 5, 1931, demanding jobs to keep from starving (Zinn, 1980); or the 1,100 people waiting in a Salvation Army bread line in New York City who attacked a nearby bakery delivery truck; or the numerous episodes of resistance to evictions which occurred in dozens of cities (Piven & Cloward, 1977).

Will Rogers, who observed that he was watching "the first nation in history to go to the poorhouse in an automobile," warned, early in 1931, "You let this country go hungry, and they are going to eat no matter what happens to Budgets, Income Taxes or Wall Street values. Washington mustn't forget who rules when it comes to a showdown" (Schlesinger, 1957: 204). The administration also worried about the restive climate. In 1931 Hoover opposed the reduction of army troop levels because the cuts would weaken government's ability to maintain domestic peace and order (Schlesinger, 1957; Manchester, 1975).

The disparity between promise and cruel reality, wealth and starvation, coupled with the breakdown in normal institutions of social control—the workplace, the family, the school—created fertile conditions for right-wing demagogues and left-wing organizing. The American Facist [sic] Association and Order of Black Shirts was founded in Atlanta and was joined by other right-wing groups. By the end of 1930, Father Charles E. Coughlin had also begun his rise to popularity with his radio program, the "Golden Hour of the Little Flower," broadcast on Sunday evenings over 17 CBS stations. Three months after joining CBS, Coughlin was receiving an average of 80,000 letters a week containing more than $20,000 and launched on his career of hatred and anti-Semitism (Manchester, 1975).

The political left took a different approach. In mid-1930 the American Communist Party made organizing the unemployed a central mission. Through direct action strategies like mass meetings, rallies, hunger marches, demonstrations, the communists built a nationwide network of Unemployed Councils (Seymour, 1937). Protests were deliberately organized, including many instances of looting of food and physical defiance of evictions. In the period between the spring of 1930 and spring of 1931, "demonstrations numbering upwards of two and three thousand persons were frequent; arrests and jail sentences were common" (Seymour, 1937: 3). Actions which began peacefully often became violent. Even though the Unemployed Councils were strongest in the largest cities, like New York and Chicago, no part of the country was left untouched. Millions of unemployed people took part in some sort of protest activity during the 1930s.

Many protests were directed at relief organizations. When survival became the issue, people felt they had a right to the income they needed. Leaders and protesters were openly derisive and antagonistic to caseworkers, supervisors, and agency directors. The physical protest tactics used in stopping evictions were also carried over to the relief offices of public and private agencies (Seymour, 1937: 13–15), where "crowds of jobless men and women . . . cornered and harassed administrators, and even took over their offices until . . . money or goods were distributed to them" (Piven & Cloward, 1977: 56). Social workers, who understood the misery behind the protests, were at first reluctant to call the police. As demonstrations grew more massive and unruly, they eventually had no other options for managing this sorry state of affairs.

Settlement house workers were among the earliest in the country to recognize unemployment as a serious social problem and to take action. Their first response was to document the struggles and defeats of the jobless in finding work through a graphic study in 1928–29, directed by Helen Hall for the Committee on Unemployment of the National Federation of Settlements. The testimony and published versions, *Some Folks Won't Work* (1930), by Clinch Calkins, a popular writer, and *Case Studies of Unemployment* (1931), edited by Marion Elderton for the NFS Unemployment Committee, spread the idea that the roots of unemployment were systemic (Hall, 1930).

Their second response was to help unemployed workers organize themselves for action. The settlements that supported more aggressive approaches to unemployment were almost entirely agencies in Chicago and New York, non–Community Chest cities where settlement staff and boards had more autonomy. Their organizing activities were fostered by Socialist Party members working on a local level to draw in liberal sponsors as well as workers. These groups consciously avoided the "open radicalism, extreme belligerence, [and] rioting" associated with their rival, Communist-inspired Unemployed Workers' Councils. More common activities included sponsorship of public hearings to elicit testimony on the effects of the Depression and follow-up of grievances by individual members against relief agency policies and regulations (Seymour, 1937: 5).

The Chicago Workers Committee on Unemployment (CWCOU), which began in the summer of 1931, was stimulated by a core group of socialists affiliated with the League for Industrial Democracy (LID). The group included Lea Taylor, head worker of the Chicago Commons and president of the Chicago Federation of Settlements; Karl Borders, a former assistant head of the Commons and resident there; Frank W. McCulloch, a Commons volunteer and son of two prominent board members (Trolander, 1975). A Workers' Committee on Unemployment was similarly organized in New York City with an advisory group of settlement workers: John Lovejoy Elliott, Grace Gosselin, Karl Hesley, Helen Harris, and Mark McCloskey. Eight locals were organized in seven settlements by 1933 (Trolander, 1975). Throughout the decade of the Depression, settlement workers and volunteers provided financial support, meeting places, supplies, leadership, and direct action for the organization of radical groups of unemployed workers, sometimes under great intimidation.

Lest the picture become distorted, most settlements were also unavoidably involved in helping neighborhood residents cope with the Depression through providing services and direct relief. Typically, they developed vocational classes, self-help programs such as community gardens, make-work activities, and employment services. Many settlement workers acted as liaisons between residents and local relief offices and, as advocates and brokers, pressured the authorities for better local and state relief policies and benefits (Trolander, 1975).

By the fall of 1931 it was apparent to public and private agencies alike that neither had sufficient resources to cope with the mounting demand for relief. Between 1929 and 1932 relief expenditures rose geometrically. William Hodson, executive director of the New York City Welfare Council testified before a Senate Committee in January 1933 to a 441% increase in unemployment relief expenditures from 1930 to 1932, a jump from $14.6 to $79 million. Free lodgings furnished in municipal lodging houses in New York City rose from 185,000 in 1928 to more than 1.5 million by the end of 1932. The city of Detroit, which spent $290,000 on 4,000 families in October 1930, was spending $2 million for 45,000 families by

January 1931. In Cleveland charitable agencies cared for 2,655 families in 1929, 7,734 families by the end of 1930, 18,978 families by the end of 1931, and by mid-1932 already had 24,843 families on the charity rolls. The essential story was the same throughout the country. The Bureau of Economic Research estimated that annual relief expenditures for the entire United States rose from $85 million in 1929 to $500 million in 1932 (A. Epstein, 1933: 167–70).

Under this onslaught private charity at first doubled and redoubled its efforts. It could not produce significant new resources. In 1930 the Community Chests raised a national total of $84.8 million in 386 local campaigns, only some $8 million more than in 1929 and spread over 33 more cities (United Way of America, 1971). The chests were running to stand still. A study of giving patterns by the Association of Community Chests and Councils (ACCC) confirmed that most contributors were making smaller gifts. Many chests actually failed to meet their goals in 1930 (United Way, 1977).

The pressure cooker of the national emergency also threatened to undermine the local federation structure. Budget cutbacks for agencies not providing relief became necessary in order to funnel dollars to the family welfare societies. But these decisions strained federation loyalties. Meanwhile, the family agencies which were providing relief with insufficient resources wanted to get some relief for themselves. To create some semblance of standards and control, they tried to limit their intake, a policy which fueled additional controversy (Hill, Hoodin, & Paine, 1930). Linton Swift, the FWAA executive, suggested that the family agencies should have more freedom to run their own supplementary fund appeals and that the chests publicize the agencies' service role rather than the relief role to promote understanding and support for more selective casework (Swift, 1930; *The Compass*, February 1932). But the chests relied heavily on the relief appeal to raise funds, fearing a loss of status and function if they left relief to the public sector (Borst, 1930). The chests also feared a loss of the considerable public subsidies which they and their member agencies were receiving to assist in handling the unemployment relief load (J. Brown, 1940).

The fall 1931 Community Chest campaigns showed the futility of private charitable initiatives to all but the most ideologically blind. A national mobilization for welfare and relief was undertaken under the aegis of the President's Organization on Unemployment Relief, chaired by Walter S. Gifford, president of AT&T. Even the popular and normally independent Red Cross joined in. A national committee was formed to enlist support from major corporations, and a nation-wide publicity and educational campaign was inaugurated by Gifford and Owen D. Young of GE with the memorable statement that "between October 18 and November 25 America will feel the thrill of a great spiritual experience . . . millions of dollars will be raised . . . and the fear of cold and hunger will be banished from the hearts of thousands" (Schlesinger, 1957: 173; J. Brown, 1940: 99). The results were disappointing, a sum total of $101.4 million from 397 local efforts. A quarter of the chests failed to reach their goals by 10% or more. Moreover, chest goals no longer represented total community needs, but estimates of what could be raised (United Way of America, 1977).

Working- and middle-class people had become the mainstay of private charity; now they did not have money to contribute.[33] With worsening conditions and the advent of public relief nation-wide, successive chest appeals continued to drop, hovering around the 1929 total for several years. The campaign did not break the $100 million mark again until 1941, when people returned to work and the mobilizations for World War II began.

With voluntary funds limited and demands multiplying geometrically, the private family agencies turned helplessly to local and state public relief agencies. The existing public agencies were overwhelmed by the deluge. Local public officials had the authority to vote more relief funds but had no funds to vote since private citizens and corporations were having trouble paying their real estate taxes, the primary source of city and county revenues. Relief money from tax sources actually decreased from 75% in October 1931 to 62% in December (United Way of America, 1977). Many cities and counties simply ran out of funds. They had reached the limit of their bonded indebtedness and could not borrow again until the state legislature raised their debt ceiling. Many municipalities verged on bankruptcy. Many paid their employees in scrip.

To meet the need public relief agencies borrowed, skipped paydays for employees, and, most of all, cut back on relief allotments and tightened eligibility requirements (J. Fisher, 1980; J. Brown, 1940). Relief payments, if one could get them, often came irregularly and provided only enough for subsistence. Based on survey responses from 461 cities, Senator La Follette told the U.S. Senate in February

1932 that relief payments averaged $6.07 per week. In many states the average was considerably less (A. Epstein, 1933).

State governors and legislators began to assume more responsibility for alleviating the crisis. With unemployment so high, revenues from state income taxes had also declined. Many states called special legislative sessions in 1931 and raised monies from special taxes and fees, or allowed localities to issue bonds or to use other funds to supplement local aid. Under the leadership of Governor Roosevelt the New York Legislature passed the first State Unemployment Relief Act, known as the Wicks Act, paying for half of its appropriation from higher state income taxes. By November of 1931 New York had a Temporary Emergency Relief Administration functioning separately from its State Department of Social Welfare which extended dollars for home and work relief to localities throughout the state on a matching basis. Twenty-four states passed similar legislation by the end of the year. Upon the suggestion of William Hodson, director of the Welfare Council of New York City, who turned the job down, Roosevelt appointed Harry Hopkins as executive director of TERA. This began a long and significant partnership in social policy and public administration.

Before the end of 1931 the people who were concerned with relief—the unemployed and their families, line workers in public and private social agencies, social work executives and lay leaders, and public officials—recognized reluctantly that the federal government had to step in. In October 1931 the combined agency boards of the 238-member Family Welfare Association of America, hardly the bastion of radical reform, took a public, modestly progressive stand. Recognizing that the unemployed were victims of "social and personal conditions beyond their personal control," they called upon "the civic and industrial leaders of America for [a] concerted effort . . . [to] ultimately bring security in employment and a more adequate distribution of purchasing power among the masses of American people" (Rich, 1956: 118).

At the National Conference of Social Work in Minneapolis, in June 1931, discussions of the unemployment situation dominated the sessions. Here the executives of the family welfare agencies went beyond their boards by soundly and publicly repudiating President Hoover and his philosophy of private responsibility. Clarence M. Bookman, director of the Cincinnati Community Chest and a national leader who was about to be anointed as incoming president of the National Conference, captured the emerging philosophy. First expressing a preference for local relief, Bookman went on to state:

> However, I should not hesitate to sanction [national and state grants] if no other way can be found to feed the hungry. It should be made clear that there is nothing unsound socially, governmentally or economically in appropriating taxes for unemployment relief purposes and that government organized to protect and promote the welfare of people has an inescapable responsibility to handle unemployment relief. (Springer, 1931: 383)

As the shift toward federal intervention gained momentum, social work leaders realized that they were confronting more than a way to alleviate massive social distress. They also faced a new opportunity to expand the realm and prestige of social work, and they could not afford to pass it by if they hoped to remain socially relevant. Gertrude Springer's summary of the 1931 NCSW Conference for the *Survey* (July 15, 1931) was titled "The Challenge of Hard Times." Its subtitle, significantly, was "Fears that Came Out of Their Holes at Minneapolis: Is Social Work Beaten or at the Threshold of a New and Great Adventure?" Karl deSchweinitz provided the answer and set the tone for the future:

> Out of our present misery will come a better organization of society. Social work was never in a better position to influence the course of events. Not in a generation have we experienced such an integration of social work, business, and politics. Social work technique will be modified in its expression by the institutions through which it will now operate, just as any skill is bound to be modified by its channels of expression. But its philosophy and its principles will prevail . . . . Social work is on the brink of one of the greatest adventures it has ever known. Overnight we are becoming public social workers with our psychology changed from the idea of individual special treatment to the idea of equalization. Now is our great opportunity to introduce social work as we know it into public thinking. This is no day for the weakling or the standpatter. The great adventure, whether we will or no, is on us. Any social worker who is worth his salt will get into it. (Springer, 1931: 385)

CHAPTER FOURTEEN

Social Work Politics in a New Social Welfare Industry

SOCIAL WORKERS FORM A NATIONAL TRADE ASSOCIATION

The leaders of the social work enterprise did not define their goals in the early 1930s in industrial terms, though unionization later forced the analogy. They only knew in the spring of 1931 that federal relief was necessary and that they had a unique opportunity to influence public policy. Politically, the opportunity came at a propitious time. The social work enterprise had developed a number of powerful national organizations whose resources and connections could be diverted to the effort, among them the newly formed Association of Public Welfare Officials (1930), which had recently been renamed the American Public Welfare Association (APWA).

APWA brought to the forefront of organized social work a segment of the profession that had been previously overshadowed, and it greatly expanded social work's expertise and credibility in the public policy arena. If the dominant private charities were organized around the nexus of the New York/New England voluntary agencies and professional schools, social workers in the public sector were identified with the long-standing emphasis on public administration and social reform at the School of Social Service Administration in Chicago under the leadership of Grace and Edith Abbott, Julia Lathrop, Sophonisba Breckinridge, Jane Addams, and other Chicago and New York settlement leaders. Frank Bane, State Commissioner of Public Welfare of Virginia, and APWA's first director, recalled the old days when "there was a section of the NCSW, Section 9, which was called Public Welfare Officials Section, and it always had the back room. . . . We were regarded if not as politicians, as people who have to handle the day-to-day routine dishwashing jobs . . ." (Kurzman, 1974: 175). In September 1931, Frank Bane opened APWA's Washington office and quickly moved to center stage in negotiating the public welfare world for social work. APWA derived a good deal of strength from its close relationships with the familiar social work organizations and a number of public administration associations affiliated with the University of Chicago, such as the Public Administration Clearing House; the American Municipal Association; the American Legislators' Association; and the International City Managers' Association. The *Social Service Review* of the School of Social Service Administration published the APWA proceedings of its annual meetings, and on April 1, 1932, APWA moved its office to Chicago (J. Brown, 1940).

Thus, as the terrain of social work shifted from private to public and from local and state to national auspices, social work was equipped to take advantage of the situation. Social workers had arrived at the path that other commercial and professional interest groups had already discovered—the use of trade associations to lobby for their interests in the halls of Congress and the offices of emergent federal bureaucracies.

Between 1930 and 1932, leaders of national social work organizations such as FSAA, ACCC, and APWA worked cooperatively with the various Hoover administration committees that were formed to deal with the unemployment crisis. Hoover's efforts were futile, but the process of collecting information, formulating ideas, preparing testimony, and working together in a national context helped prepare and mold a cadre of social work leaders who could effectively advocate their special interests.

After the bitter winter of 1931, the NCSW meetings in Minneapolis became a springboard for organization and action. In June 1931 the American Association of Social Workers formed an Unemployment Commission in the belief that "all kinds of social work [sic] are unified in centering their interests in the problem of reasonable standards of living" (*The Compass*, December 1931). The commission soon overlapped with and gave way to a much broader social work effort which got underway in October 1931, the Social Work Conference on Federal Action on Unemployment.

Formed by representatives from several national social work agencies under the umbrella of the National Social Work Council (NSWC), the conference included 157 members from 28 states and

50 cities. Its express purposes were clearly political, namely, to collect information and mobilize social work groups behind its proposals on the design and administration of federal unemployment relief and public works programs during the forthcoming Congressional session (Colcord, 1943; Rich 1956). Its steering committee, chaired by Linton B. Swift (FWAA), consisted of: Frank Bane (APWA); Howard S. Braucher (NSWC); Allen T. Burns (ACCC); C. C. Carstens (Child Welfare League of America); Joanna C. Colcord (RSF); Helen Crosby (on loan to the FWAA by the Metropolitan Life Insurance Co.); John A. Fitch (New York School of Social Work); David H. Holbrook (NSWC); Paul U. Kellogg (Survey); Harry L. Lurie (Bureau of Jewish Social Research); John O'Grady (National Conference of Catholic Charities); Walter M. West (AASW); and Benson Y. Landis, Secretary (American Country Life Association).

The availability of organizational resources made the work of the conference possible (Colcord, Ibid.) Since the conference had no budget, its constituent national agencies lent staff support and picked up all the operating costs, such as clerical work, travel, postage, and wires. The AASW, which could not afford to give financial assistance, provided an important network of relationships which linked the conference leaders and nearly all of its members in a common pursuit.

Throughout the fall of 1931, conference members met informally with senators Edward Costigan and Robert La Follette, Jr., and Representative David J. Lewis, who were drafting a federal relief bill. The conference group was organized enough to be able to present a united front in favor of federal aid through home and work relief. Its chief recommendations were incorporated in the first Costigan–La Follette bills introduced in January 1932, and formally endorsed by AASW's Unemployment Commission. Two of these recommendations became central features of all future public welfare legislation: the principles of federal grants-in-aid to states on a matching basis, and state disbursement of relief through state and local agencies rather than by the Federal Government or any single nationwide agency (*The Compass*, December 1931: 3).

Throughout the 72nd Congress, conference members actively promoted federal legislation on unemployment relief by meeting with legislators and organizing data and social work testimony. The four executives who did most of the social work lobbying, Allen Burns,

Linton Swift, Walter West, and William Hodson, spent enough time in Washington to be nicknamed "the Four Horsemen" (Colcord, 1943). The still Republican controlled Senate defeated the Costigan–La Follette bill in February 1932. All that could be passed was a version of Senator Wagner's Emergency Relief and Reconstruction Act at the end of the session in July 1932, for which social work could not take direct credit. The act set up Hoover's ill-fated Reconstruction Finance Corporation, an admission, all the same, of the need for federal aid. Nonetheless, social workers had acquitted themselves well as knowledgeable advocates and able politicians.

During the fall of 1932 and winter of 1933 social workers resumed their interest in group activities on behalf of federal relief legislation.[34] Both the AASW and the APWA presented and coordinated extensive testimony on a new Costigan–La Follette bill. Again the bill was defeated, but the Hoover administration was also on its way out. The recommendations which emerged from the testimony and the process of organizing it gave social workers a critical headstart in influencing the more amenable Roosevelt administration which took over in March 1933.

HARRY HOPKINS AND THE POWER OF BUREAUCRATIC POLITICS

The election of Franklin Roosevelt set the stage for a new level of social work influence on federal social welfare policy. Roosevelt won the election by more than 7 million votes and brought with him substantial Democratic majorities in both the Senate and the House of Representatives. Much of Roosevelt's strength was centered in the major cities of the country where unemployment had hit hardest. The distribution of social workers followed a similar pattern.

During Roosevelt's administration, federal relief legislation would not be denied again, but the social work enterprise wanted more than relief measures. Social work salaries in the private sector were being cut back, and trained workers still did not command better salaries than untrained workers. The public sector, on the other hand, represented social work's avenue for growth (The Compass, October 1931; February 1932). Thus the enterprise wanted a federal relief system which would buy into and enforce the standards of professional social work, a system which would employ trained social workers, in short, a system where social work technology would be preferred. At the APWA sessions of the NCSW in May 1932, Stanley Davies, then associate secretary of the State Charities Aid Association of New York and incoming president of AASW, stated the position plainly:

Public social work has become so much the larger part of social work that it must inevitably be our primary professional concern. Social work cannot develop into a profession of great significance in our national life until our professional standards embrace the public field. This does not mean a leveling down of standards but a constant, patient process of leveling up until one professional standard on a common high level is attained for both public and private social work. (1932a: 449)

The elevation of Harry Hopkins to national prominence in the Roosevelt administration assured social work of a place in national social welfare planning and programs. Though he had not graduated from a professional social work school, Hopkins was a social worker with a long list of credentials. He had practiced on the line and as an administrator in child welfare, with the Red Cross in the South, with the Association for the Improvement of the Condition of the Poor in New York City, and with the New York Tuberculosis and Health Association. He had early on served as president and treasurer of the American Association of Social Workers (1923). As director of Roosevelt's Temporary Emergency Relief Administration (TERA) in New York, Hopkins had worked closely with organized social work to bring professionally trained social workers into his state administration (Davies, 1933; J. Brown, 1940). He had testified on the federal relief measures that social work supported.

Hopkins's experience at TERA and his close ties to social work provided the connections and schooling for his move to Washington as federal relief administrator. At TERA Hopkins got to know Frances Perkins, a state industrial commissioner and progressive aligned with social work causes, whom Roosevelt appointed as his Secretary of Labor after the presidential election. After the inauguration Perkins arranged for Hopkins and William Hodson to meet with Roosevelt to present their ideas on how to deal with the national unemployment emergency (H. Adams, 1977). They sold Roosevelt on social work's legislative package, but with the TERA model for administration by an independent Federal authority.

When Roosevelt turned to the relief question in the spring of 1933, he asked Senator La Follette to draft a new version of the previous Costigan–La Follette bill along the TERA lines. La Follette called for assistance from his old allies, the "Four Horsemen," with Hopkins replacing Walter West who was unavailable at the time. According to Colcord's account, "Hodson, Hopkins, and Swift put everything else aside and stayed in Washington till the bill was drafted and introduced in the Senate, while Allen Burns then took up the ball for the House, assisting Representative Lewis in its introduction, organizing testimony at the hearings, and being himself on call for testimony during four straight days of committee discussion" (1943: 393). Congress passed the Federal Emergency Relief Act on May 8 and 9, 1933. The act established a Federal Relief Administration (FERA) and a $500 million appropriation to meet emergency relief needs, half to be made available to the states on a one-for-three matching basis, half to form a discretionary fund for states unable to meet the match.

The establishment of the FERA "nationalized" public relief and irreversibly imprinted the public welfare system. The formative process also set into motion a whole new politics of public bureaucracy in which Hopkins was a central actor and consummate teacher. The FERA's administrative independence and its ability to grant or withhold relief funds badly needed by the states enabled Hopkins to resist or bypass political demands and traditions and to exact compliance with FERA policies and regulations. Through Hopkins and its national trade associations, social work got in on the early construction of the corporate social welfare state. Hopkins provided organized social work with the legitimacy, prestige, access, and many of the resources that it needed to advance its enterprise, especially decently paying jobs.

In exchange the social work enterprise gave Hopkins a unique source of political power within the Roosevelt administration, one that other key social policy makers (Perkins excepted) such as Ickes and Tugwell lacked: a ready-made, loyal, and organized constituency. Even Congressional leaders came to dislike and fear Hopkins because, as the *Baltimore Sun* commented, "they think he is capable of building up an organization in their individual districts to fight them, if they do not vote according to his orders" (H. Adams, 1977: 119). In organized social work Hopkins recognized that he had a machinery in place with potential for addressing the unemployment crisis, one that he could draw on to support, advocate, and loyally implement his decisions.

Hopkins installed social work in the public sector in several different ways, generally, through staff appointments and consultation, specific policies and regulations, and the allocation of funds for social work training. Just as he had done as head of TERA, Hopkins moved quickly to include professional social workers in his administration. He consulted with the AASW and APWA and brought social work leaders such as C. M. Bookman, William Hodson, and Frank Bane into his circle of decision making. In his own office Josephine Brown from the voluntary sector was an early assistant; Aubrey Williams, head of the Wisconsin Conference of Social Work, became a right-hand assistant administrator of the FERA in charge of the critical Division of Relations with the States. A field staff was appointed almost immediately, and regional offices were later established, with major responsibility and authority to get out to the states to communicate and enforce FERA decisions and to bring back pertinent information on needs and resources. Many of these staff members were also social workers, such as Robert Kelso, an influential Fund and Council executive. The director of the Transient Bureau was a social worker. The federal staff of the Social Services Division that provided technical supervision to the State Social Service Divisions were social workers. Although the FERA never had more than twenty social workers on its Federal staff at any one time out of a group that gradually grew to over 400 nonclerical employees by July 1, 1935 (J. Brown, 1940), the social work presence was powerful.

With a half-billion-dollar budget to oversee, an enormous sum for 1933, Hopkins set up an extensive administrative structure to implement the FERA legislation and enforce his authority. He issued numerous administrative policies and regulations to mold the program to his views, such as policies establishing a uniform minimum wage, and preventing discrimination due to "race, religion, color, non-citizenship, political affiliation, or . . . membership in any special or select group" (J. Brown, 1940: 199). Several of these directives specifically reinforced social work's position in the public relief system. Among them were requirements that trained social workers be hired to administer relief operations, that personnel employed by the states be approved by the FERA, and that only public agencies were to be responsible for the expenditure of public funds.

The requirement to employ trained social workers applied to the decentralized Social Service Divisions that had been operating in states and localities since the FERA's inception. The Social Service Divisions (SSD) were social work's exclusive domain. As the point of entry for recipients to the entire relief program, they lay at the heart of FERA implementation. SSD staff members determined eligibility for individual and family relief and the amounts of relief to be given out; they did follow-up investigations on recipients; and they made referrals to work programs and other sources of assistance.

In July 1933 the FERA issued Rules and Regulations No. 3 requiring every local relief administration to have "at least one trained and experienced investigator on its staff," and for larger public welfare districts with several investigators, further directed that "there should be not less than 1 supervisor, trained and experienced in the essentials of family casework and relief administration" for every 20 staff workers (J. Brown, 1940: 218–19). These rules constituted the authority for the operation of SSDs wherever FERA funds were accepted. Since the need was massive, the FERA quickly spread into every county and town in the country, bringing social workers and social work technology into hundreds of rural areas on a scale even greater than occurred in the extension of Home Services by the American Red Cross during World War I. By October 1934, social service staffs existed in more than 3,000 county administrative units and more than 1,000 additional town and municipal units. In sheer numbers the social service staff totaled more than 40,000 workers, exclusive of clerical staff, to administer relief to 4–5 million families (J. Brown, 1940). About a quarter of the state administrators appointed at the beginning of the FERA were also social workers, and many states hired social workers as local relief administrators.

Hopkins's policy that federal dollars were to be administered by public agencies also promoted social work in public welfare. It clarified once and for all the principle of governmental responsibility for relief. It also effectively separated the emergency relief program from the whole field of privately sponsored social work which had advocated the notion that in times of depression it was preferable for the "best qualified," read "private," agencies to carry the relief load rather than setting up a new apparatus. The practical effect of the new policy was to stop the widespread practice of giving subsidies to private agencies to administer public relief. In June 1933 at least 175 voluntary sector agencies, including about 20% of the FWAA member organizations, had been receiving these funds. As a result, jobs for trained social workers were cut back from the private sector and added to the public. Ideologically, the new public relief system challenged the powerful myth of the efficiency and effectiveness of the voluntary sector (J. Brown, 1940).

Hopkins also supported organized social work by setting aside approximately $420,000 of FERA funds for professional social work training. Without this support the SSDs in many parts of the country would not have been able to find professional workers to fill their supervisory positions. The training project was established in the summer of 1934 in consultation with the AASW and the American Association of Schools of Social Work (AASSW) who stipulated the use only of accredited, graduate social work programs. Funds were allocated to support professional training in 21 schools of social work for 912 relief workers from 39 states. Quotas for states were set up based on need.[35] State relief administrations supported training for another 225 students bringing the participant total to 1,137. Completion of the program did not lead to a professional degree, but some schools added enough fieldwork hours to enable graduates to meet the qualifications for junior membership in the AASW (J. Brown, 1940; Kurzman, 1977). The FERA's support of graduate social work education for relief workers was a powerful act of public legitimation for professional social work. With market demand high other choices could have been made, such as support for undergraduate-level training. (See Chapter 19.)

Hopkins's support of social work advanced the interests of its leaders and simultaneously served expedient ends. The administration was faced with a massive need for assistance requiring what Mary Richmond had once called "wholesale" measures. Hopkins was primarily interested in reducing unemployment by getting people back to work, not extending "the dole" (Salmond, 1983). Emergency relief was a humane, temporary measure to tide people over until a huge public works program could be put into place and economic recovery took hold. The skills and functions of social work with its "retail" casework philosophy that interpreted problems in terms of individual needs and behavioral characteristics could be readily adapted to Hopkins's ends. Social workers could use their "skills" to determine eligibility, to separate employables from unemployables, "continuously to investigate families to see to it that no one obtained relief who could get along without it" (Hopkins, 1936: 101). With the aid of FERA funds and regulations, social workers would be trained and placed as mid-level bureaucratic functionaries dedicated to implementing the FERA program, the epitome of Porter Lee's prescription of a social work commitment to function. These attributes plus social work's long-touted claims of professional integrity, impartiality, and "scientific" attention to efficient and responsible stewardship of the public's dollars made social work technology attractive for a social welfare industry. They were the bases on which social work expansion could be "sold" to public sponsors at that particular moment in history.

If Hopkins was the darling of the NCSW meetings in Detroit in June 1933, he also made clear his position on relief and the expansion of social work. Ever the pragmatist, Hopkins viewed unemployment relief as a "makeshift" program to keep people from starving until employment programs were functioning, and not a social work boondoggle or a means to build "a great social-work organization throughout the United States" (Hopkins, 1933: 69–71). Social work, meanwhile, had committed itself to the public sector and begun to adapt its casework methods to treating the "victims of unemployment" following "the same general patterns as that applied to other disasters in the field of human relations" (Bruno, 1933: 12). While social insurance and employment were certainly desirable ends, the FERA had ensconced social workers in the public relief business where necessity and invention made them difficult to dislodge.

Social Security Secures an Industry

As the national sense of crisis abated with the FERA and other programs, and the Roosevelt administration could get its political bearings, Hopkins and Roosevelt moved to dismantle the FERA. It had been a temporary structure. In most locales state and local emergency relief agencies were not integrated with existing public welfare organizations. Neither Roosevelt, nor Hopkins, nor Congress, nor state politicians for that matter, wanted an extensive federal relief system. The principles of state's rights and local responsibility were too well engrained. It was politically timely to be finished "with this business of relief," as Roosevelt outlined in his January 1935 State of the Union address.

In 1934, Roosevelt, who had shown some sympathy for public sector involvement in social welfare as governor of New York, was pushed further in this direction by some of his advisors and by the budding populist and socialist sentiments for Townsend's old-age pension scheme, Huey Long's "share the wealth" movement, and socialist Upton Sinclair's End Poverty in California (EPIC) program. The Democratic sweep of the 1934 Congressional elections gave Roosevelt the mandate he needed for advancing social legislation. An elated and politically astute Hopkins remarked to Aubrey Williams and a car-pool contingent en route to the Laurel racetrack: "Boys—this is our hour. We've got to get everything we want—a works program, social security, wages and hours, everything—now or never. Get your minds to work on developing a complete ticket to provide security for all the folks of this country up and down and across the board" (H. Adams, 1977: Salmond, 1983). The first priorities, then, were for an employment program to stimulate the economy and a social insurance program to protect against the hazards of unemployment and old age. Reform of the public welfare system and additional social services were secondary.

The groundwork for "social security" was laid by a mix of liberal officials, social work and public welfare leaders, and technical experts, who were mindful of the President's political needs but also understood the inadequacies of state and local public welfare and temporary relief. Between June and December of 1934, they worked together under the aegis of the President's Committee on Economic Security, chaired by Frances Perkins.[36] She was assisted by Deputy Secretary Arthur Altmeyer and Dr. Edwin Witte as Executive Director.[37] Probably more to broaden political support for the forthcoming legislation than to serve any other function (Chambers, 1971), Perkins also appointed an Advisory Council that included top-level representatives from labor, business, and social work. Other advisory committees were soon added, though the foremost American authorities on social insurance, Abraham Epstein, Isaac Rubinow, and Paul Douglas, were conspicuously absent from these forums (A. Epstein, 1933: 672; Lubove, 1968).

For reasons noble and narrow, social workers were interested in both social insurance and public welfare. At the AASW Conference on Governmental Objectives for Social Work in February 1934, they had endorsed the "creation of a permanent, comprehensive, well-coordinated and adequate system of welfare services" and social insurance financed through increases in taxes in the higher income brackets, excess profits, and inheritance (The Compass, March 1934). In the Committee on Economic Security, social workers advocated the idea of a Federal Department of Welfare and grants to the states for general public assistance. The political climate made these and other more progressive recommendations unfeasible. Instead, the committee spent most of its time drawing up the social insurance programs, and these along fairly narrow lines, notwithstanding the protests of Paul Kellogg from the Survey and his supporters (Chambers, 1971). In the end, despite many misgivings, when the administration's social security measures were introduced into Congress, the social work enterprise saw little alternative but to lend its support (Altmeyer, 1966). More radical factions in social work led by Mary van Kleeck endorsed the socialistic alternatives embodied in the Frazier-Lundeen Bill. (See Chapter 15.)

The passage of the Social Security Act in August 1935, imperfect as it was, furnished the legal underpinnings for the inchoate national welfare industry. Though its categorical public welfare measures fell short of social work's goals, they were sufficient to "secure" a burgeoning enterprise.[38] And, some sort of welfare legislation was necessary. The Depression had carried the nation philosophically past the point of return to the poorhouse. Nor could the relief bureaucracies be easily dismantled. Millions of people still needed relief, and thousands of white-collar workers, social workers in this case, needed to be kept employed if the federal government meant to contribute its share to the recovery. Organized social work understood its stake in this enormous market, and its leaders by then were well positioned to take advantage of the opportunity.

Social work's payoff came through the creation of the Social Security Board (SSB), an independent federal agency, which was to oversee a state-operated public welfare system. Although Congress had imposed limitations over the "selection, tenure of office, and compensation for personnel" by the SSB,[39] and hence requirements for hiring professional social workers were not neatly written into the law, this did not prevent social work entrée through administrative regulations. Frank Bane, the capable leader of APWA, was appointed as the first executive director of the Social Security Board. This was the sensitive, strategically central position through which federal authority and control over public welfare standards could be exerted.

The board quickly acknowledged that public assistance fell into social work's domain and placed the administration of the three titles of the act providing categorical assistance into a Bureau of Public Assistance under a single director responsible to the board's executive. Jane Hoey, a social work graduate of the New York School, a former assistant to Hopkins, and an acquaintance of many prominent political figures including Franklin and Eleanor Roosevelt, was chosen for this position. On Hoey's insistence, the bureau was staffed by social workers hired under the "expert" provision in the Social Security Act until a Civil Service Commission was established. The bureau's main function was to approve and monitor the states' public welfare plans. Through its interpretations of the act, the bureau influenced the States to establish "minimum qualifications" and hire "qualified staff members," i.e., social workers. They also arranged for the use of federal administrative funds by states to pay for salaries of staff members on educational leave in schools of social work. The 1939 merit system amendment to the Social Security Act later solidified social work's hold on the public welfare system (J. Brown, 1940).

Between the vagaries of the economy and the New Deal's programmatic responses, the nation endured a consistently high level of social distress until World War II. However, the year of transition from the FERA to the Works Progress Administration and Social Security Act programs starting January 1, 1936, was particularly chaotic. The WPA was set up to accept "employables" drawn 90% from the FERA relief rolls, but its funds were insufficient to employ all of the people who were certified for WPA jobs. The unemployed who had not been on the relief rolls were basically not eligible for WPA jobs at all. In January 1936, this meant that about 8.8 million of the 11 million unemployed were excluded. The "unemployables" in the

FERA program plus all the others in need of relief were supposed to be handled by the narrow categorical assistance programs of the Social Security Act and state and locally funded general assistance programs. The slow start-up time of the programs and lack of funds left millions of people without assistance. To no avail organized social work vigorously protested administration and Congressional unwillingness to grant additional transitional funds for relief and enlarged work programs (Fisher, 1936a: AASW, 1936; Clague, 1936; Williams, 1936). "The end of the F.E.R.A.," wrote Edith Abbott (1940: 764), "has been one of the tragedies of the Administration program. Our most promising experiment in public welfare has been destroyed in the house of its friends."

In the long run, the shutdown of the FERA forced the now-bereft states to participate in the Social Security Act programs to obtain federal funds. The process of passing state legislation to conform to the stipulations of the act and to provide for general assistance took several years. Since the states still had a great deal of say over administrative arrangements, determination of need, and the size of the assistance grants, the results were uneven. Still, in 1938 the total number of recipients of general and categorical assistance exceeded 4.4 million, 40% of whom received Old-Age Assistance, and nearly 37% of whom received General Assistance (U.S. Bureau of the Census, 1943: 192). The cost for these programs ran to nearly $2 billion, $3.2 billion if the various federal works programs are added in, which was more than the cost of operating the entire federal government for the year 1931 (Fink, 1942). By June 30, 1939, all 48 states, Alaska, Hawaii, and the District of Columbia were participating almost fully in the public assistance programs of the act.

During this transition period many untrained social workers lost their jobs in the FERA cutback. Many others, trained and untrained, left due to the stressful work. Efforts were made to maintain the trained and experienced social workers, among them those who had gone to school on FERA funds. With wide variations in administrative views of social workers' roles and needed skill levels, and with insufficient funds, social workers continued to carry out "the dirty work" of public welfare. They became increasingly unpopular in the community as they investigated need, searched for fraud, certified eligibility for WPA work, applied the "means tests" for the new categorical programs and general assistance, granted and denied assistance, and generally buffered the sponsors of the inadequate public welfare system from the despair of its needy applicants. From 1935 onward "relief had come to big business" (Fink, 1942: 349). But for rank and file social workers, what kind of business was it?

CHAPTER FIFTEEN

The Radical Challenge to Professional Social Work

THE RANK AND FILE MOVEMENT: OVERVIEW

Between 1931 and 1942, rank and file social workers exerted a strong, politically progressive counterforce to the profession's attempts to control the emerging national social welfare industry.[40] Through its various forms of organization—discussion clubs, practitioners groups, and protective organizations—and its journal, *Social Work Today*, the Rank and File Movement helped push social work to accept political action as a legitimate professional function, to support a national system of public social protections, and to modify its earlier antiunion biases.

At its peak in 1936, the Rank and File Movement numbered some 15,000 members, the majority of whom worked in public relief agencies and lacked professional social work credentials. This did not mean the movement was peripheral to organized social work. Professional social workers, though disproportionately from the Jewish welfare field, like Jacob Fisher, Joseph Levy, and Harry Lurie, sparked the movement and gave it vigorous leadership. Others of national repute, such as Mary van Kleeck and Bertha Reynolds, joined them. Many more professional social workers from both public and private agencies simply enlisted in the ranks.

The roots of the Rank and File Movement were chiefly economic, another facet of the response to the Depression, but within a particular socioeconomic stratum—the fast-growing white-collar, professional, technical, and managerial sector—and a specific occupational sphere, the social services industry. This Depression had reached far beyond the traditional victims of economic slumps, the poor and working poor. Engineers, teachers, architects, chemists, journalists, motion picture actors, and lawyers were all affected. Social workers were no exception. Unlike social workers, some of these occupational groups had organized trade unions before the Depression; now all found the need for protective organizations much more urgent.

The movement arose first and foremost out of a heightened consciousness among "trained" and "untrained" social workers alike of their particular relation to the means of production. In the earlier years of the Depression, it was a consciousness forged from countless distressful working experiences in overextended private and public relief agencies wherein social workers served as operatives of an inadequate relief system and as victims themselves of the economic crisis. Strongly influenced by the parallel growth and struggles of the American labor movement and the American political left around them, social workers sought to protect their own economic security in their workplaces and to shape the larger social policies affecting all working Americans.

As temporary federal relief and public works programs yielded to a more permanent system of public welfare and social insurance, the huge and disorderly expansion of the social service work force further created the objective conditions for raising working-class consciousness and building social work unions. Essentially these conditions were: (1) the employment of large numbers of social service workers under one roof in a multiplicity of public bureaucracies performing similar functions; (2) a majority of workers with no professional social work training and hence who had not been socialized into the profession by their educational experiences; (3) few strong experiences of socialization into the agency since these organizations were new, quickly overburdened, and often mismanaged; (4) extremely taxing working conditions and lack of job security; (5) unrewarding eligibility and investigation work that often elicited client and community hostility; (6) inadequate resources for helping clients which fostered workers' sympathy for their plight; (7) few workers from upper-class socioeconomic backgrounds. Social work activism was also stimulated by external national and international events, particularly the spread of fascism and the outbreak of war abroad and U.S. involvement in it.

When the conflicts created by these conditions were gradually resolved, the Rank and File Movement began to decline. Internally, the establishment of the welfare system under the provisions of the Social Security Act foreclosed more radical policy options. Its stabilization created permanent social service positions covered by civil service regulations and controlled by the social work enterprise at the upper levels. Professional and movement interests converged around the narrower protective concerns of raising the standards of service through job classification, salary schedules, training, and personnel practices. Externally, as fascism and war increasingly demanded national attention, the political left, including Rank and File opinion, was forced closer to the growing center. When World War II finally captured public priorities in the early 1940s, it channeled the energy of a reunited nation, heated up its economy, and buried the visible remains of America's worst economic depression. *Social Work Today* stopped publication in 1942, symbolizing the end of the Rank and File Movement.

GROWTH OF POLITICAL CONSCIOUSNESS: 1931–33

Social workers' radical consciousness of themselves as workers rather than elite professionals grew out of their economic plight and particular relation to the means of production. After the market crash, social workers, like many other working people, experienced the pangs of economic loss, job insecurity, and personal hardship. To respond to the massive demand for relief, between 1931 and 1933 public and private social agencies across the country retrenched professional staff members, reduced salaries by 5% to 25% or more, hired nonprofessional replacements on subsistence wages, and increased workloads (*The Compass*, November 1930, October 1931; Clague, 1933; Committee of the Case Workers Group, 1933; *Bulletin* of the AFW, 1933; Rosen, 1933). The budgets of many agencies were sliced to the bone by Community Chests and other sponsors, particularly those of hospitals, child-care institutions, special schools, and character-building agencies (*Bulletin* of the AFW, March 1933: 5). Some agencies went out of business altogether. Some private agencies further cut staff and curtailed services as relief caseloads were gradually transferred to the public sector.

Meanwhile, to deal with their growing caseloads, the overburdened and resource-poor public agencies hired large numbers of unemployed white-collar and professional workers at lower salaries to temporarily expand their on-line work force and, in some instances, to replace more costly trained social workers. Many came from the ranks of unemployed college graduates and other professionals such as teachers, nurses, and engineers (Jeter, 1933; Committee of the Case Workers Group, 1933). But cheaper labor did not solve the financial exigencies of the public agencies. Consequently both the new workers and their professional counterparts were faced with irregular paychecks, overwork, payless vacations, and uncertain employment.

In New York the position of the public relief worker was further undermined when the Emergency Home Relief Bureau, serving 130,000 families, hired almost its entire field staff at submarginal wages from the rolls of unemployed workers in the Emergency Work Bureau, a public work-relief program (*Bulletin* of the AFW, March 1933). This means of reducing unemployment, it should be noted, had implications for workers far afield of social work. The threat was that work-relief programs (and potentially other relief efforts) designed to help the unemployed would be used to depress the salary standards of already employed workers by circumventing prevailing wage scales. Thus would the working classes inequitably be forced to suffer the burdens of a malfunctioning economic system. This was the kind of pressure that spawned protective associations where none existed, that triggered the defenses of labor unions where they were already organized, and that pushed toward the logic of industry-wide rather than guild organization in the larger labor movement.

To the professional enterprise the use of cheap labor signified a loss of control over the production and distribution of its specialized commodity, the services of the trained social worker. Thus the AASW maintained requirements that automatically excluded the new "untrained" workers, and the executive committee (*The Compass*, October 1931) formally urged its members "to resist salary reductions for themselves and their colleagues." They argued that professionals should have protected status (the *Survey*, Nov. 15, 1930), and that short-run austerity measures would only aggravate the scarcity of social workers, erase years of effort to raise standards, and lead to inefficient and inferior services for clients (Kelso, 1930; Beck, 1930, Benjamin, 1930; *The Compass*, October 1931). But all to no avail. For, as Beck (1930: 226) pointed out, ". . . social work can regulate the supply (and thus salaries) by the creation of standards which require advanced educational preparation, but in the final analysis the salaries will be determined by the competitive demand for workers."

As the Depression gained momentum the ratio of social work jobs to applicants sank to about one in ten (Rosen, 1933). The flood of new, untrained workers could not be stemmed. People needed jobs, relief needed to be given out, and it was by no means clear that this service function could only be furnished by workers with specialized training from a professional school. Inasmuch as the new workers shared the stressful working conditions, economic circumstances, and, often, the social class backgrounds of their professionalized colleagues, many naturally joined hands in a search for explanations and solutions to their economic predicament.

The frustrations of actual practice during the Depression hastened social workers' radicalization. "The casework methodology and the careful budgeting of standards, built up during a generation of patient work, had to be completely abandoned. Relief was reduced to such a level that it was not sufficient even to hold body and soul together" (A. Epstein, 1936: 172). Helpless to meet the expectations of their clients, the public, or their profession, social workers were forced to question the efficacy of their professional training (Kelso, March 1931: 647–48).

Rank and file social workers bore the brunt of their clients' rage and despair. Dispensing relief could be nearly as painful for the social worker, "trained" or "untrained," as it was for the client. Thus the experience of the young, professional county caseworker in 1933, as recounted to Studs Terkel some 35 years later (1970: 481–82), was undoubtedly not unique:

I was twenty-one when I started and very inexperienced. My studies at school didn't prepare me for this. How could I cope with this problem? We were still studying about immigrant families. Not about mass unemployment. The school just hadn't kept up with the times. We made terrible blunders. I'm sure I did.

There was a terrible dependence on the case worker. What did they feel about a young girl as their boss? Whom they [sic] had to depend on for food, a pitiful bare minimum? There was always the fear of possibly saying the wrong thing to her. The case worker represented the Agency. We seemed powerful because we were their only source of income. Actually, there was little we could do. . . .

There was a lot of waiting around the relief offices. Where they came to pick up their food orders. These places were mostly old warehouses, very dismal. That was another thing, dispiriting. Sitting around and waiting, waiting, waiting. . . . The case worker was often the object of their anger. Where else could they give vent to their feelings? So they took it out on us. They didn't know the cause of their problems. . . .

I'll never forget one of the first families I visited. The father was a railroad man who had lost his job. I was told by my supervisor that I really had to *see* the poverty. If the family needed clothing, I was to investigate how much clothing they had at hand. So I looked into this man's closet—(pauses, it becomes difficult)—he was a tall, gray-haired man, though not terribly old. He let me look in the closet—he was so insulted. (She weeps angrily.) He said, "Why are you doing this?" I remember his feeling of humiliation . . . this terrible humiliation. (She can't continue. After a pause, she resumes.) He said, "I really haven't anything to hide, but if you really must look into it . . ." I could see he was very proud. He was so deeply humiliated. And I was, too. . . .

From such experiences came a new political consciousness, an understanding no longer obscured by a class-ridden professional ideology, that existing institutional arrangements were simply insufficient to preserve the human spirit, to provide social protection and a decent way of life.

After the bleak winter of 1931 social work leaders were compelled to resurrect the "cause" orientation they had largely abandoned in the 1920s. Many social workers joined their call for federal relief. But the awakening political consciousness of rank and file social workers required solutions more consistent with their changing social reality. Dissatisfied with the ideological assumptions of professional social work, they turned toward a Marxian analysis of the political economy, affiliation with labor, and the use of direct action strategies and tactics.[41]

The earliest organizational manifestation of the new movement came in the form of Social Workers Discussion Clubs beginning in New York City in the spring of 1931. The New York Discussion Club was organized by private agency employees, many of whom worked for Jewish (Welfare) Federation affiliates and belonged to the Association of Federation Workers (AFW). (The AFW was an early protective association of Jewish agency workers that had been reorganized in the winter of 1931–32 after a threat of layoffs and salary cutbacks.) In a short time discussion clubs extended well beyond the borders of the Jewish communal service field.[42]

Discussion clubs, in fact, varied as to size (from 100 attendees on the average to as many as 1,000 people on a hot issue in the New York club), mix of public and private agency workers, membership composition—clerical employees, case aides, unskilled line workers, trained social workers—and radical perspective. Sympathetic to progressive causes and leftist ideas, the clubs did not advocate any particular political program in their early stages (Fisher, 1936a; Spano, 1982; Levy, 1934). Instead, they sought to broaden their understanding of political-economic events and include all social service workers, not just "professionals," in their discourse. Along with lectures and debates from "critics of the status quo," the clubs also shared a belief in taking action. Their activities included: support for labor and dissident groups protesting hunger, unemployment, fascism, racism, and other social concerns; legislative proposals on social issues such as unemployment insurance, birth control, lynching; and pressure for improvement in salaries and working conditions of social agency employees.

By 1932 clubs had spread to Chicago, Philadelphia, and Boston; by 1933 to St. Louis and Cleveland. With further cross-fertilization at the NCSW, by 1935 discussion clubs also had formed in Kansas City, Pittsburgh, Los Angeles, and San Francisco. As the movement matured and emergency relief workers developed a real stake in public social-service employment, the discussion clubs increasingly stressed workplace issues and promoted protective organization. Some discussion clubs actually became protective associations—St. Louis, Cleveland, Los Angeles. This emphasis brought the movement into a new phase of development which saw the gradual decline of discussion clubs as such by the end of 1935 and the growth of practitioner groups, protective associations, a national coordinating body, and *Social Work Today* as a vehicle for dissident expression.

MATURATION: 1933–36

Between 1933 and 1936 the Rank and File Movement reached a peak membership of about 15,000, almost twice the size of the American Association of Social Workers. Its maturation was also exhibited in other ways. *Social Work Today* and activities at national conferences gave the movement a national identity and presence and stimulated widespread public debate over social and political policy options. Movement leaders articulated clearer, more unified positions on professional and political matters which could not be discounted by affixing labels of radicalism or youthful impetuosity. Movement organizations, allied with labor, improved wages and working conditions. And, most telling of all, the professional enterprise softened its opposition to unionization of social workers.

The formation of Practitioner Groups between 1933 and 1936, while not central to the movement, represented one measure of its influence on organized social work. Practitioner Groups were "rank and file groups which develop[ed] in a professional setting" (Fisher, 1936a), such as within the Chicago (1933), New York (1934), and St. Louis (1934) chapters of the AASW, or the National Caseworkers Council of the Family Welfare Association of America, or the Association of Practitioners in Jewish Social Agencies of the National Conference of Jewish Social Work. While oriented toward social action, in a certain sense these groups also reflected some of professional social workers' ambivalence about it. This ambivalence was exhibited, on the one hand, by younger AASW members, who were dissatisfied with the AASW's political conservatism, domination by executives, and ineffectiveness in improving salaries and working conditions, but who also did not want to completely cut their professional ties. At the same time, it was manifested by the leaders of various AASW chapters, who recognized the need for change, but who tried to maintain control through a strategy of accommodation, negotiation, and cooptation (SWHA, Archives, NASW b22, note 253, "Report of Committee on Practitioners' Movement"; SWHA, Minutes, Joint Meeting-Social Work Forum and AASW, NASW b22, note 253; Leighninger, 1981: 61–67). For all intents and purposes, Practitioner Groups fizzled out during 1935 with the growth of *Social Work Today* and social work unions, and as the AASW chapters themselves became more involved in action on social and professional issues (Fisher, 1936a, 1980).

The heart of the Rank and File Movement was really located outside of the professional enterprise, among the 31,000 social workers who had entered the field of public service by 1934 (about four times the size of the AASW membership) and who were ineligible for professional affiliation. For the AASW, the threat of this huge rank and file membership base made it "hard to decide which was worse; the potential of strong rival social work organizations or the danger to standards and current organization policies if these workers were let into the AASW" (Leighninger, 1981: 67). AASW leaders elected to compete rather than modify membership standards, hardly surprising, given their influence over the federal relief programs of the Roosevelt administration.

Between 1933 and 1936 the Rank and File Movement caught fire in the large, urban, *public* relief agencies in the form of protective associations and trade unions. Professional norms did not hold sway here, working conditions were deplorable, and precedent for unionization of public employees did exist (e.g., teachers and government employees). In the voluntary sector, where lower caseloads and norms were strongly antithetical to unionization, the growth of unions did not move beyond the Jewish Federation agencies in Detroit, Philadelphia, Boston, and Brooklyn (Alexander, 1977) until 1936.

In the fall of 1933 the Social Workers Discussion Group of Chicago organized the first Social Service Workers Union among staff in the Cook County Department of Public Welfare and its Unemployment Relief Services division. The Illinois Emergency Relief Commission responded with firings, red-baiting, and harassment. Such tactics, however, could not stem the powerful forces driving relief workers to organize in virtually every major city in the nation. Even as Chicago workers were struggling, in December of 1933 workers in the New York Emergency Home Relief Bureau were beginning the largest and most successful city-wide protective association in social work, eventually named the Association of Workers in Public Relief Agencies. In January the association won wage increases for all its members, workmen's compensation, greater leeway in absenteeism, and an end to means-testing of employees, all of whom had been hired from the relief rolls (Fisher, 1936a).

Employee organizing soon followed in relief agencies in other cities, some of which had more than one association. In 1934 new associations of relief workers formed in Chicago, Cincinnati, Cleveland, Minneapolis, Newark, New York, Philadelphia, Pittsburgh, and several Pennsylvania counties. In 1935 protective associations took root in Baltimore, Denver, Detroit, Los Angeles, Milwaukee, Oakland, St. Louis, St. Paul, Washington D.C., and additional countries in Ohio and Pennsylvania (Fisher, 1936a), bringing the total to 21. Their creation was helped along in no small measure by the Roosevelt administration's decision to quit "the business of relief" in 1935 and the insecurity and chaos which followed the reorganization. Another 14 protective organizations in public agencies were added the following year.

By 1936 protective organizations were also beginning to affiliate with the American Federation of Labor (AFL). Since governmental employees were already organized, protective groups in the public agencies could not establish a national union of social workers, the original hope of Rank and File leaders. Instead they obtained charters as lodges of the American Federation of State, County, and Municipal Employees (called the American Federation of Government Employees in 1935). Nine such unions were chartered by the summer of 1936.

Ironically, employee groups in the voluntary sector fared better in maintaining a social work identity. In November of 1936 the AFL chartered two unions of private agency employees in New York and Chicago (Social Service Employee Unions, Nos. 20334 and 20335). These were "federal unions," a misnomer which meant they had their own "federal charter" directly tied to the Executive Council of the AFL (Fisher, 1936a, 1937). Unattached to any other national union or occupational group, the SSEUs could develop a strong sense of identification among members who shared their social work practice concerns and experiences.

On the debit side, the SSEU ranks were smaller and more vulnerable to the blandishments of professionalization, and the conservative AFL limited their autonomy by requiring consultation before actions could be taken that might interrupt service to clients, i.e., a strike (Alexander, 1977: 91). Moreover, the diffuse structure of the service delivery system and the small size of private agencies significantly limited the spread of unionization in the voluntary sector. Of the 12,000 Rank and File members in protective groups in 1936, 90% were public agency employees (Fisher, 1937).

Programmatically, protective organizations devoted much of their energies to the bread-and-butter issues which had stimulated their formation. They struggled with some success for higher salaries and standardized salary schedules, longer vacations and sick leave, workmen's compensation, a five-day work week, lower caseloads and other improvements in working conditions, proper grievance procedures, and recognition of the union as a collective bargaining agent. To strengthen job security Rank and Filers also joined social work leaders in seeking civil service coverage.

The strategies and tactics that protective organizations used to achieve their goals were consistent with other union struggles, though the New York groups were probably the most consistently militant. They included: grievance meetings, media publicity, mass meetings, demonstrations, petitions, and delegations to local, state, and even national authorities. The AFW in the private sector added to these tactics torchlight parades, street meetings, mass picketing, neighborhood conferences, and on two occasions two-hour work stoppages or strikes (Fisher, 1936a). Firings due to involvement in organizing activities or protests against relief policies were frequent and generated more grievance hearings and protests to obtain reinstatement. The labor tactics of the protective groups sharply separated them from traditional white-collar workers and professionals. Their hard-won successes, however, spoke to the potential of the union alternative.

Protective organizations also fought for principles beyond immediate self-gains. In a show of solidarity with the labor movement many associations contributed funds to assist other trade unions in their struggles. Many also actively supported broader social reforms through direct action, joint activity with clients and unemployed groups, and legislative testimony at all governmental levels. Such reforms included: an end to discrimination against blacks in hiring and promotions in public agencies, anti-lynching legislation, continuing allocations of federal relief to the states and opposition to the regressive state sales tax as a means for supporting public assistance, adequate relief standards, a federal Department of Welfare, the Frazier-Lundeen Bill, and federally financed, socially productive job programs at union wage scales for all the unemployed based on need (Fisher, 1936a, 1937, 1980).

The rapid organization of public welfare employees helped to propel the Rank and File Movement onto a national stage, a forum which in turn spurred further organization. The April 1934 launching of *Social Work Today*, edited by Jacob Fisher, further strengthened national discourse. Its commentary on social and professional issues offered a perspective not usually found in other social work publications. It criticized the New Deal, supported left-wing political analyses and proposals, advocated civil rights legislation, and promoted labor organizing and direct action in and out of social work. The journal's many prominent authors and supporters—e.g., Abraham Lourie, Mary van Kleeck, Bertha Reynolds, Paul Douglas, Grace Coyle, Benjamin Glassberg, Forrester B. Washington, Eduard C. Lindeman, Gordon Hamilton, John Fitch, Wayne McMillen, Roger Baldwin—cloaked the Rank and File Movement in a mantle of respectability and legitimacy.

Mary van Kleeck, Director of the Department of Industrial Studies at the Russell Sage Foundation, became a principal exponent of Rank and File ideas. Attracted to the Soviet experiment, she persistently advocated a more planned economy and redistributive reforms that would undo firmly entrenched group interests (*The Compass*, May 1933: 20). In May 1934, van Kleeck carried the Rank and File critique to the NCSW in Kansas City where it erupted with full force and galvanized the movement. Accurately gauging the temper of the conference, she challenged organized social work's uncritical endorsement of the Roosevelt administration. She contended that social workers were laboring under the illusion that government was a benign instrument of the public interest instead of seeing government as it really was, a tool of the groups with the greatest economic power. The important question for social work, she asserted, "is not whether social work is changing its base from private to governmental sources, but whether this reliance on government commits social workers to the preservation of the *status quo* and separates them from their clients. . . ." (*Proceedings*, NCSW 1934: 474). To achieve more radical ends, van Kleeck urged social workers to ally themselves with their clients and with other workers in making demands and taking action in support of a new economic order.[43]

Van Kleeck's stirring paper at the NCSW attracted an overflow crowd and had to be repeated for those who could not get into the session. It was reproduced in the *Survey*, and excerpted in *The Compass*. Along with a complementary paper by Eduard Lindeman (1934), the NCSW Editorial Committee voted it the Pugsley award for "the paper or papers adjudged to have made the most important contribution to the subject matter of social work" (*Proceedings*, NCSW 1934: vii). Considering the acclaim given to Porter Lee's conservative "cause and function" speech only five years earlier, the recognition given to the radical views of the Rank and File Movement was nothing short of astounding.

At the conference dinner the night after van Kleeck's paper, William Hodson, NCSW President, and then Commissioner of the New York City Department of Public Welfare, responded to the challenge. His action set off a storm of protest for "criticizing and opposing . . . a single paper read before and at the request of one division . . ." (Springer, 1934: 179). Hodson noted "the repudiation of the present national administration" by "a distinguished member of the conference" and went on to defend social work's liberal stance of support for the Roosevelt administration (Springer, 1934), despite its imperfections, as the only realistic option. Rejecting a path of no action, he also strongly rejected a more radical course which might "destroy the present economic and industrial order" and result in Fascism rather than Communism (*Proceedings*, NCSW 1934: 11, 12). Hodson's was not an altogether idle fear at that time, as the political right, led by the popular Senator Huey "Kingfish" Long, Reverend Gerald L. K. Smith, and Father Coughlin, was massing for political battle in the 1936 elections. Nevertheless, van Kleeck's paper had touched a vital nerve. The NCSW had heard "an evangelist" and liked it, wrote Gertrude Springer (1934) in the *Survey*.

Bolstered by their growth and national visibility, Rank and File leaders began to form the national organization that the Case-Workers Section of the National Conference of Jewish Social Work (NCJSW) had first proposed in June 1933 (Rosen and Fisher, 1933). Two delegate conventions of Rank and File groups, the first in Pittsburgh, February 22–24, 1935, and the second in Cleveland a year later, drew the movement together. The Pittsburgh convention attracted 45 representatives from 30 different organizations in 11 cities and counties, most from employee groups in public-relief agencies. They represented a combined membership of 8,200 workers. The Cleveland convention attracted delegates from 29 affiliated organizations from 15 different cities (Fisher, 1936a, 1980), representing a total membership of about 12,000.

Of the two conventions the Pittsburgh meeting was probably the more significant because of its timing in relation to national events, its effect on spreading the movement, and the challenge it immediately conveyed to "the AASW's claim to speak for the whole of social work" (Fisher, April, 1935: 5). At that point the course of American social policy was still maleable since the cornerstone legislation of the New Deal was pending in Congress. Furthermore, on January 5–7, 1935, the Unemployed Councils of America had mobilized a massive effort in Washington to get the more radical Lundeen Bill passed (Fisher, 1980).

The Pittsburgh convention enabled Rank and File groups to put local issues into national perspective and to formulate a unified program for action. Its platform translated a ripening political awareness that the country's economic plight was tied to fundamental flaws in the capitalist model into a specific corrective program. The convention also formed the National Coordinating Committee of Rank and File Groups in Social Work (NCC) with the mandate and authority to promote employee organizing and national action on the convention positions.

The discussion and final platform resolutions of the Pittsburgh convention reflected many of the positions already accepted and acted on by local Rank and File groups regarding adequate salaries and personnel practices, better training opportunities, improved relief standards, genuine social insurance provisions, guaranteed civil rights, and protection from repressive activities. Delegates also endorsed the Workers Unemployment and Social Insurance Bill (also called the Workers' Bill or the Lundeen Bill), a politically left alternative to the Administration's social security provisions. The Workers' Bill featured universal coverage for all unemployed workers, better benefit levels, funding from general revenues through taxing incomes over $5,000, immediate payment without waiting for reserves to accumulate, and administration by workers' and farmers' representatives (Spano, 1982; NCC, 1935; Fisher, 1980).

As for the National Coordinating Committee, this was not the type of organization ultimately desired by Rank and File leaders. The NCC was only to serve as an interim body en route to a national membership association structured as a "national union of social service employees to be formed by amalgamation of the groups in the field" (Fisher, 1936a: 40). However, convention delegates rejected as premature the first step in this direction, local affiliation by Rank and File groups with the American Federation of Labor. NCC leaders feared that the AFL structure would "divide social work employees among the craft unions" and destroy the solidarity developing between professional and non-professional employees, thereby preventing the emergence of a single, strong national organization (Fisher, 1936a: 40).

Unfortunately, events moved too fast for the NCC to control. The retrenchments and turmoil of the FERA phase-out pushed local protective associations into the arms of the AFL. Once the huge New York Association of Workers in Public Relief Agencies decided to affiliate, the NCC Committee on Constitution had no option at the 1936 Cleveland convention but to encourage local affiliation with the AFL on an individual basis. It could only hope that an independent international charter for social service employees could be obtained in the future through a joint application of the locals (NCC, October 1935; Fisher 1936a), a strategy which was never realized.

The recommendation for local AFL affiliation symbolized the difficulties that the NCC experienced in the year between the Pittsburgh and Cleveland conventions. There was too much to do—organize the unorganized, guide new groups, coordinate the struggle against relief contraction, amass materials on the AFL, maintain alliances, and weld a national movement together—all in a social maelstrom while operating without budget, staff, or office (NCC, October 1935; Fisher 1936a). That it did many of these things successfully if not as extensively as desired is a credit to NCC leaders' dedication and talent. At the 1935 NCSW meetings in Montreal the NCC was officially recognized as an associate member of the conference.[44]

Inasmuch as the hopes for a national membership association had to be deferred, the Cleveland convention reaffirmed the continued organizing work of the National Coordinating Committee. It also brought the publication of *Social Work Today* under the NCC aegis. Politically, the NCC platform endorsed many of the kinds of measures it had supported in Pittsburgh, including the Marcantonio Relief and Work Project Standards Bill and the Frazier-Lundeen Social Insurance Bill. Finally, the Cleveland convention officially blessed the Rank and File marriage with organized labor, setting into motion a new phase of movement life.

By late 1936 the Rank and File Movement had established itself as a clear alternative to the voice of organized social work. It was identified with unions and the use of labor tactics, and with radical reforms stemming from a Marxist perspective. Its politics were a product of life experiences, not just the reflexive rote of Communist rhetoric. Rank and Filers believed that only a $75-a-month job separated the relief worker from the client (Fisher, 1935) and hence that their welfare was tied inextricably to the welfare of the people as a whole rather than to the fortunes of any elitist segment. Thus identified as workers, rather than professionals, Rank and Filers saw a class struggle between capital and labor in which government could be trusted neither as the impartial mediator nor as the protector that liberals of a bygone Progressive Era had imagined. The new bureaucratic apparatus threatened to make social workers the obedient instruments of state-enforced inequities. The social control of a planned economy in which labor would be an influential participant offered the only hope for broader economic and social justice. Despite these lofty ideals, however, the decline of the Rank and File Movement was not far off, and could perhaps have been anticipated by the astute political observer in the softening of the Communist Party line—the Popular Front policy—toward democratic values, Roosevelt and his second New Deal programs, and the common enemy of Fascist aggression abroad.

A MOVEMENT IN DECLINE: 1937–42

After 1936 the Rank and File Movement could not sustain its radical stance toward social work and social welfare. Although the movement continued to grow into the 1940s through unionization, first within the AFL and, from 1938, within the CIO, with the 1936 presidential election the movement began to peter out ideologically. Its historical moment of influence had passed.

Roosevelt's landslide reelection in 1936 affirmed the solidity of the emerging democratic political coalition—organized labor and farmers, ethnic and racial minorities, intellectuals and administrators—and with it the pragmatic design of the new welfare state. It was no longer realistic to expect more radical changes in the political-economic structure. Forced to abandon its strident critique of liberal New Deal policies and programs, and hence its critique of organized social work as well, and unable to find a unified position on U.S. involvement on the war in Europe, between 1937 and 1941 the movement gradually lost its followers. United States entry into World War II completed the decline. Publication of the final issue of *Social Work Today* in the summer of 1942 marked the end of the Rank and File Movement in social work.

The 1936 election assured the movement's acceptance of the unfinished welfare state. Roosevelt campaigned against the ultra-reactionary Liberty League more than the Republican Party, sensing that polarization would unite a maturing Democratic coalition. As for Landon, the Republican candidate, the "Kansas Coolidge" whose symbol was to be the Kansas sunflower, Roosevelt deftly dismissed him, noting that the sunflower "was yellow, had a black heart, was useful only as parrot food, and always died before November" (Manchester, 1975: 140).

Rank and Filers had no other political option but to support the Democratic slate. New Deal initiatives had preempted the development of a viable, progressive third party of farmers and labor. Nor did the Communists under Earl Browder or the Socialists under Norman Thomas attempt a serious campaign. Fearing conservative backlash at home and fascism abroad, the Communist Party developed a Popular Front strategy which sought to coalesce liberals and radicals of all persuasions. In the election this strategy translated into attacks on Landon, support for Farmer-Labor Party efforts at local and state levels, and non-criticism of Roosevelt (Olson, 1972; Haynes, 1975; Spano, 1982). Influenced by the logic of the Popular Front, labor's support of Roosevelt, and the real-politik of a New Deal already in place, the Rank and File Movement added its endorsement as well (*Social Work Today*, October 1936: 4). (See ahead for Popular Front and foreign policy.)

The movement's basic support for the Roosevelt administration continued throughout the later 1930s (*Social Work Today*, April 1937: 3; June 1938: 4), shifting again in the fall of 1939. "The New Deal is Our Deal" wrote the editors of *Social Work Today* in June 1939. And it was, because social workers in and outside of the movement were firmly entrenched in government programs. From this advantageous position social workers sought to hold the administration to its social commitments and to expand the welfare state by extending social security benefits, the minimum wage, health care coverage, and public employment programs.

The shared self-interest of Rank and Filers and professional social workers on matters of wages, working conditions, and higher standards via civil service made it harder to distinguish the positions of the two groups. The idea of trade unions for social workers gained relatively wide acceptance in professional circles, recognized and endorsed even by the American Public Welfare Association. By the same token, between 1936 and 1942, a new preoccupation with professional issues found its way onto the pages of *Social Work Today* in the considerable space devoted to current debates in casework practice, technical issues, and attempts to reconcile casework with more radical perspectives.

The successful attainment of civil service coverage for public social workers in 1939, ironically, further weakened the movement. Social work unions had fought for merit system requirements, but because the professional enterprise had control over the channels of upward mobility in the public welfare agencies, merit in the form of salary differentials and promotions required more professional training. Inclusion under civil service regulations also meant less need for the protective functions of public social work unions.

If, in 1935, Rank and Filers had defined government as an instrument of capital, by 1938 Rank and Filers were "committed to making it an instrument to improve the living conditions for workers" (Spano, 1982: 156). Social work unions no longer regarded awakening the class consciousness of social service workers as a primary aim. On domestic issues, the *Survey* and *Social Work Today* argued a similar liberal line (Olson, 1972). Remarkably, self-interest and the public interest had now become identical.

The movement experienced difficulties of a different sort in the area of foreign affairs. From their beginnings, Rank and Filers had been stimulated by the Soviet experiment, and uncritically supportive of social engineering in Russia, evidently unaware of the massive extent of the Stalinist purges in the 1930s. Although the Moscow trials between 1936 and 1938 did provoke disenchantment with the Soviet Union among many communist fellow-travelers, including movement sympathizers like Harry Lurie, the influence of the Popular Front strategy and Nazi militarism abroad temporarily forestalled any mass exodus and deflected the harshest criticisms of the Soviet system.

The movement had also repeatedly expressed its opposition to international fascism. Therefore, between 1937 and 1939 *Social Work Today* generally took an anti-isolationist stance toward U.S. involvement in developments in Europe (especially in Spain), China, and Africa (*SWT,* May 1937; November 1937). These positions against fascism and U.S. neutrality did not sharply distinguish Rank and Filers from the liberal social work establishment. For example, the *Survey Midmonthly* and the *Survey Graphic,* led by their staunchly progressive editor-in-chief, Paul Kellogg, and John Palmer Gavit, the *Graphic's* foreign affairs editor, also strongly opposed United States neutrality in the face of fascism in Spain, Italy, Germany, and the rising militarism of Japan (C. Chambers, 1971; Olson, 1972).

Harmony among liberals toward interventionism and collective security finally fell apart in August 1939 with the signing of the Soviet-Nazi Non-Aggression Pact. The American Communist Party shifted rather abruptly to an isolationist stance, now ignoring the spectre of world fascism and condemning American interference in an imperialist war. Many of its supporters, Jewish and non-Jewish, Rank and Filers among them, gave up their affinity for and affiliations with the party.

Among social workers, the pact obviously hit Rank and Filers the hardest. Suddenly the movement's position favoring both the Soviet Union and the struggle against Nazi fascism had been rendered untenable. The paradox was resolved by cautiously advocating a neutralist position that stressed social progress at home as the best safeguard against the threat of fascism and opposed any mindless submission to a "save-the-world-for democracy" impulse as had happened in World War I. The theme of reform at home struck a chord with socially minded, liberal intellectuals who were searching for a way to maintain their progressive principles.

In the January 1940 issue of *Social Work Today*, 75 leading social workers signed a "Statement of Principles" arguing the case for nonintervention. The statement opposed the decision to go to war as a way of dealing with unsatisfied social and economic needs and "any developments having in it the possibility of giving the United States an economic stake in the present hostilities." It also advocated continued funds for domestic programs, protections of civil rights, and the taxing and redistribution of war profits (*Social Work Today*, January 1940: 5–6). Three months later van Kleecks's (*Social Work Today*, March 1940) more convoluted argument against intervention in an imperialist war arrived at a similar position of "constructive neutrality."

At the May/June 1940 National Conference of Social Work over a thousand social workers signed the Statement of Principles that had appeared in *Social Work Today*. These noninterventionist sentiments were strongly reiterated in the speeches of NCSW president Grace L. Coyle and Max Lerner, educator, author, and former editor of *The Nation* who was particularly alarmed at the rise of fascist activity in America (*Proceedings*, NCSW 1940: 66–68).

The noninterventionist position did not go unchallenged. In the same 1940 NCSW conference, Vera Micheles Dean of the Foreign Policy Association forcefully argued the need for U.S. responsibility to aid its allies in the face of totalitarianism and the threat to American democracy of a German and Japanese victory. She was applauded by the *Survey Midmonthly* (Olson, 1972; Dean, 1940). Katharine Lenroot (1940), former NCSW president, and Chief of the Children's Bureau, made a similar plea. By the fall of 1940, after Germany had invaded Denmark, France, Belgium, and Holland, social work sentiments, like those of other Americans, began to turn in favor of allied support to Britain and a strong national defense.

Social Work Today's continued noninterventionist position in late 1940 and the first half of 1941 was now putting it at odds with the rest of the social work community. When the Joint Committee of Trade Unions in Social Work continued its unmitigated noninterventionist line at the June 1941 NCSW, the movement was viciously attacked from within. The assault came from the Committee of Social Work Trade Unionists for Britain and Democracy, which was organized by John Fitch and Philip Klein, professors at the New York School. Both had supported the Rank and File Movement and signed the neutralist *Social Work Today* Statement of Principles. Fitch's committee made clear that not all unionists were noninterventionists and accused the Rank and File leadership of having allowed the unions and *Social Work Today* to be used by the Communists "as channels for propoganda against defense measures, and against aid to the enemies of totalitarianism" (Haynes, 1975: 96; Olson, 1972).

For the bulk of NCSW attendees the bitter rift in the movement was anticlimactic. They had already swung away from domestic reform, social action, and the internal defense of democracy to support of preparations for the war effort (Olson, 1972). Still committed to nonintervention after the German invasion of Russia in June of 1941, when Japan attacked Pearl harbor in December, the Rank and File Movement finally joined in the call for mobilization and national unity to win the war (Spano, 1982). *Social Work Today* ceased publication in June 1942, giving way, as it ultimately had to, to political forces far beyond its sphere of influence.

The Rise and Fall of Social Work Unions

During the latter half of the 1930s and the 1940s the union movement in the United States reached new heights of power and public regard. Some of the main factors contributing to this rise were: widespread labor strife and the organizing of the blue-collar, mass-production industries by the Committee (later Congress) of Industrial Organizations (CIO) under John L. Lewis in the mid-1930s (Brooks, 1964); the severe economic recession of 1937–38 which raised unemployment past the 10 million mark and did not begin to abate significantly until war spending heated up the economy in 1940–41; Supreme Court validation of the Wagner Act in 1937; and the economic expansion caused by World War II, followed by an unparalleled peacetime prosperity.

By 1939 blue- and white-collar union membership had soared to 8–9 million persons, almost triple the 1929 figures. Nearly half the members were affiliated with the CIO whose militance spurred a major resurgence in the still larger AFL between 1939 and 1941. By 1945 union growth reached 13 to 14 million members and was still rising at a fast rate, with organizing in industry leading the white-collar sector. The American Communist Party grew alongside the labor movement in these years, the success of each intertwined with the other. Within the labor movement, communist influence was stronger in the CIO unions than the AFL, and particularly in its white-collar segment (Alexander, 1976). Unions of rank and file social workers arose out of this same yeasty soil, reached their heights in the mid-1940s, and declined precipitously in the early 1950s.

Between 1936 and 1950, the spread of unions in social work somewhat paralleled the remarkable growth of the larger labor movement. In 1936 Rank and File protective associations began to affiliate with the AFL, as has already been discussed. In 1937 and 1938 most of the social work unions in public and private agencies switched their affiliation to the more politically progressive CIO. The State, County, and Municipal Workers of America (SCMWA), chartered by the CIO in 1937 to organize all nonfederal government workers, quickly picked up most of the (AFL) AFSCME public welfare locals. The United Office and Professional Workers of America (UOPWA), chartered by the CIO to organize white-collar workers not covered by other CIO unions, picked up all of the AFL federally chartered Social Service Employee Unions in the private agencies.

By mid-1938 the CIO's SCMWA represented 8,500 workers in 28 public welfare locals among its total of 35,000 members. About 1,000 public welfare members stayed with AFSCME (Fisher, 1980). In the voluntary sector, nine SSEU locals had been established by June of 1938 representing about 2,000 members, three-fourths of whom belonged to Local 19, the old AFW in New York City. Though strongest in the Jewish agencies, the SSEUs were by no means a sectarian union. By 1940, for example, 43% of Local 19's membership was based in nonsectarian agencies (Alexander, 1980).

During the war years, public social work unions shrank slightly, while private sector unions maintained a slow growth. As of the summer of 1944, the SCMWA had 43,852 members in 257 locals, 25 of which were social work locals with a membership of 6,518. As for the UOPWA, out of a total of 51,000 members, 4,000 were employees of social agencies, affiliated with SSEUs in 28 cities, and grouped under the National Social Services Division of the UOPWA (Reynolds, 1945). Most of these locals had fewer than 50 members, except for Local 39 in Chicago, which reached a couple of hundred (Haynes, 1975), and Local 19 in New York, which alone had more than 50% of all the members. Collective bargaining agreements were not widespread, but had been negotiated successfully with several private agencies, especially in New York and Chicago, such as: the Russell Sage Foundation, the National Council of Jewish Women, the National Refugee Service, Hull House, and the Jewish Social Service Association, which was the largest Jewish family agency in the country (Haynes, 1975; Fisher, 1980). At its peak in the mid-1940s, the social work membership of the UOPWA numbered some 6,500 professional social workers (plus an additional number of non–social work personnel), about half the size of the AASW during that same period (Alexander, 1980).

Thus, between 1936 and 1945, as unionization slowly gained ground, it seemed that it might become a viable alternative to professionalization as a way of protecting the social work commodity. Or, if not an alternative, at the least unions and professional associations might collaborate and prosper together, as the ideology of each found common expression in the rhetoric of concern for high standards of service to clients and high standards for employment practices. However, after World War II, unions in social work faded, while the professional enterprise dramatically expanded its hold over the social work field. The explanation for this turn of events is complex.

It can be attributed in part to a series of structural obstacles to building social work unions inherent in national and state labor laws, the rules and composition of the sponsoring AFL and CIO labor federations, and the ideology and organizational pattern of voluntary social work. In the public sector, national and state laws prohibited strikes and the legal status of collective bargaining was unclear. Without these potent weapons, unionized public employees, including public welfare workers, were forced to rely on moral suasion, legislative lobbying, and favorable public opinion to achieve their ends (Moore, 1949). Union recognition was difficult to achieve in the private sector because national and state laws did not require employers of nonprofit organizations to bargain collectively with their organized employees, though they did not prohibit it. Similarly, the use of strike tactics in the private sector, though not illegal, was not easily accepted in the social work community.

The structure of the labor federations added to the difficulties of building social work unions. Federation rules would not allow a separate social workers union covering both public and private agency practitioners. Unionization therefore unwittingly contributed to the persistent division between public and private workers, as Rank and File leaders had originally feared (Fisher, 1936a). Ironically, the federation structure submerged the largest segment of social work rank and filers, public relief workers, in a governmental employees organization where it could not establish a distinct identity as a social work body. At the same time, labor federation rules permitted that distinct identity (e.g., through the SSEUs in a National Social Service Division) for private sector rank and filers where the potential for union membership was weakest.

As for the impediments posed by the structure of private social work, Haynes (1975: 86) has summarized these succinctly. Private agency boards suffered no pecuniary losses from labor tactics such as strikes. Therefore workers had to generate pressure by the difficult route of swaying agency donor and public opinion. Agency staffs were small and relations with the executives often friendly. The executives also tended to be hostile to collective bargaining, which they were not legally forced to accept. And, hardest of all, a pattern of many small agencies spread far afield scattered potential membership and forced the union to deal with many separate boards and executives.

Larger environmental forces also contributed to the decline of social work unions and the corresponding expansion of the professional enterprise. Essentially, in the 1940s, the political and economic conditions that generated social work unions disappeared. The new conditions fit the interests of professional social work better.

During the Depression, when the market for professional social work contracted, the professional enterprise could neither protect its members adequately against loss of income and jobs, nor its occupational sphere against encroachment by "unqualified" workers. Unions gave rank and file social workers a trenchant analysis of their plight, an instrument for protecting their livelihoods, and a measure of control over chaotic working conditions. As economic stability slowly returned, during the mid-1930s, the interests of unions and the professional enterprise coincided for a short time around raising practice and employment standards. Meanwhile the professional enterprise continued to perform its main functions—commodity definition, marketing, and sustaining elite sponsorship—in order to establish social work as a distinct occupational specialty.

Then, in the 1940s, World War II and the revitalization which followed significantly altered the political and economic landscape for social work. The social work market expanded rapidly again, but unlike the Depression period, now an abundance of voluntary and public sector funds flowed into "professional" social work positions. Drawn by war needs and higher salaries, trained social workers flocked to defense agencies and wartime emergency services (e.g., the American National Red Cross, the United Service Organizations, military hospitals and mobile armed forces field units, emergency service units of public welfare agencies and other newly created government organizations, and welfare departments of defense factories). As a result, the demand for "professionally qualified" public and private agency personnel outstripped the supply, and social work employment opportunities were opened up to recent college graduates with no experience and/or graduate social work education (Johnson, 1943). Graduate social work education, the source of social work's distinctive commodity, was devalued.

After the war private and public sector markets for social work continued to grow, prompting the observation that "personnel in the field [was] more mobile than ever and choices on the part of both professional workers and agencies [were] more opportunistic than at any time in social work history" (Kahn, *The Compass*, June 1946: 24). With opportunity calling and a sizable investment already in place, professional social work leaders again moved to regulate social work's unique commodity market. In 1955 their renewed drive for professionalization culminated in the birth of a consolidated, national professional association, the National Association of Social Workers.

On the political front, the need for unity during the war had muted leftist critiques from labor and other progressive groups. Social work unions came under fire for their leftist positions. After the war communist hysteria led many individuals and groups, social workers included, to disavow any left-wing sentiments altogether. In this climate of expanding economic opportunity and political conservatism, unions were neither suitable nor necessary for promoting and shaping specialization in social service work.

In 1950, the union movement in social work experienced a sudden deflation. Up through 1950 Local 19 in the private sector and Local 1 in the public social service sector, both CIO affiliates from New York City, were the strongest and most successful of the social work unions. In the Cold War aftermath of World War II, both the UOPWA and the United Public Workers of America (the successor of the SCMWA which merged with the United Federal Workers of America in 1946), and nine other unions, were purged from the CIO because of their alleged domination by communists (Alexander 1978, 1980; Brooks, 1964). Many social agency leaders used this excuse to repudiate their agreements with workers and bury the union movement in disrepute. The union idea did not gain respectability in professional social work circles again till the 1970s.

CHAPTER SIXTEEN

The Professional Enterprise Prevails: Reshaping the Social Work Commodity

THE AASW CLOSES RANKS

By the time of the Depression, social work had achieved a measure of public recognition as a profession. Urban, private agency–styled casework was its primary commodity. Social group work, community organization and administration, and research held lesser status. Yet many tasks remained if social work was to model itself after other established professions. There was a need to raise salaries which averaged less than teachers and about par with nurses and urban ministers, to put an end to non-uniform apprenticeship training in the agencies, to establish greater uniformity in educational requirements, and to attract a larger body of students with B.A. degrees so that education could truly be considered graduate level (E. L. Brown, May 1932). The Depression provided the impetus and the opportunity to achieve many, though not all, of these interrelated tasks. Through it all, despite multitudinous pressures, casework remained social work's dominant professional modality.

While in the early years of the Depression professional social workers temporarily lost ground, enterprise leaders envisioned a better day, for social workers were hardly in a position of "enforced idleness" (*The Compass*, October 1931: 2). In preparation, social workers fortified the membership requirements for their professional associations, a policy of "greater selectivity." Stricter educational qualifications gave organized social work a more legitimate claim to unique skill and knowledge and provided an easy test to distinguish the professional from the nonprofessional in employment classification and legal certification proposals.

The promulgation and enforcement of increasingly more exclusive requirements—some would say, "higher standards"—for membership in the American Association of Social Workers (AASW) and the American Association of Schools of Social Work (AASSW) served as the major means of perpetuating the casework definition of social work.[45] For the former, these requirements entailed, by 1933, some prescribed mix of undergraduate college education and/or experience in an approved agency and/or course work in an approved school of social work (graduate).[46] The thrust of the requirements was to establish a uniform educational baseline and to move gradually but firmly toward academic education over agency experience as the avenue for professional standing. For the AASSW, the requirements entailed a minimum recommended curriculum (1932), and a fateful 1937 decision that by 1939 all member and applicant schools needed to offer a full, two-year graduate course of study. In both instances the implementation of these membership requirements excluded most of the thousands of newly employed public service workers from AASW membership and "professional" social work training opportunities in graduate and undergraduate programs, even though they were publicly identified as social workers by virtue of their roles and functions.

Social workers had ample opportunity to modify their selective membership criteria and consciously chose not to do so. Between their adoption in July 1929 and their implementation in July 1933,[47] the National Membership Committee (NMC) of the AASW had carefully considered the potential impact of making the new standards operational. At the NMC meeting of November 7, 1931 (SWHA, NASW, f6, #50: 2–4), a study subcommittee indicated that "only 18.8% of seniors admitted to membership in 1929 and 1930 would have been eligible under the new requirements." (See also, *The Compass*, July 1931; March 1932; Davies, June 1932.)

The subcommittee also clearly spelled out the pros and cons of modification. Without modification, thousands of new public relief workers would never be able to meet the membership requirements, thereby intensifying the division between public and private agency workers and weakening the association by not "having the majority of persons doing social work belong to it." On the other hand, the new requirements were "lower than for any other professional group." Modifying or postponing them "would remove the present impetus to higher standards" in social agencies and among new workers, while "strong backing of the A.S.P.S.W. by the A.A.S.W. would do for standards of social work training what the backing of the medical schools by the A.M.A. did for standards of medical education" (SWHA, NASW, f6, #50: 2–4).

Moreover, AASW leaders and members knew that 65% of its membership consisted of caseworkers compared to 17% in community organization and 6% in group work, that this had resulted from previous membership requirements, and that the new qualifications would likely exacerbate the disparity in this mix (*The Compass*, August 1929: 4; February 1933; West, June 1933; Pettit, July 1933). They were aware of the problems and needs of the flood of untrained workers coming into the public relief agencies, including salaries, job security, and working conditions. Despite all of the foregoing, the AASW members voted overwhelmingly to put the new standards into effect. Twenty AASW chapters favored adoption as is, nine favored adoption with modifications, two favored postponement (Pettit, July 1933: 10).

Just as the political consciousness of rank and file workers had reflected their particular relationship to the means of production, a position which led them to a radical critique and militant protective organizations, so the decisions of professional social workers reflected theirs. Professional social workers grasped the potentially favorable implications of the opportunistic employment market in public welfare. The path of greater selectivity fit their *weltanschauung*. Walter West (1933: 12–13), executive secretary of the AASW, expressed this outlook perfectly, as always equating the profession's self-interest with the public interest:

It seems clear that social workers have been retained in their positions because their importance in this crisis has been recognized. If that is true, it bears on a fundamental policy of the A.A.S.W., namely, that the first objective is to improve social work personnel and consequently to improve the services performed. . . .

Raising the standard of personnel, broadening professional education, providing better interpretation of the significance of problems and services and by degrees achieving a status for social work and the social worker—these are the steps in securing professional recognition. That status in turn yields job safeguards of all kinds and enables the worker to make his intellectual contribution to the program of which he is a part. . . .

Many social workers evidently agreed with West's analysis. In 1933, applications for membership in the AASW increased three-fold over each of the previous four years, respectively from 1929: 889, 791, 680, 975, and 3,048 (Minutes of National Membership Committee Meetings, March 28, 1931; April 15, 1934: SWHA, NASW, b6, f#50, 51).

The swell in AASW membership did not continue apace throughout the decade, however. Ten years later, in 1942, membership had increased only by some 3,500 to 10,830 (Johnson, 1943). For this and other reasons the issue of membership requirements continued to be debated (*The Compass*, April 1940). Still, in both 1940 and 1942, when the matter was put to a vote, the members again affirmed their policy of greater selectivity, setting the stage for a long period of internal divisiveness about the nature of the social work commodity and the point of entry to professional practice. The membership issue also heightened the problems of attaining social work certification.

THE DILEMMA OF CERTIFICATION

State registration or certification can be defined as "the act by which a governmental unit endorses by definition or by examination the qualifications and competence of certain persons to perform a function in which this government recognizes an interest in the quality of performance" (West, 1932: 6). The terms are very nearly interchangeable, certification being a bit stronger by connoting "a more active governmental function than does registration, which may be limited to keeping a list of certain types of individuals" (West, Ibid.) By implication, uncertified individuals are unqualified to practice. Professional licensure goes the next step by legally restricting the right to practice only to persons officially certified in some specified manner.

In private industry the company that can institute its commodity standard for the industry as a whole has achieved a major marketing advantage. With professions state certification establishes an industry-wide standard for that political jurisdiction. If social work certification were achieved state by state, based on standards set by the professional enterprise, it would gain extensive control over the social work commodity and pave the way for a single national standard. Wherever the hiring of professional social workers is stipulated, these standards would hold.

Understandably, then, social work leaders were very interested in legal certification. Beginning in 1928 when the California League of Women Voters introduced the first social work certification bill in the country into a state legislature, they have continually sought its establishment. Since certification requires a set of easily measurable objective criteria, it precluded and reinforced the establishment of other selective professional standards, such as educational requirements for membership in AASW.

In the 1930s and 1940s, social workers viewed certification as a way to protect their domain from the assault of untrained emergency workers and to assure their dominance in the growing public sector (*The Compass*, September 1933). But social workers failed in their efforts to gain legal certification. By 1945 certification was legally mandated only in Puerto Rico (1934). None of the 48 states had established certification by law, though California (1932) and Missouri (1934) had each set up plans for voluntary registration of social workers (Anderson, 1945). The failure illustrates a fundamental dilemma which aspiring social workers encountered during the Depression and helps us understand some of their other struggles and decisions.

In order to fulfill their professional ambitions, social workers required both a sizable number of practitioners and a group with certifiable expertise based, at the very least, on educational standards. Both of these requisites could not be met simultaneously in the 1930s. The logic and culture of professionalization pushed toward greater selectivity; this was the paradigm of other professionalizing occupations. But greater selectivity reduced the number of persons identified with the professionalizing group. Alternatively, the logic of industrial unionization pushed toward mass organization. Here inclusion of the broadest possible number of workers raised the political potency of the occupational group by virtue of its size, but weakened claims to special expertise.

Between 1930 and 1940 the number of persons holding social work positions according to census enumeration had grown from approximately 40,000 (*The Compass*, September 1933) to 70,000. Some 11,000 of these belonged to the AASW, a gain of about 5,000 since 1930. "Professional" social workers represented only about one-seventh of the total population of social workers. Less than 50% were estimated to have had any technical training in social work at all. Moreover, compared to other professionalized occupational groups such as physicians (165,000), lawyers (178,000), nurses (365,000), or teachers (1,000,000 plus), even the most inclusive count of social workers was still relatively low (Johnson, 1943). As social workers, conscious of their territory, stratified their occupation to gain better control of it, their rigid standards also preordained small size and an exceedingly slow growth rate for professional social work for many years to come.

The failure of social work's certification efforts should by now be plain. Since legal certification must be enacted by state legislatures, inclusion of the huge numbers of social service workers in the public system would have given the professional enterprise a mass organization with substantial potential for influence at the state level. At the same time, since the criteria for determining who was a social worker would have been broadened, the argument for certification based on special expertise would have been undermined. In choosing the route of greater selectivity over mass organization, organized social work lacked the political power to lobby successfully for its cause.

Was any compromise possible? For example, could social workers have established different levels of certification based on different degrees of experience and education as they had once done with junior and senior membership in the AASW, and as is the situation in many states in the 1980s? Once social workers proceeded to affirm and reaffirm their AASW membership criteria, they locked themselves into their dilemma. They fought any proposals on standards that might have led to compromise, such as the possibility of entrée to a professional degree at the undergraduate level. The struggle over the status of undergraduate social work programs in the 1940s, taken up later, was probably one of the least well known yet fiercest battles in the field.

RETOOLING SOCIAL CASEWORK

Casework practice by social workers who belonged to the AASW in the 1930s did not fully incorporate the psychiatric insights and treatment principles presented in the social work literature (Field, 1980; Alexander, 1972). The diffusion of innovation progressed slowly, and a sizable number of AASW members still had had only minimal exposure to casework training in a professional school. This reality did not diminish the ideal of casework treatment nor its hold on the field. The ideal was well promoted by social work leaders and educators who took responsibility for raising social work's prestige as a scientific profession.

The prominence of social work as casework treatment eventually gained from the growth of federally sponsored public assistance. When the federal government was forced to take over material relief, many caseworkers moved from the shrinking private sector to administrative and supervisory positions in the growing public sector. They brought the assumptions, tools, and philosophy of social treatment along with them. Large-scale federal relief also freed up the private family and children's and mental health agencies financially and philosophically to concentrate on and refine their counseling technologies (Rich, 1956; French, 1940). As the public sector solidified, these technologies were gradually refitted to the contours of this enormous market. Adherents of casework in positions of influence in the professional enterprise and the emerging social welfare industry provided a crucial push for this interpretation of social work by their insistence on professional training and standards. During the 1940s the unusual stresses of World War II also increased the market for medical and psychiatric social workers to counsel members of the armed forces and their families.

Whether or not professional social workers ever convinced the citizenry of the value of their treatment expertise for the public welfare agency remains in doubt to this day. The machinations of bureaucratic politics seem to account better for the profession's hold in the public sector. Nevertheless, professional social workers in the 1930s invested considerable energy in adapting their private agency practices to the requirements of the public setting. To say that this endeavor was a necessary, though not sufficient, condition for capturing the public sector market for social work services in no way demeans the sincerity of the social work leaders who were so engaged. They, more than anyone else, had to believe in their product in order to successfully persuade others of its value.

The professionalization of public welfare had long been an interest of the leadership at the School of Social Service Administration at the University of Chicago, e.g., Julia Lathrop, Grace and Edith Abbott, and Sophonisba Breckinridge, and of various kindred organizations like the Association of Public Welfare Officials (later APWA), the AASW and its predecessors, and others. A major objective was to protect public welfare agencies from the evils of the political spoils system (Abbott, 1936). The concept of civil service and a merit system for hiring public welfare administrators and social workers had its genesis here, and was fought by many local, state, and federal elected officials because it interfered with their patronage customs.

Another objective was to bring knowledge and skill to bear in the fulfillment of a public responsibility—the planning, administration, and delivery of social welfare services. For social workers like Gertrude Vaile this meant that public welfare services should encompass both financial assistance and social treatment by competent caseworkers, in accordance with the "higher" standards of the more professionalized private sector. Said Stanley Davies in 1932, "As between public and private agencies, it is inconceivable that we shall be content for very long to accept two sets of standards. ... It is perhaps truer of social work than of any other practice that there can be only one standard, namely, what is for the best interests of the individual and the group."

The difficulty with applying the single standard and providing individualized treatment derived from the nature and precipitous growth of the national market for public social work. In economic terms, the exigencies of the Depression required the rapid construction, almost from scratch, of a massive, labor-intensive, undercapitalized social welfare industry. The costs of its major product, material relief, were unprecedented; the costs of administration and production, namely staff costs for management and delivery, were similarly huge. Tremendous demand and the temporary state of emergency relief created an oversupply of jobs for unskilled workers at low salaries. Since the private agency job market was decreasing, skilled workers moved into the new public field, but at necessarily depressed salary levels. Nor was there much place for individualized casework treatment if any headway was to be made in stemming the relief epidemic. Where, then, did casework treatment fit in and who should provide it?

As for who should provide it, the strategically situated leaders of the new welfare industry, who had come from professional social work, had little doubt that experienced administrators of casework services and skilled caseworkers were necessary and desirable. Harry Hopkins and his appointees at the FERA, Katharine Lenroot, the protégée of Grace Abbott at the Children's Bureau and her successor in 1934, and Jane Hoey, Director of the Bureau of Public Assistance, all played key roles in promoting professional social work standards and training (Leighninger, 1981).

The public agency staff members who were sent for social work training, and the professionals the industry sought to hire were largely taught social casework. Though courses in community organization, group work, public welfare administration, child welfare, and research were prescribed by the minimum curriculum of AASSW member schools adopted in 1932, classroom education was dominated by the philosophy and methodology of private agency casework. The Northeastern schools, in particular, stressed psychiatric casework, which by the late 1930s had developed far enough to arouse conflict between advocates of a Freudian-based diagnostic model and a Rankian-based functional approach.

Fieldwork, the potent experiential aspect of professional training, was carried out primarily in private agencies, even for the 1,137 federal and state relief workers who participated in a grant-supported training program in graduate schools of social work. Many of the family societies that had been forced to curtail training activities in the early years of the Depression resumed them in the mid-1930s. In 1935, 867 students from 36 schools of social work did fieldwork in 59 family service societies. In 1936, 92 family service agencies accepted 1,010 students (Rich, 1954: 133–34).

Adapting casework treatment to the public welfare agency was difficult, since the majority of clients, in crushing numbers, sought relief because of social factors beyond their control. Social work educators devoted considerable attention to this matter. Seldom in doubt about the basic worth of individual treatment, they found many ways to support the role of caseworkers and to rationalize the utility of psychiatric concepts "in maintaining morale, in emphasizing the connection between mental health and economic health, and ... lessening the stigma in accepting help on personal problems" (Day, 1936: 333; Rich, 1937). This is not to say that casework theorists were politically naive, conservative, or socially insensitive. On the contrary, many prominent educators such as Antoinette Cannon, Gordon Hamilton, Bertha Reynolds, and others who supported social action from a variety of political perspectives all saw a place as well for social casework in public welfare.

Bertha Reynolds, who agonized over the role of the social caseworker in a social order she believed to be unjust, spoke eloquently, for example, of the need for public assistance caseworkers to "*individualize* a program planned for the average or the mass," and "to serve their clients with the same dignity and mutual respect as in the private practice of a profession" (1934: 39; 1935). Mindful of the dangers of intrusive authority in public assistance, Reynolds also saw a political value in counseling, "if it frees men from crippling accumulations of fear and hate so that they may have energy to use what intelligence they possess," to work for "a better social order" (1934:27).

Within the constraints of public assistance, then, casework treatment had the potential to be useful with all manner of clients, though all clients might not need, want, or be able to make use of such a service (Fink, 1942). Under positive circumstances, casework would respect self-determination, and draw on skill and knowledge in the management of human relationships to promote personal growth and constructive activity (Hamilton, 1937; Vaile, 1940). In meaner circumstances casework would be abused by forcing it into the mold of investigation, means testing, or hunting for chiselers (Siegel, 1935). Psychological concepts, easily subject to misinterpretations of behavior and motivation, would be used to limit eligibility; clients would be manipulated through the coercive power inherent in the caseworker's authority; and economic injustice would be perpetuated. Professional training presumably increased the likelihood of sensitive treatment, but gave no guarantee that it could withstand the pressures of inadequate budgets and bureaucratic demands. Caseworkers and their technology could fit either set of conditions. In any event, since most public welfare workers either lacked the desire or the credentials for admission to graduate social work schools, the true value of professional casework in public agencies could not be fully tested.

In the private sector, casework treatment continued its development along psychiatric lines almost without interruption. As early as 1925 family society leaders had recommended a division of responsibility for relief among public and private agencies, such that "the private society doing family casework of a high order may extend its services to clients who can pay, even as visiting nurse associations do" (Rich, 1956: 100). Ten years later the Depression had brought about the first recommendation and set the stage for the second. Freed from the main responsibility for providing relief, private agency caseworkers could be more selective about the problems they treated and more oriented to a middle-class clientele. Private sector leaders such as Linton Swift staunchly advocated for public programs, public/private agency cooperation, and social work's continued commitment to the poor. Even so, differences in the kinds of problems and needs of their clientele inexorably widened the distance between public and voluntary social work practice.

One form of distancing came with the establishment of fees for service. The payment of fees had been going on for some time in medically controlled host settings such as child guidance clinics. The development of fee payments for casework services in purely social work agencies began with the Jewish Family Service in New York City in 1943 (Levenstein, 1964). By 1945 fee payment had been established in 15 family societies and was well on its way to institutionalization. The Committee on Current and Future Planning of the Family Welfare Association of America that examined this development at the time said:

> . . . First, the principle of paying for goods or services is an integral part of our American culture. Second, family casework, as a method of helping families with personal difficulties, is available only within the setting of the family agency, and, therefore, it is neither sound nor just to discriminate against those willing and able to pay and who would not feel free to use the service unless given the opportunity to pay. (Rich, 1956: 157)

Payment of agency fees for service also paved the way for another such "nondiscriminatory" activity, the practice of social work outside of agency auspices supported by client fees, i.e., private social work practice. This idea had been on the edge of professional consciousness since the 1920s awaiting the right political-economic conditions to flower.[48] Aided by agency fee payments, the market for private practice began to open for social work in the late 1940s and early 1950s and really took off in the 1970s and 1980s with the success of licensing legislation and third-party vendor payments.

SOCIAL WORK'S LABOR MARKET PROBLEMS

The segmentation of the market for casework services seemed to hold the promise both of higher professional status and correspondingly better salaries. If the "psychiatrization" of social casework raised social workers' status, however, it did little for their pay. Salary improvements, dependent as they were on tax dollars and voluntary philanthropy, were delayed by the stifling impact of the Depression on wages in the United States in general and its particular effects on the social work field. In the larger society the average weekly earnings of industrial employees did not reach their 1929 rate of $28.55 until 1939, an annual rate of $1,485 (*Statistical Abstract*, 1943: 148). These depressed salaries, in turn, depressed the levels of giving to Community Chests, the funding source for many private casework agencies.

Social work salaries followed the general pattern of other industrial workers, professional aspirations notwithstanding. (See Table 1.) According to Hurlin's study of 255 family societies, in 1932 median salaries for caseworkers in family welfare organizations ranged from $1,400 for cities under 25,000, to $1,632 for cities above 500,000; casework supervisors ranged from $1,950 to $2,820 (E. L. Brown, 1936: 107). An updated study by Hurlin in 1936 found almost no change; the median casework salary was $1,500 for cities under 25,000, and $1,635 for cities above 500,000 (E. L. Brown, 1942: 178).

In Chicago a 1932 study of the largest public and private agencies—the United Charities, the Jewish Social Service Bureau, and the Unemployment Relief Service and Field Service Division of the Cook County Bureau of Public Welfare—did not reveal significant differences in the salary ranges of caseworkers by agency auspice, e.g., between $1,200 and $2,040. The median salary for all caseworkers in the Chicago study was $1,620, somewhat lower than reported

Table 1. Social Work Salaries During Depression Years
(All are annual median salaries unless indicated otherwise.)

SETTING	YEAR					
	1931	1932	1933	1936	1937	1946
Hurlin study family soc's N = 255		caseworkers $1400–$1632		caseworkers $1500–$1635		
UJC's of Chicago Jew. Soc. Serv. Bur. Cook Co. DPW		$1620				
AAPSW psych. and med. soc. wkers.			$2000			
JVS study psych. soc. wkers.	$2100				$1828	
L. French study child guid. clin.						
ment. hygiene			$2100		$2100	
ment. hosps.			$1800		$1800	
family welfare			$1800		$1800	
child welfare			$1800		$1800	

SETTING	YEAR					
	1931	1932	1933	1936	1937	1946
AASW members Worc. Mass. Chpt.			$1500			
Boston, Mass. 4 public and 50 priv. agens.						
female cwkrs.				$1543		
family agens.				$1553		
childs agens.				$1657		
medic settgs.				$1430		
public agens.				$1809		
Steele & Blatt prof'l. salaries						
starting wkers.						$1500–$1800
expermcd. wkers.						$1800–$2400
NY state entry					$1800–$2300	

for family agency workers in Cleveland, Pittsburgh, and Los Angeles (Jeter, 1933), and not far different from what other industrial workers were earning.

Among psychiatric social workers, a highly professionalized segment of casework along with medical social workers, the median salaries of members of the AAPSW between 1930 and 1933 was $2,412 (actually dropping to $2,000 in 1933). But, it should be noted that these salaries do not distinguish beginning workers from supervisors (French, 1940: 101–5). A study of salaries offered for positions in psychiatric social work registered with the Joint Vocational Service showed that between 1926 and 1931, the median salary was $2,100; in 1937 it was $1,828. Again, these figures cover all positions, not just entry-level jobs; they also show how static the field was (French, 1940: 105).

Furthermore, according to French, salaries did not vary a great deal by different types of agencies within the psychiatric social work field, though mental hygiene and child guidance clinic positions led the others. Median salaries in 1937, about the same as for 1933, were respectively: child guidance clinics, $2,100; mental hygiene clinics, $2,100; mental hospitals, $1,800; family welfare, $1,800; child welfare, $1,800 (Ibid., 105–6). After careful study of the psychiatric social work field, including the above figures, French (1940: 101) indicated in an optimistic tone that beginning workers with a college degree plus two years of graduate study in a professional school "may be assured, after training, of an annual salary of from $1,500 to $1,800 and may reasonably hope, within a few years, for a remuneration of $2,000 to $3,000."

In Massachusetts, the Worcester Chapter of AASW found in 1933 that the median salary for staff workers in their city was $1,500; by comparison, for elementary school teachers it was $2,000, and for high school teachers, $2,475 (E. L. Brown, 1936: 102). Three years later, Boston salaries were not much better. A study of 4 public and 58 private agencies in July 1936 found that the median salary for female caseworkers was $1,543. Broken down by public and private auspices, it was $1,553 in family agencies; $1,657 in children's agencies; $1,430 in medical settings; and $1,809 in public agencies. These salaries were considered to be $100 to $200 lower than the median salaries for caseworkers in other Eastern cities (The Compass, February 1937).

Finally, in a book on social service careers published in 1946 (Steele & Blatt), the authors indicate that social workers with complete professional training but no experience could expect beginning salaries of between $1,500 and $1,800 a year. With experience, the salary range was between $1,800 and $2,400; supervisory and executive positions began at $2,400 and ranged to $5,000, going all the way to $10,000 or more for executives of large agencies and public welfare departments. Salaries in the psychiatric social work field were slightly higher. Salaries in public assistance agencies were also comparable to those mentioned above, varying a great deal by size of population served and scope of program, e.g., from $1,200 to $2,600 for positions with primary responsibility for carrying caseloads. In New York, by way of illustration, entry positions for state-employed social workers commanded from $1,800 to $2,300, with an annual increase of $100. The entry salaries of senior social workers (positions requiring graduate social work education and/or experience beyond the B.A.) ranged from $2,400 to $3,000, and social work supervisors, from $2,760 to $3,360 (Steele & Blatt, 1946: 189–90). The extent of professional social work training required for these entry positions is not clear.

Taken together, all of these data on salaries—spotty, unsystematic, and difficult to compare as they are—seem sufficient to provide a picture of the financial remuneration for professional social work from the beginning of the Depression through World War II. They suggest that social work salaries did not really begin to recover from the cutbacks of the early years of the Depression until after World War II, and then not very dramatically. Neither union activity nor professionalization had much effect on salaries during this period.

The rapid creation of an unskilled, tax-supported social welfare industry helped to keep social work salaries low for much of the 1930s. When private casework agencies, the most professionalized segment of social work, had to give up the responsibility for providing relief, they lost some of their capacity to define what social work was and who could practice it. They also lost some actual dollars previously allocated to the private sector for the administration of public relief. In addition private-sector funds suffered from consistently low levels of voluntary charitable giving.

Private agency caseworkers concentrated on fashioning a more exclusive social work commodity and fitting it to the public market and to middle-class, private markets. As the private agency model of casework treatment was gradually incorporated into the public sector, social work leaders could ideologically justify requirements for trained personnel. Passage of the 1939 merit system amendments to the Social Security Act increased social work's control of the public sector market and hence the potential for higher social work salaries.

Before significant improvements could take place, however, the need for trained social workers during World War II generated new opportunities and new shortages. Between 1938 and 1940 the number of social work positions had almost doubled, and in the next two years war-connected agencies such as the Red Cross and the USO created 5,000 new social work jobs (Leighninger, 1981: 194). Demand again outstripped supply, opening the door for unskilled workers and volunteers, i.e., lower standards and lower salaries (Anderson, 1945).

Slow to respond at first because of internal conflicts within the AASW (Leighninger, 1981), in 1943 leaders of the professional enterprise took steps to assert better control of social work's markets through concerted planning and action. Two coordinating bodies were created: the Wartime Committee on Personnel in the Social Services, which was a joint effort of several professional associations, and the Interim Committee for Joint Planning in Social Work, which included lay leaders as well as association representatives. The former had the common purpose of increasing the supply of trained social work personnel during the war and reconstruction. The Wartime Committee successfully obtained a classification for psychiatric social workers in the armed services, followed later by a classification for commissioned officers. When the war ended, more than a 1,000 enlisted and commissioned men and women had served in the social welfare program of the armed services (Cohen, 1958). The Interim Committee saw its mission as developing the means for mobilizing social work opinion "on matters of broad social concern and policy" (Leighninger, 1981: 191–92). Both initiatives contributed to the consolidation of professional social work in 1955 under the banner of the National Association of Social Workers.

Expanding the Enterprise: Social Group Work, Community Organization, and the Formation of NASW

THE RESISTANCE TO SOCIAL GROUP WORK

Once professional social work became defined as casework, other practitioners historically identified with social work had great difficulty expanding the social work commodity. To do so required more than a tested body of knowledge and proven effectiveness as a helping medium. It also demanded a capacity for political struggle and influence, control of a sizable labor/commodity market, and adaptability to the casework model. In the 1930s and 1940s social group workers succeeded in gaining recognition of their work as a social work specialty. Community organization practitioners did not.

Group workers entered the 1930s with strong but unfocused claims for professional recognition. They had a historic stake in social work turf, a sizable employment market, influential members already credentialed as social workers such as Eduard Lindeman, Grace Coyle, and Clara Kaiser, and a foothold in various professional schools. In the pre-professional world of social work there had long been persons who worked with groups under auspices identified with charitable social service, e.g., YM/YWCAs, Boys' Clubs, settlement houses, churches, Boy Scouts and Girl Scouts, Camp Fire Girls, Jewish Community Centers, YM/YWHAs, and playground and recreation departments. In 1929, agencies such as these employed more than 11,877 group workers (Williamson, 1929), a fairly large proportion of the 40,000 social and welfare workers estimated by the 1930 census (as adjusted by Hurlin). A group work curriculum had been operating in the graduate social work program at Western Reserve University since 1923, and courses and institutes were also being taught at Carnegie Institute of Technology, at Northwestern University, at George Williams and Springfield colleges (both of which were training schools for the YMCA), and by numerous national agencies. A group work literature had begun to develop, based on the work of authors like Lindeman, Follett, Sheffield, and on studies such as Coyle's influential *Social Process in Organized Groups* (1930). Practice covered a wide range of informal education, recreation, and civic activities across all age groups, though increasingly oriented toward children and youth.

On the liability side coming into the 1930s, group workers had not yet developed a collective consciousness about themselves as a professional group, nor an organizational vehicle for communication and joint action. Many group workers who naturally gravitated toward social work were not equally as attracted to graduate social work training because casework dominated the curriculum and employers did not require it. Even in Chicago, at the center of the settlement movement, Gertrude Wilson recalled how "faculty members at the School of Social Service Administration of the University of Chicago minced no words in their exclusion of any study of an activity remotely connected with recreation. The general population of the country was still dominated by the 'protestant ethic'" (G. Wilson, 1976: 25). In fact, the training program for recreation workers at Northwestern University, developed by Neva Boyd in the 1920s, had originally been an integral part of the Chicago School of Civics and Philanthropy (Kaiser, 1953).

The AASW, too, had been formed primarily by caseworkers, and catered to their interests (see Part 3). Group workers were both left out and left themselves out. When the AASW's new membership requirements were instituted in the 1930s, many group workers could not meet the educational qualifications. About the time these went into effect, however, group workers began to organize themselves, setting off a long internal struggle for recognition within social work.

Group workers' organization began with local associations such as the Chicago Committee for the Study of Group Work Methods and the New York Conference on Group Work in Education. During the summer of 1934, representatives from these and other groups coalesced at a weekend meeting at Ligonier, Pennsylvania, near Pittsburgh. Among the twenty persons present, mainly from the Northeast and Midwest, were Neva Boyd, Henry Busch, Grace Coyle, Charles Hendry, Clara Kaiser, Joshua Lieberman, Eduard Lindeman, Wilbur Newstetter, Claudia Wanamaker, and Goodwin Watson (Hendry, 1947). The efforts of this nuclear group influenced the development of a Section on Group Work and reorganization at the National Conference of Social Work in Montreal in 1935.

The following year, at the NCSW in Atlantic City, about 50 group workers from around the country launched the National Association for the Study of Group Work, later changed to the "American" Association (AASGW) in deference to Canadian participation (Hendry, 1947). Having recognized that the time was ripe for formal organization, but not yet for a professional association, AASGW leaders set out to change their situation. Charles Hendry (1947: 162–65), one of the AASGW leaders, candidly outlined their tactics: "a deliberate effort to enlist and involve national-agency personnel" who had both influence and physical mobility; "the studied cultivation of group workers at local, state, and national conferences of social work"; attention to publishing group-work material and getting it "out into the main stream of professional development"; and "a deliberate cultivation of leaders in fields other than social work," e.g., the Progressive Education Association, the Society of Recreation Workers, and the Orthopsychiatric group. Among the many connections cited by Hendry were: Shelby Harrison, director general of the Russell Sage Foundation; Gertrude Springer and Bradley Buell of the *Survey*; S. M. Keeny of the Association Press; L. K. Hall and Ronald Lippitt, and the Society for the Psychological Study of Social Issues; Wilma Shields and the Junior League; and other national figures in recreation, camping, health and physical education, youth work, and labor education.

Both group work and social work as a whole also benefited from the early actions of settlement leaders in publicly testifying to the dire effects of the Depression, pushing for reforms, and organizing and coordinating relief among the unemployed. Group workers had been in tune with the times and continued to be so as social work practice unfolded during the Roosevelt administration.

The group work approach lent itself to the goals of individual personality enhancement and socialization as well as to the promotion of democratic values and collective action to address social inequities. "The underlying social-philosophical assumption is that individualized growth and social ends are interwoven and interdependent; the individuals and their social environment are equally important" (Newstetter, 1935: 297).

Group work's ideological roots were affected by its churchly social-action origins, the ethnic/sectarian diversity of its personnel and agencies, and the "normalcy" of its "leisure-time settings." It espoused a seemingly neutral, "preparation for informed and responsible citizenship" type of democratic pluralism, rather than any particular political ideology, conservative or radical. However, the value placed on active participation did speak to a kind of populist sentiment that was far different from the casework perspective of the day. Group work's assumptive world was built on rational problem-solving, cooperation, and inclusiveness. In a tumultuous time, its philosophy was reassuring. It provided a middle ground where most social workers could feel comfortable between the importance of the individual and social action.

By the mid-1930s group work had been defined as a conscious helping process akin to casework and community organization (Newstetter, 1935)—helping the individual to grow, to learn, to manage complex civic responsibilities and social roles, and helping society to manage forces that would tear it apart. Advocating this perspective, Grace Coyle's paper at the 1935 NCSW on "Group Work and Social Change" won the Pugsley award, just as van Kleeck's and Lindeman's had the previous year. If the majority of group work papers at the NCSW had attested to a compatibility with casework, Coyle's paper had done this and more. It had spoken to the higher purposes of social work and carved out a vital niche for group work therein.

To gain full acceptance of their practice as a bona fide social work method, group workers also had to penetrate the privileged portals of the professional enterprise. Foremost this meant cracking the AASW's formidable membership barrier. These efforts were only partially successful, and their frustrations as much as any positive professional identity led the group workers finally to form their own professional association, the American Association of Group Workers, in 1946.

The main line of strategy available to group workers was shaped by the existence of a loophole in the AASW's membership policy. Known as Section 6 of the AASW's bylaws dealing with membership (Article IV), the loophole provided an "Exceptional Clause" whereby "the Executive Committee may in exceptional circumstances elect to membership persons who do not technically meet the requirements specified above" (SWHA, NASW, #7, f 58, May 26, 1938). For about a year, beginning in April 1935, there seemed to be some receptivity within the AASW to use this loophole to bring some balance to its membership. Aware of the lack of access to professional education for some social workers, the Sub-Committee on Section 6 of the National Membership Committee (NMC) applied the "exceptional clause" to three groups: "(1) Those who have made an outstanding contribution in their own field of social work and in the community; (2) Those who are discriminated against in securing training (Negroes in the south); (3) Those in fields of social work for which training opportunities in the accredited schools of social work are lacking" (SWHA, NMC Minutes, December 7, 1935: 1).

Under class (3), particular consideration was given to group workers because of their large numbers, growing collective consciousness, and lack of social work training opportunities. The NMC favored a plan to admit "approximately 50 leaders in the group work field with the idea of stimulating training from within the professional association" (Ibid.: 2). Group work leaders, however, countered with a much more inclusive proposal that "for a period of three years the present membership requirements for the admission to the AASW be waived for group workers," subject to an alternative set of specified criteria. These were: "Four years' experience in a recognized group work agency; endorsement by two members of a local chapter of AASW; and one year of graduate study in the social sciences, education or psychology in a university; or one year of graduate study in a school of social work; or a two year period of combined study and field experience" (Ibid., attached proposal). In the interim, training standards for group work would be developed and the number and quality of courses would be increased. Clara Kaiser presented the case for a temporary membership waiver to the NMC. But the committee feared that amending the bylaws would raise the issue of exceptions "for other fields such as public health, vocational guidance, etc." Rather than open the door, the NMC approved its own more limited proposal.

Between 1935 and 1944, group work gained increasing prominence in the profession; the AASGW was formed, 17 group work courses were added to schools of social work by 1939, and Grace Coyle was elected president of the NCSW in 1940 and of the AASW between 1942 and 1944. In this same period internal AASW controversy continued to rage about the AASW membership requirements and the use of Section 6. In 1939 and 1940 the National AASW Board asked the NMC to appoint a series of local subcommittees of AASW members to examine the problems created by the membership requirements for their specific subfields—group work, public welfare, community organization, probation—and to make recommendations accordingly. The 1940 Delegate Conference of AASW meanwhile recommended that the National Board abolish Section 6.

By October 1942, the NMC had reached the same conclusion and said so in a forceful report to the National Board (SWHA, NMC Report to Board, October 9, 1942, #739: 4). This action undercut the work of the appointed subcommittees who had not yet issued their recommendations. When the group worker subcommittee, chaired by Margaret Williamson, did report, its members prudently upheld the AASW's membership standards for all group workers who had entered the field within the past five years and henceforth. Nor did they argue to maintain Section 6. Instead, in a fallback to their 1935 proposal, they again asked for a temporary adjustment in requirements for a five-year period to bring experienced group workers into the fold. As an added bit of pressure, they accompanied this request with a veiled threat that the group workers might separate themselves from their fellow social workers and form their own, independent professional association (SWHA, ibid. #740: 7).

In February 1943, the National AASW Board, acting on advice of the NMC, recommended the abolition of Section 6 to the membership (to be determined by a mail vote).[49] Even though the action on Section 6 did not technically affect the group worker's proposal, the National Board's acceptance of the NMC's recommendations also meant acceptance of the NMC's position against the special provisions proposal of the group work subcommittee. Just as it had in 1935, the NMC feared that a special provision for group workers would open the door to similar requests from other fields. Without a common educational base and membership standard, the Association would then become "a weakly federated group of specialties" (SWHA, Report of the NMC, #781: 20, February, 1943). A request for reconsideration contained in a minority report of the NMC also fell on deaf ears (Ibid., 25–27), as did the threat of a separate professional association for group workers.

After nine years of struggle to crack the AASW membership barrier, group workers had precious little to show for their efforts. Even with Grace Coyle as AASW president during the period of the association's major membership study, the group workers had not been able to gain any ground. Coyle, for her part, had taken office at a point of crisis in the association (see below), and felt she could not champion the needs of any particular subinterest because the whole was in danger of falling apart (SWHA, letter to Kaiser, August 25, 1944). Consequently, at its annual meeting, in Cleveland in May 1944, the AASGW appointed a Steering Committee, chaired by Nathan E. Cohen and representative of the various interests within the group work field, to develop a plan for "an inclusive profession" (Rowe, 1946).

At the same time, with Dr. Coyle leaving the AASW presidency, the group workers again tried to open the AASW to the full range of social work practitioners. On July 18, a committee of AASW members chaired by Clara Kaiser sent their president a letter for board action. They advised that group workers were exploring the need for an inclusive professional society which would not be oriented exclusively to the field of social work, but they also wanted to continue to explore how the AASW could be more responsive to their interests. They formally requested the National Board to appoint a committee of group workers in AASW to collect data on their numbers, encourage chapter recruitment and retention, and reexamine how to overcome the obstacle posed by AASW's membership requirements (SWHA, Minutes of AASW Exec. Comm. Mtg., July 1944). Perhaps because a spirit of unification was in the air with the ending of World War II, or because the pressures of growth in the various sub-sectors were getting too strong, this time the conference committee delegated by the board to recommend action agreed with the request.

The favorable recommendation of the conference group in early 1945 carried significance beyond the field of group work. The AASW had never been structured to recognize and devote organizational resources to functional fields within social work. Up to that point, as far as the AASW was concerned, casework and social work were synonymous. The implications of the special functional subcommittees that the National Membership Committee had previously appointed had been resisted in 1943–44. Now the group workers had opened the way for a broadly inclusive professional association, an umbrella that could cover medical, psychiatric, and school social workers, as well as group workers, community organizers, and others. For both the AASW and the AASGW this direction was consistent with their joint participation on the Wartime Committee on Personnel in the Social Services, and other interprofessional committees, along with representatives of the other existing professional social work associations. It took another ten years, however, for the AASW to actually become a more inclusive organization.

In the meantime, the group workers continued to pursue their own professional interests independently. The publicity between 1944 and 1946 about a pending transformation of the AASGW to a professional association attracted 1,100 new members. In April 1946 a majority of the 2,043 AASGW members voted to become the American Association of Group Workers (AAGW) (G. Wilson, 1976).

The establishment of an independent group work association did not remove group workers from social work's orbit nor excise its social work heart. To actually establish an autonomous profession would have been an extremely arduous and dubious undertaking given its small numbers, composition, and historic affiliations. In 1944 Harleigh Trecker wrote that "group work is a *method in social work* . . . not a profession—social work is the profession" (*The Compass*, March 1944: 4). Even though it was to be an inclusive organization within the group work field, the AAGW was dominated by leaders whose education and professional identification was in and with social work. Nearly all taught at schools of social work or administered major social work agencies where group work flourished; the list is too long to present here. Harleigh Trecker was president of the AAGW when it joined the other social work associations to form the NASW in 1955.

The social work imprint and the emphasis on becoming professional inevitably led the new AAGW to a concern for developing standards of competence and a body of concepts and techniques which would help to steadily raise its stature. "There was less emphasis upon program and social action in other areas of common concern" (G. Wilson, 1976: 30). This direction was not inconsistent with group work's evolution in the mid-1940s as a versatile and "apolitical" method of helping or problem solving, relevant both to social treatment and to a myriad of intergroup, community, national, and even international problems (Somers, 1976). Some members of the AAGW with greater interests in planning and social action left the group work body to work with the newly formed American Association for the Study of Community Organization (1946). By the time the formation of NASW was in the offing, group work had long been ready to become part of the social work commodity line.

COMMUNITY ORGANIZATION MUST WAIT

During the 1930s and 1940s community organization began to emerge as a distinctive method of social work akin to casework and group work. In December 1932 the minimum curriculum adopted by the American Association of Schools of Social Work included community organization in its first grouping of courses. By 1940 a basic literature on community organization in social work had been clearly established (Dunham, 1940). In 1944, community organization was included as one of eight basic areas of generic social work content in the revised minimum curriculum of the AASSW, along with casework, group work, and research. But recognition of this area as a separate and legitimate method of specialization did not come from the Council on Social Work Education until 1962. As with the group workers, the delay had much to do with political-economic factors—a late start in collective self-identity and organization, an inability to establish a sufficient market for their service commodity, insufficient political power to open the doors of the professional enterprise to another specialty, and insufficient conformity to the dominant casework model.

Community organization originated less as a specific method within social work than as a means by which social service providers could develop programs within a given community and mobilize the resources needed to support and sustain them. Although early proponents of community organization like Mary Parker Follett and Eduard Lindeman connected this work with the expansion of democratic principles into local community life, and others like Florence Kelley and Jane Addams identified it as an aspect of social reform, by the late 1920s community organization was largely applied to the planning and delivery of social services within the context of existing social agencies. "Community organization had barely emerged as a cause before it had become a function absorbed into the administrative structure of social work" (Lubove, 1965: 80). This absorption exacerbated preexisting dilemmas concerning the boundaries of community organization. As the impulse toward professionalization grew among social workers, "to the extent that [community organization conformed to this impulse] it [was] harder to integrate it with broader societal efforts and social change. To the extent that it [was] more integrated with such efforts, it [became] harder to identify its distinctive professional base" (Gurin, 1971: 1326).

In the 1920s, community organization's claim as a social work specialty was weakened by the decline of social reform in settlement house work, its continued redefinition by financial federations, and the establishment of casework as the core social work commodity. The decline of the settlement movement after World War I reduced a significant employment market for community organization practitioners. During the 1930s settlement houses dwindled to about 230 agencies (Trolander, 1975), little more than half of the 413 houses estimated for 1910 (see Part 3). By 1940 the National Federation of Settlements had only 155 member organizations (McMillen, 1945). Some grass-roots organizing and neighborhood development work continued during the Depression and World War II (Dillick, 1953; R. Fisher, 1984), but the settlements were not really revitalized until the late 1950s and early 1960s with the resurgent neighborhood movement and the War on Poverty programs.

The council and fund field followed a somewhat similar pattern. In the 1930s, the small but growing voluntary sector market for professional social workers as planners and fund-raisers was stymied by the Depression. The subsequent revitalization of the chest agencies in the 1940s which stabilized this career line was too small by itself to establish community organization as a distinctive social work commodity. Professional education for federation work was also closely controlled by federation executives and tied to training for this specific field rather than for the broader field of community organization in social work. The two schools of social work that served the federation movement almost exclusively from the 1930s to the 1960s, Ohio State University and Boston College, each received substantial financial support from federation organizations (United Way of America, 1977).

Outside of the federation field, the 1930s offered new opportunities for employment in national and state planning, coordination, and policy and program development positions. These jobs enlarged the career possibilities for community organization practitioners in social work and created the potential for a distinctive, yet compatible community organization commodity. Unfortunately, these positions were also immediately subjected to competition from the rapidly professionalizing fields of public administration and city planning that were responding to the same market contingencies. In the narrower social welfare industry, where career lines for professional social workers with community organization skills could have been written into civil service job classification requirements, this was not done. Nor did the radical Rank and File Movement of the 1930s expand the market for community organization, despite the sympathetic support it received from politically liberal and "radicalized" social workers for its progressive social agenda and union organizing.

Throughout the thirties and forties social workers debated the place of social action in their profession. Confusion existed as to whether or not social action was simply an individual civic responsibility, a professional responsibility for all social workers (and if so, how it should be exercised), or a specialized function of professional social work akin to casework. The fact that these possibilities were not mutually exclusive only confused the issue further. Prominent social workers supported all of these positions at one time or another (SWT, June 1936; Lurie, 1937; Fitch, 1940; Lane, 1939; McMillen, 1944; A. Johnson, 1945; Pray, 1945, 1947).

The separation between community organization and social action, each of which had its own organizational section at the NCSW between 1935 and 1945, also reflected the division of sentiment and outlook among social workers. While community organization had something of an independent and durable organizational base to support a professional career line, social action did not. Without that, its proponents would always have difficulty establishing social action as an aspect of community organization and community organization as a social work specialty.

The resolution of the commodity dilemma for community organizers did not begin until the 1939 Lane Report at the NCSW. The activities of the planning committee for the Community Organization Section of the 1939 NCSW and the discussion groups which it initiated in six different cities culminating in the 1939 report marked the beginning awareness of a professional identity among community organization practitioners. The report was drafted by Robert P. Lane, Mary Clarke Burnett, and Arthur Dunham. It identified community organization as a process of social work whose aim is "to bring about and maintain a progressively more effective adjustment between social welfare resources and social welfare needs" (Lane, 1939: 499). Its conceptualization drew heavily from the field of councils and funds but also tried to be more encompassing, for instance in the notion that community organization was practiced on local, state, and federal levels. Its appeal was that as a process, community organization could be readily compared to casework and group work, while its aims sought to promote social welfare services, hence the creation and expansion of social work markets. The latter was especially clear in the listing of secondary objectives such as developing "a better public understanding of welfare problems and needs, and social work objectives, programs, and methods," or developing "public support of, and public participation in, social welfare activities." Its concern for meeting and eliminating social needs also projected an image of institutional reform, though with no specific program for social change.

In 1940, Robert Lane presented a follow-up report at the NCSW. At that time he estimated that the study of community organization stood "approximately where the study of casework stood in 1923 and the study of group work stood in 1935," and recommended the creation of a small, nation-wide committee "to assume responsibility, not for directing, but for focusing the continued study of the concept and practice of community organization" (Lane, 1940: 459). It took until 1946 for community organization practitioners to form the Association for the Study of Community Organization (ASCO). In 1948, ASCO had 1,000 members around the country and at least

13 local discussion groups that reported at its annual meeting (Hollis & Taylor, 1951).

During the mid- and late-1940s, amid much rhetoric about the need for social reform (Pray, 1949), social work leaders in all of its specialties shied away from outright political action and social advocacy except on the narrowest, professionally oriented issues (Olson, 1972). The community organization literature, like group work and casework, stressed the more acceptable idea of community organization as a helping process in the context of a democratic value base (McMillen, 1944; Pray, 1947). This approach enabled community organization in the late 1940s and 1950s (McMillen, 1945; Ross, 1955) to be developed in conformity with the social work commodity as defined by casework, and to fit with the prevalent postwar belief in the abiding soundness of American social and economic institutions. Perhaps the only exception, the Social Workers Action Committee, organized by Harry Lurie in 1945 "to engage in militant action without the impediment of carrying the entire group along with it" (Olson, 1972: 310), failed within a year, out of step with the conservative bent of postwar profession-building.

Community organization practitioners followed the same route as group workers to penetrate the AASW in the late 1930s and early 1940s. They tried to crack the AASW's rigid membership barrier through the route of the Section 6, "exceptional" clause, and related strategies. When the National Membership Committee (NMC) of the AASW undertook its major membership study in 1940, it established a Subcommittee on Community Organization, chaired by Isabel P. Kennedy of Pittsburgh, along with similar bodies on group work, public welfare, and probation and parole. The subcommittee's assignment was to see how applicable the membership requirements were for the field of community organization and to devise some means for identifying professionally competent, but technically ineligible community organization practitioners.

The subcommittee presented its report in October 1942. It identified community organizers only as persons practicing in agencies whose primary function was in the field of community organization, that is, "planning and coordinating agencies, . . . usually known as councils of social agencies, or . . . agencies operating in a similar manner on a state-wide or national basis" (SWHA, Sub-committee on Community Organization, Appendix 10, NMC Report, October 1942: 1). Workers involved in social action groups, neighborhood organizing in settlement houses, and the like were thereby eliminated from consideration. The subcommittee also aligned community organization with casework and group work and did a creditable job outlining its distinctive knowledge and skills. Like the group workers, it then went on to support the AASW's membership requirements for new workers, but recommended special provisions during a five-year period for community organization practitioners with five or more years of professional experience. Their competence, however, was to be determined by a special examination "similar to the unassembled examinations used by civil service authorities." These recommendations were roundly rejected. Without a strong organization of their own to advance their interests, community organizers probably had little chance to succeed.

The fortunes of the community organization wing of social work were probably also set back in the 1940s when Wayne McMillen was forced to resign from the presidency of the AASW in February 1942. (Our brief review of this conflict follows a much fuller account by Leighninger, 1981: Ch. 6; also Leighninger, 1987.) McMillen was a respected professor of social economy at the University of Chicago School of Social Service Administration where he taught courses on community organization, research, and statistics. He had been president of the Chicago chapter of AASW from 1936 to 1938, the second largest chapter in the country with nearly 10 percent of the AASW members, and a chapter noted for its social activism. He was actively interested in public affairs, supported the Rank and File Movement, ran for public office, and promoted the views of public welfare advocated by the Abbotts and their supporters. Backed by the Chicago chapter, McMillen became national president of AASW in 1940.

McMillen brought to the presidency a strong commitment to an organized AASW role in promoting social reform. He also advocated a more decentralized decision-making structure for the AASW which would increase the strength of the membership through their chapters and decrease the power of the national office staff and national board. McMillen had encountered resistance to his ideas about national priorities for social action and AASW structure a number of times over the years from Walter West, the AASW national director. While West was by no means opposed to social action, his order of priorities placed the development and maintennance of professional standards first. West had the support of the "New York-Eastern social work establishment" that continued to dominate AASW thinking. McMillen, of course, represented a "Chicago-Midwestern/other-outsiders" social work faction. The understated conflict between these loosely structured groups on a number of topics—decision-making structure, membership representation, chapter support, public welfare policy, social action—had been a source of tension in the professional enterprise since its inception.

Soon after McMillen took office, for whatever the reason, he filed formal charges with the AASW Board against Walter West on grounds of "Executive Office inefficiency, failure to get the mail out on time, taking 'impulsive action', taking too strong a hand in Association affairs, subverting the President's right to appoint committees, and delay in carrying out national Board policies promoting closer relations between the national committees and the chapters" (Leighninger, 1981: 181). The ensuing conflict and investigation tied the association up in knots for months at a crucial time in its life. After hearing the recommendations of the special study committee, headed by AASW Vice President Kenneth Pray, the National Board essentially upheld West's performance and found that McMillen had "overstepped his role as President" and that "his conduct [was] unprofessional and damaging to the integrity of the organization." The board voted to ask for McMillen's resignation, and at the same time, also asked for West's resignation, fearing the crisis had rendered him ineffective. Kenneth Pray, a West supporter, also decided to resign.

McMillen was replaced on an interim basis by former AASW President Frank Bruno (1928–30), who served as acting president between February and October 1942. Grace Coyle then took over the presidency—a group worker to the breach—and she, in turn, opened the way for Joe Anderson, a colleague from Western Reserve University, to come on as the new Executive Secretary. Whether or not McMillen's fall from grace actually retarded the development of community organization as a social work specialty is obviously speculation. But it is hard to see how it could have been anything but detrimental. McMillen's interests in community organization practice spanned the field—planning at all levels, political and social action, interagency coordination, neighborhood development.

He saw all of these activities as a legitimate part of the social work process requiring specialized expertise. With McMillen as AASW president, community organization practitioners would have had an influential internal advocate for their position.

THE FORMATION OF NASW

On October 1, 1955, the National Association of Social Workers came into being, an amalgamation of seven separate membership associations. Five were formal professional organizations: the American Association of Social Workers (AASW), the American Association of Medical Social Workers (AAMSW), the American Association of Psychiatric Social Workers (AAPSW), the National Association of School Social workers (NASSW), and the American Association of Group Workers (AAGW); two were still informal study groups: the Association for the Study of Community Organization (ASCO), and the Social Work Research Group (SWRG).

A number of factors contributed to this consolidation, including: the positive outcomes of joint action on professional issues during World War II, the push by various membership associations for inclusion in the AASW, the formation of the Council on Social Work Education in 1952 (see Chapter 18), and the apparent benefits of expanding organizational resources so as to influence local and state legislation and the postwar market for social work services. Perhaps with the exception of the AASW, none of these organizations had a politically influential corpus of members. For example, in 1950 the membership figures for the largest of these groups were: AASW, 12,000; AAMSW, 2,250; AAGW, 1,900; AAPSW, 1,200; ASCO, 900; and NASSW, about 600 (Leighninger, 1987).

Furthermore, although "professional" social work within the field was primarily identified as casework in medical, psychiatric, child welfare, and family service settings, in the public's mind social work was still strongly identified with public welfare work. About 40% of the nation's 75,000 social workers worked in public assistance, and few were professionally trained (Ibid.) Untrained workers were also common in other areas of practice identified with social work, such as group work, community organization, and corrections. These workers had been systematically excluded from social work's professional organizations, yet their practice activities were defining the social work commodity, for better or worse. Greater unity in the field might give social workers a greater opportunity to control the definition of their specialized product.

Naturally, the professional bodies potentially interested in forming a single association varied in their motivations. The better-established groups—AASW, AAPSW, AAMSW—had the highest membership standards, clearer public recognition and acceptance of their special expertise, and hence higher status within social work's occupational sphere. Still, they could benefit from the political and financial advantages that larger numbers would afford. The lesser-established and/or smaller groups would benefit from size, but also from affiliation with a more widely recognized professional body. In all cases, however, there would be a natural tension between loss of identity and autonomy as a specialty group and the advantages of being able to speak out with one professional voice on issues of professional concern (Ibid.).

Growing out of an AASW delegate conference, in January 1949, six professional associations—the AASW, AAMSW, AAPSW, NASSW, and the American Association of Schools of Social Work (AASSW)—formed a Committee on Interassociation Structure to explore the concept of creating a single professional social work association. A few months later it recommended formation of a single, merged professional body with subdivisions to accommodate specializations and particular professional concerns, as contrasted to a federation structure where each member association would maintain its own identity. On the matter of membership, the committee proposed gradations of classification (for a five-year period) from workers with a B.A. plus one year of practice experience to those with degrees from a two-year graduate social work program. These gradations were designed particularly to bring public assistance workers into the professional fold (Ibid.; Cohen, 1958).

With enough consensus to maintain the initiative, but without full agreement, in 1950, the Committee was reconstituted into a Temporary Inter-Association Council of Social Work Membership Organizations (TIAC), consisting of four representatives from each of the five formal professional associations. Representation from the Association of Schools, as well as from the SWRG and ASCO, was excluded at that time. As usual, the main conflicts in the group came over membership standards: exclusiveness versus inclusiveness. Without any means of organized representation, public welfare workers were destined to be kept out by TIAC's proposed membership requirements. After further negotiation and pressure by TIAC on the SWRG and ASCO to adopt membership standards for their own groups, these two organizations were finally admitted into the deliberations.

In the spring of 1953, a proposal for a unified professional association was accepted in principle. Formal action on a proposed organization and bylaws was taken by the membership of all seven associations by mid-February 1955. The new organization, the National Association of Social Workers, was structured as a single body with a single membership standard—two years of graduate study, after blanket acceptance of the members from each of the founding bodies—divisions for the specialties, six commissions on professional and policy issues, and Delegate Assembly with authority to define the broad policies of the organization (Leighninger, 1987; Cohen, 1958). NASW began operations in October 1955 with 20,000 members. Joseph Anderson, director of the AASW, was selected as executive secretary.

The membership standards of NASW reinforced the accreditation requirements of the Council on Social Work Education, which had been formed a few years earlier, for retention of the graduate degree as the entry level to the profession. (See Chapter 18.) Perhaps the AASSW's early participation in the Committee on Interassociational Structure had sufficiently alerted the other members to the dangers of professional recognition for practitioners holding B.S. degrees. If NASW had allowed a B.A. membership category, it would have provided an avenue of legitimation for undergraduate social work schools, thereby undermining the hard-won CSWE structure. Taken together, these two professional associations represented the twin towers of a modernized professional social work enterprise, built primarily to private agency, casework specifications.

CHAPTER EIGHTEEN

Social Work Education

THE BATTLE FOR UNDERGRADUATE RECOGNITION

Even more than professional associations, professional schools determine the nature of the service commodity by the students they choose to prepare, and the content and manner of their preparation. They also affect the price of the service commodity in the market, i.e., the size of fees and/or salaries, by their role in the balancing of supply and demand. Professional schools, working in tandem with professional associations to set standards for an occupation, are its true guardians of entry.

During the 1940s a critical battle over social work standards took place in the educational arena. Its outcome had major political and economic ramifications for social work as a profession. The crux of contention was whether undergraduate social work education would be recognized as professional education, making the undergraduate social work degree the first point of entry to the profession. The main protagonists in the battle were the American Association of Schools of Social Work (AASSW) representing the older and established graduate social work schools, and the National Association of Schools of Social Administration (NASSA) representing the less-established undergraduate social work programs.

The stakes of the battle were high. Politically, the control of the professional social work enterprise was on the line, since more undergraduate than graduate schools offered social work courses. Economically, the nature and price of the social work commodity were at risk. Undergraduate programs were more generic in their approach—many were located in college and university sociology departments—and they reached a much larger and broader cross section of the college student body.

The Depression and the construction of a nationwide social welfare industry fueled the struggle. As federal emergency relief and categorical assistance programs spread across the country, public agencies faced a tremendous shortage of trained workers. Rural and small town social service departments felt the shortage most acutely due to the uneven distribution in the supply of trained social workers—located primarily in the northeastern states, parts of the Midwest and Pacific coast, and a few southern states—and state and local policies that stipulated the hiring of residents and unemployed persons, qualified or not (J. Brown, 1940; Harper, 1948).

The demand for social workers generated by the Roosevelt administration program created a bullish market for all levels of social work education. Undergraduate colleges and universities throughout the country set up numerous training programs for social workers in response to thousands of young men and women seeking relevant social work and sociology courses. They were a boon to social service departments suffering from the deficits of inexperienced personnel. Several of these courses were approved by the AASW as "random courses" in social work that could be used to meet the eligibility requirements for AASW junior membership. But offering AASW-approved courses did not constitute the basis for accreditation by the American Association of Schools of Social Work (AASSW). The vast majority of these undergraduate institutions had no connection to this organization.

The market also rose dramatically for graduate professional schools of social work, stimulated by the demand from college graduates who could not find employment. Full-time and part-time enrollment in graduate schools of social work virtually doubled between 1933 and 1934, jumping from 1,981 to 3,910 (SSR, June 1941: 337–41). This favorable market situation helped social work leaders establish hiring policies in the public sector that were preferential to social workers with graduate-level training.

Starting with the FERA-funded training program in 1934 which was instituted and controlled by leaders of the social work enterprise, federal- and state-sponsored social work training and work-leave opportunities, a major source of social work students from then on, began to be used to feed the schools accredited by the AASSW (J. Brown, 1940). The 1,137 federal and state subsidized students in this first program accounted for more than half of the part-time students enrolled in AASSW member schools, and represented nearly 30% of the total enrollment, full- and part-time, for 1934. Requests from unaccredited state universities to be included in the FERA-funded training effort were turned down on grounds that their programs could not be evaluated (Ibid.). Furthermore, since the FERA training program was designed for graduate study, applicants had to be able to meet graduate admission requirements. These requirements automatically excluded the bulk of the staff members in rural and smaller social service departments, and many others.

AASSW policy decisions over the next eight years tightened its control of social work education by tying it exclusively to graduate study. Before 1930, when the market could not support graduate-level education, training for social work had been primarily an undergraduate endeavor. In 1933 the AASSW decided that eligibility for admission to the association required a school to offer at least one year of graduate study, and this standard was applied to all the member schools in 1934. In 1936 the AASSW ruled that after October 1, 1939, membership in the AASSW required schools to offer two years of graduate study. In 1938, 23 of the 32 member schools offered only graduate courses, while the remainder, mostly undergraduate schools, offered both graduate and undergraduate courses. By 1942, all of the 42 member schools in the AASSW offered only graduate programs, with a special provision for seven one-year programs (E. L. Brown, 1942).

The AASSW's protectionist behavior provoked opposition on several fronts, most particularly from organized sociology. As a professionalizing group dominated by undergraduate faculty members, the sociologists needed to find ways of attracting students in a declining college market. They were widely involved in social work education. Outside of the AASSW member schools, in 1941–42, 54 different institutions of higher education offered a relatively full sequence of social work courses; 44 of these were in undergraduate schools, primarily in sociology or social science departments. Another 94 college and university departments of sociology offered at least one course surveying the social work field, and several offered second or third courses (Ibid.).

In 1934, the American Association of Sociology appointed a "Committee on Opportunities," whose purpose was to foster outlets for "applied sociology" in federal and state research, planning, administrative, and other public service positions. After three years of effort, the committee discovered to its dismay that social workers and other organized professions had gotten there first (Rhoades, 1980). But the sociologists were not about to surrender their claims easily. One of the committee members, Ernest Harper, became a prime actor in the future NASSA/AASSW skirmishes.

College and university administrators, especially in the South and West, were also disturbed about the growing exclusivity of social work education. They believed that: (a) the graduate social work curriculum had too much material of an introductory nature, was too sharply separated from the undergraduate, was too narrow and rigid, and did not address rural and small town needs sufficiently; (b) graduate teaching faculties lacked proper academic credentials; (c) the AASSW was dominated by Eastern social work and large urban schools, several of which had no university connections, and not enough collaboration had gone on with the colleges and university officials who were affected by the standards the AASSW set up; and (d) state universities should train state and county workers paid with public funds (Harper, 1948; Leighninger, 1981).

The concerns of the sociologists and university officials culminated in two preliminary moves to curtail the AASSW's power to define professional social work. In January 1938, the year before the AASSW's two-year graduate curriculum requirement was to go into effect, the president of the University of Oklahoma, W. B. Bizzell, invited 40 non-AASSW state universities to form an alternative accrediting body. Bizzell's memo carried much weight because he was also president of the National Association of State Universities at the time. Early in the spring of 1938, representatives of several state universities and land grant colleges also met in two separate regional conferences about the problem of social work education (Harper, 1948; Leighninger, 1981).

The AASSW members were duly alarmed. Under the leadership of Wilber Newstetter, AASSW president, they formed an Advisory Committee on State Universities and Membership Requirements to negotiate with a newly formed, counterpart group of the state university and land grant schools, the Joint Committee on Accrediting, headed by President John J. Tigert of the University of Florida. The AASSW also undertook a study, funded by the Rockefeller Foundation for the fiscal years 1938–40, to assess the readiness of the schools to prepare students for the public social services. Directed by Marion Hathway, the new executive secretary of the AASSW and a devotée of Abbott and Breckinridge, the study enabled a field staff to visit all the schools in order to directly assess the "revolt" in the field.

The AASSW's appraisal and negotiations produced some concessions. More state universities and other public institutions were admitted to the AASSW after 1938. This expansion was aided by the creation of a new category of AASSW membership for schools offering only one-year graduate programs, Type I schools. They would be allowed to grant a Certificate in Social Work, and its holders could then, if desired, complete their second year of graduate work at a Type II school with the full two-year program. A half dozen institutions came into the AASSW under this cooptive strategy, including the University of Oklahoma, whose program, headed by sociologist J. J. Rhyne, had been repeatedly rejected up to then. In addition, the AASSW required its members to be an integral part of a recognized college or university. Lastly, the AASSW established a Committee on Preprofessional Education to continue to address the problems of undergraduate training and the needs of rural communities (Harper, 1948; Leighninger, 1981). All of these modifications were compatible with the final report of the Rockefeller study, published in 1942 as *Education for the Public Social Services* (Chapel Hill, University of North Carolina Press). The study unreservedly supported professional social work education at the graduate level for public social service personnel, despite the thousands of untrained workers who could neither qualify for nor afford masters degree training.

Between 1938 and 1942 dissatisfaction with the AASSW grew more bitter. The AASSW's concessions still meant denial of membership and legitimation for undergraduate programs even though 90% of the social service positions in the country, public or private, did not require educational preparation beyond the bachelor's degree level (SWHA, Maxted Papers, Porterfield letter, March 4, 1942). The consequences were that "most of the recruits, especially in the public assistance and employment service programs, [had] no social work training whatever," a situation which was "in danger of doing a great amount of harm to the recipients of these services" (Ibid.). Moreover, as undergraduate advocates saw it, so long as the public identified social work with untrained public service workers, professional status was sure to remain elusive, whereas, "with a recognition of the different levels of social work and a coordinated program of training, much could be done to raise the present standard and to make social work a profession in fact as well as in theory" (SWHA, Maxted, January 26, 1945).

Under the leadership of Austin Porterfield at Texas Christian University, Mattie Cal Maxted at the University of Arkansas, and others, the undergraduate schools—state universities, land grant colleges, and denominational and private schools—formed a rival educational association called the National Association of Schools of Social Administration (NASSA), in November 1942. Austin Porterfield was elected president, and J. J. Rhyne, then under AASSW pressure to discontinue Oklahoma's undergraduate component, became secretary (SWHA, Maxted Papers, Minutes, April 3, 1942). The still-active Joint Committee on Accrediting of the Association of Land-Grant Colleges and Universities gave the new association its seal of approval.

NASSA's formation was warmly received among undergraduate institutions. By the time of its second meeting in April 1944, it had 28 member schools in 27 states. A constitution was ratified which recognized graduate as well as undergraduate instruction and established minimum requirements for membership, namely, "twelve semester hours in social welfare courses considered as the basic preparation for any one of some 12 closely related professional courses" (Harper, 1948: 17; SWHA, Maxted Papers, NASSA Second Annual Meeting, April 22, 13, 1944; Constitution and By-Laws, April 22, 1944).

In December 1943, the Joint Committee on Accrediting and the National Association of State Universities formally recognized NASSA as an accrediting body in social work (Harper, 1948, Leighninger, 1981). This action brought AASSW leaders back to the negotiating table, but bore precious little by way of results. After six months of meetings between the associations during the latter part of 1944, the only point of agreement was approval of the concept of the B.A. degree with a major in social welfare, though not as an entry-level professional degree.

More serious negotiations began after January 1945, when each educational organization authorized the appointment of three members to a Joint Committee on Social Work Education (JCSWE). Dr. Esther Lucile Brown, of the Russell Sage Foundation, served as the

impartial chair. A year of deliberations led the committee to recommend the creation of a single social work accrediting body—an
inclusive council or commission on social work education—to be
formed after completion of a comprehensive study of social work
education (Leighninger, 1981). However, the recalcitrant AASSW rejected these proposals at its annual meeting in January 1946. Feeling
betrayed, the Joint Committee on Accrediting observed, "We are
now back where we started with the AASSW. For two or three years
they have apparently been stalling. We now have no agreements
with them" (SWHA, Maxted Papers, Report of Joint Comm. on Accrediting, National Association of State Universities, April 26–7,
1946: 1, 2).

Mistrust of the AASSW reached a new high among undergraduate
leaders, and with good reason. Sensing the NASSA's weaknesses, the
AASSW deliberately acted to undermine its rival even as it engaged
in joint deliberations and other openly cooperative ventures (Leighninger, 1981). One strategy, begun in 1945, was to use paid field con-
sultants to visit NASSA institutions and recommend the AASSW
model of "pre-professional education for admission to the graduate
schools rather than 'junior professional' preparation for either jobs
or advanced training," a more technically oriented approach (Harper,
1948: 22). In a confidential letter to Ernest Harper, Mattie Cal
Maxted lamented that "this move of the AASSW to put Miss Branch
on as a consultant in pre-professional education is a master stroke
on their part. The AASSW and its graduates fill the influential positions in social work. The AASSW is getting letters about pre-
professional education—not us" (SWHA, Maxted Papers, Maxted
letter to Harper, June 15, 1945).

Another effective AASSW strategy was to weaken and divide
NASSA by members with one- or two-year graduate programs to join
the AASSW and withdraw from NASSA rather than develop five-year
M.A. programs (Harper, 1948). The loyalties of NASSA Secretary
Rhyne at Oklahoma had already been divided (Ibid., Maxted letter,
1945), rendering him ineffective. Since 1945 Wisconsin had with-
drawn; South Carolina was in process; Colorado was only prevented
by intervention of its president. When informed by Dr. Coyle Moore
in January 1948 that Florida State had just arrived at the same decision, Ernest Harper, then chair of the membership committee, expressed his dismay:

Practically all of our NASSA institutions as they have come to establish a graduate curriculum have deserted the Association. . . . It's easy to fathom the strategy of the AASSW. They defied the recommendations of the Joint Committee and refused to negotiate with the NASSA. Why shouldn't they since they are 'biting off' each of our larger and better institutions one by one! (SWHA, Maxted Papers, confidential letter from Harper to Moore, January 10, 1948)

The breakdown in negotiations and the climate of mistrust left the joint committee at a loss as to how to handle accreditation. Neither educational association deserved to be designated as the sole accrediting body for social work education. The AASSW with 2,000–3,000 students in its member institutions was willfully ignoring the 40,000–50,000 public service employees who did not need graduate training nor a singular emphasis on casework (Maxted papers, Report of the Joint Committee on Accrediting, April 26–27, 1946). The NASSA really dealt only with undergraduate programs and was not yet sufficiently developed to take on the responsibilities, a fact they themselves recognized (SWHA, Maxted Papers, letter from Harper to Maxted, June 23, 1945). NASSA's membership campaign conducted in 1947 produced only a total of 35 schools.

To break the impasse in social work education, in November 1947, the Joint Committee on Accrediting threatened "that unless the AASSW and the NASSA agree on an accreditation program for social work by January 1, 1948, there [would] be no recognized accreditation in this field" (Harper, 1948: 23). In March 1948, with no breakthrough in sight, the Joint Accrediting Committee, representing most of the colleges and universities in the country, decided that no accrediting agency in social work should be recognized for an indefinite period of years (Harper, 1948).

A COUNCIL ON SOCIAL WORK EDUCATION:
UNEASY RESOLUTION

The necessary resolution of the problem eventually began to take shape through the auspices of the National Council on Social Work Education (NCSWE). The council was an outgrowth of one of the

JCSWE's proposals in 1946 that had been accepted by both educational bodies. It called for an Interim Committee sponsored by both associations, the American Public Welfare Association, and the federal social welfare departments to plan for a study of social work education and to create a National Council on Social Work Education (NCSWE). The National Council was established in New York on August 26, 1946, with representatives of 13 associations and organizations, and its study committee began to plan for implementation of the research. The broad composition of the NCSWE and the task of mounting a study eased the strain between the rival groups and kept the prospects for compromise alive. The question was, what sort of compromise could be reached?

The NCSWE moved quickly to get its study on social work education underway with a $31,000 Carnegie Corporation grant. The study committee was chaired by Harriett Bartlett after Kenneth Pray resigned due to illness. Mistrust and political tensions surrounded the project from its inception. The members could not even initially agree on an outline of areas of study (SWHA, Maxted Papers, Minutes of NCSWE Meeting, January 14, 1948: 4). Under pressure from the Carnegie Corporation, in the summer of 1948 the committee appointed a director from outside of social work who would not be partial to the aims of the AASSW, Dr. Ernest V. Hollis, Chief of College Administration in the Office of Education of the Federal Security Agency (SWHA, Maxted Papers, letter from Harper to Cape, February 17, 1948). Hollis chose a social worker, Alice L. Taylor, Training Consultant for the Bureau of Public Assistance, as his assistant director.

A primary purpose of the study was "to build a framework of principles within which existing programs of social work education might be examined" (Ibid.). However, this impartial-sounding approach could not produce a final report that would entirely satisfy all the various social work factions. The framework that emerged from the study envisioned a continuum of social work education with undergraduate and graduate programs working closely together. After this innocuous idea, choices had to be made, and these clearly favored existing arrangements. The graduate degree was retained as the entry level for the profession, though graduate social work education was conceived more broadly "to provide a one- or two-year undifferentiated basic [generic] program," and for social workers with the basic requisite education and experience to provide "curricula that prepare for service in the several specializations of advanced practice . . ." (Hollis & Taylor, 1951: 397).

The undergraduate schools were assigned the role of laying down a preprofessional foundation to prepare students for graduate study, "a concentration in the arts and sciences basic to the more advanced study of social work" (Ibid.: 396). Bowing to pressure from AASSW members in the NCSWE, recommendations on the preparation of technical and semiprofessional workers in undergraduate programs also were put off on grounds that further study was needed to clearly distinguish between professional and semiprofessional functions in social work (Leighninger, 1981; Ibid.: 397). Again the bias toward graduate education appeared.

Advice from the federal agencies likewise apparently supported the graduate degree when push came to shove. By the time of the study, graduate social work education had already been written into federal civil service requirements for many positions. After the Hollis report came out, Jane Hoey, head of the federal Bureau of Public Assistance and a member of the NCSWE, expressed her disapproval of any further consideration of an undergraduate social work concentration (SWHA, Maxted Papers, letter from Hoey to Steininger, January 3, 1952). Writing to a colleague at the APWA whose committee supported undergraduate social work training, Hoey argued it would be detrimental to "a broad liberal education." Besides, it was now time to close ranks behind the report and support the order in social work education that it had helped create. Said Hoey (Ibid.):

> . . . Since the study of *Social Work Education in the United States* by Ernest Hollis and Alice Taylor is now available, I thought it was very important that your committee not include anything that was in contradiction to the recommendations made in this study. I think the findings in this report will be very generally accepted, after many years of discussion and controversy, and, therefore, I would not like to see the APWA committee report reopen this conflict.

The Hollis study's aim of placing social work education on firm conceptual ground could not be accomplished without putting its house in order politically. An avowed objective, therefore, was "the development of a comprehensive structure within which the accrediting bodies, schools of social work, practitioner organizations, and employing agencies could achieve a working agreement on what constituted acceptable programs of social work education for the immediate present and for the future" (Hollis & Taylor, 1951: viii). The process of planning and conducting the study achieved as much along these lines as the actual recommendations in the report (Ibid.: 354–62).

NASSA had entered into a cooperative venture on unequal terms as the composition of the NCSWE tilted toward the social work establishment. Since it did not have the organizational strength to put up much resistance, in effect, NASSA had allowed itself to be co-opted. Thus, as the study progressed, NASSA participated with other NCSWE members in developing the organizational structure for a new Council on Social Work Education, a structure that for the immediate future would politically parallel the educational proposals in the "Hollis Report."

In the summer of 1951, President Mattie Cal Maxted reported to the NASSA members on the plans for a new Council on Social Work Education:

> A tentative constitution provides for the following structure: A council of delegates of 78 members which meets annually, a board of directors which meets twice a year, and four commissions.
>
> The Commission on Accrediting consisting of fifteen members will accredit graduate schools of social work. Undergraduate departments will not be accredited but will have membership requirements. The Commission on Schools and Departments of Social Work will have a division of graduate schools and one of undergraduate departments. The other two Commissions are Program, Planning and Services; and Research and Publications. (SWHA, Maxted Papers, Memo to NASSA Members, c. July 1951)

The structure that Maxted outlined was officially ratified by a Constitutional Convention in the Hotel Roosevelt in New York on January 28, 1952 (SWHA, Maxted Papers, CSWE By-Laws, January 28, 1952). After more than a dozen years of hard labor, a single body, a Council on Social Work Education, had finally been born, to coordinate, accredit, and generally establish educational policy for the profession.

The new organization had room for participation for all parties interested in social work education—the graduate and undergraduate schools, professional practitioner associations, and major employing agencies. Still, NASSA representatives feared that the AASSW "was planning to dominate the new organization" (SWHA, Maxted Papers, letter from Harper to Maxted, February 2, 1952; letter from Wetzel to Maxted, February 15, 1952), and correctly so. The structure of power initially favored the graduate schools and their supporters over the undergraduate programs. NASSA was authorized to appoint ten delegates to the Council of Delegates compared to 20 for the AASSW. Its member schools would form the nucleus of the Division of Undergraduate Departments in which membership was open only to "departments offering programs with social work content introductory to professional social work." It had no designated seat on the Commission on Accreditation.

But the political compromise embodied in the council structure also contained the potential for future realignments of power. If undergraduate institutions had not attained the professional status they originally sought, nevertheless they had been grudgingly brought into the social work education family. By the summer of 1951, some 400 schools were teaching undergraduate courses in social work. Maxted had already reached out to this group and foreseen "that the Undergraduate Division of the Council should become a real force in social work education" (SWHA, Maxted Papers, Maxted letter to F. S. Whatley, January 11, 1952). Constitutionally, in the future, 30 of the 78 seats on the Delegate Council were to go to representatives of social work educational institutions. The CSWE Board required representation from educational institutions represented in the Council of Delegates. Three of the 15 members on the accreditation commission could potentially come from the undergraduate members. With vigilance and organization, the undergraduate institutions could eventually have their day.

The social order in social work education that was endorsed by the Hollis Report and the formation of the Council on Social Work Education buoyed up the entire professional enterprise and lasted some 17 years. In the late 1960s societal and market forces and internal professional struggles generated the conditions that gradually brought the undergraduate schools to power. The full effect of this shift is still being played out in social work's educational circles, its various professional associations, and its employment markets.

Whether or not the political and economic standing of professional social work was improved as a result of the 1952 compromises is an open, if moot, question. In the 1930s and 1940s professional social work had a unique opportunity to improve the quality of social work practice as it was carried out throughout most of the field, namely, by social service workers without B.A. degrees. The ubiquitous presence of this work force in undiminishing numbers was, and still is, an undeniable reality for much of the public, though one which the profession tried to avoid. It has contributed significantly to the continually low level of social work salaries and weakened social work's professional status. If social work leaders had fully developed undergraduate social work education and recognized professional entry at the baccalaureate level *early on*, the profession might have improved its public standing and gained immense political power through the added numbers. In hindsight, organized social work seemed to have postponed the inevitable. At what cost remains to be seen.

CHAPTER NINETEEN

Continuing Dilemmas of Profession Building

OMISSIONS AND COMMISSIONS

Twenty-six percent of the population of Washington D.C. in 1932 was black, the highest rate of any American city. Yet in the sweltering heat of that Washington summer, the black laborers who were digging the foundations of the new Justice Department building on Pennsylvania Avenue had to go two miles down Seventh Avenue to find a restaurant which would serve them a drink of water (Manchester, 1974). Segregation was a way of life in this Southern city, seat of rulers pledged "to establish justice, . . . promote the general welfare, and secure the blessings of liberty"—home of a national government that would soon establish a modern welfare state. The noble words of the Constitution had not been applied to blacks in the United States. Neither wealth nor misery were distributed equitably. As a result, blacks suffered hardest during economic setbacks.

In 1933 blacks made up 18.4% of all the families on the relief rolls, while they constituted less than 10% of the entire population. The discrepancy should have been higher, since, contrary to federal rules, many blacks could not get relief due to local racial discrimination. These figures for blacks did not arise from individual character deficiencies any more than did the figures for whites. Their disproportionality signified something else—the workings of racism that permeated American society. Blacks were being forced onto the relief rolls by private agriculture and industry's displacement of black labor and by discrimination and institutional racism in the operation of government programs (Washington, 1934; Ross, 1978; Salmond, 1983).

In industry, North and South, blacks were fired to give jobs to unemployed whites. In some cities, whites openly organized to promote such policies. Some municipalities passed ordinances to this effect. Many unions did not admit blacks and insisted that union members be hired first under recovery programs. Even black domestics were displaced in large numbers so that whites could be "taken on"; menial jobs no longer offered blacks refuge (Washington, 1934). Relief was being used to subsidize discrimination and underemployment.

With public programs, blacks had a harder time qualifying for relief, and did not get the same share of work relief jobs or the same types of jobs as whites when they were employed (D. Hamilton, 1984). Blacks in the federal service held mostly lower-level positions and were less likely to be accepted into in-service training programs for upgrading (J. Fisher, 1980). Black sharecroppers had difficulty securing credit under the Farm Credit Administration (Washington, 1934). The Federal Housing Administration permitted racially restricted covenants in housing which it insured (J. Fisher, 1980; Granger, 1945).

Nor was much consideration given as to how the design of new programs would affect blacks as a group, given their place in the employment market; they suffered the painful indignity of white disregard. In the South, before the Depression, blacks had already been badly hurt by declines in agricultural production, their chief source of livelihood. In the 1930s, the deterioration in agricultural markets plus New Deal crop reduction policies under the AAA programs led to the eviction of millions of blacks from farms throughout the country (Manchester, 1974; Piven & Cloward, 1977). N.R.A. codes, especially in the South, led many blacks to be discharged, rather than to be paid wages equal to whites; hence they were driven onto relief (Washington, 1934).

Forrester Washington, Director of Negro Work of the FERA, and later Dean of the Atlanta School of Social Work, warned the social welfare community of "the danger of making the Negro, as a race, a chronic dependent" and "developing racial friction through creating resentment on the part of the majority public against the presence of so many Negroes on the relief rolls" (1934: 185). He pointed out, ". . . Already community-chest executives in certain cities have stated that they are averse to publication of data touching on the number of Negroes on relief rolls because, in spite of the fact that community-chest agencies are not carrying Negroes on relief, nevertheless, certain of their large contributors have indicated an intention to discontinue their contributions if so many Negroes continue to be supported on relief" (Ibid.).

Social workers whose mission was to help the poor were ill equipped, and generally not predisposed to deal with the plight of blacks in American society. Why? Overt prejudice does not explain enough. The AASW was ahead of other professional associations in barring racial discrimination, compared for example, with the American Bar Association, the American Medical Association, and the National Education Association, all of which condoned white state and local affiliates or considered blacks separately (J. Fisher, 1980). The American Associations of Medical Social Workers and Psychiatric Social Workers in the mid-1940s specifically set up projects to assure that social work jobs in their fields could and would be filled by black, professional social workers.

Neither was social workers' indifference due to a lack of awareness of the tribulations of blacks. Others besides Forrester Washington had brought racial matters to the attention of the profession. The Rank and File Movement had publicized and railed against discrimination in the relief agencies; it had continuously fought for anti-lynching legislation, which the New Dealers buried to mollify the Southern Democrats in Congress whose votes they wanted; it had pushed the NCSW to select conference sites, as it did, where non-segregated accommodations would be assured. NCSW planning committees had generally responded favorably to this latter pressure, though when urged on appeal to extend its policy to cover bars, in 1937 NCSW President Edith Abbott replied tersely that "the business of the conference required that attendees be assured the availability of food and housing, not recreation" (J. Fisher, 1980: 166).

Some settlement houses also were highly sensitive to the needs of blacks. Located in many of the nation's largest cities, most of these agencies were established for the express purpose of working with the black community, hence segregated in their specialization (Trolander, 1975). Phillis Wheatley House in Minneapolis, which began in 1924, exemplified this approach as the only black settlement in the city. Its director until 1937, W. Gertrude Brown, held a B.S. degree from Columbia University and had attended two summer terms at the New York School of Social Work. However, Brown's extensive involvement in activities outside the settlement on behalf of blacks and civil rights eventually led to unjust criticism by the Council of Social Agencies in 1936 and to Brown's resignation a year later. In white ethnic enclaves, settlements generally eschewed interracial activities and outreach to the black population that was replacing the original immigrant settlers. Many simply closed down when they could not adapt to their changing situation. As for why settlements did not do more during the Depression, in her study of settlements during this period Trolander (1975: 146) concluded that "the United States of the 1930s was [an] openly racist society" in which some settlement workers, "blind to racial problems, . . . still thought of their movement primarily in terms of white middle-class workers living in poor white neighborhoods."

Trolander's explanation also fits the rest of social work fairly well. Mainstream professional social work was racially blind, mainly a white, Protestant, status-conscious enclave, dominated by case-workers and administrators. Although various white ethnic and religious groups, as well as non-white minorities, notably blacks, developed important sectarian services that greatly contributed to the growth and diversity of American social work, they did not define the professional social work commodity. But also, those leaders who did had a different agenda, a different consciousness. Professionalization itself had become a cause.

Social work in the 1930s and 1940s devoted itself almost single-mindedly to maintaining and extending its professional enterprise. Even as it advocated a public interest, it shaped its public concerns to fit its self-interest. In this social work was no worse than other professions. Status insecurity coupled with enormous opportunity kept the center of social work fixed on the course it had begun in the 1920s. Caught up with internal and external struggles for control over markets, redefinition and expansion of its service commodity, and enhancement of its public image, mainstream social work largely ignored the racial and social class problems of minorities. Tackling them meant "rocking the boat," creating a dilemma for a group professing concern for the poor.

Social work came into the 1930s with a professional enterprise already in place and a stake in its preservation and growth along particular lines. Thus poised, organized social work benefited from the Depression because of the widespread need for its service commodities when many other occupations and industries were going under. It had sufficient power to capture a preferential place in the public sector market ahead of any other serious professional challengers. Social work benefited again from the economic recovery, because now it had an opportunity to refine its original private sector commodity and expand again. With all of this, social work could not establish enough market control to improve salaries.

Social work's attempts to gain an exclusive foothold in the rapidly expanding service industry created other dilemmas. The profession was dominated by a casework technology fashioned in the voluntary sector around counseling. The public desperately needed relief and a system for its distribution. In order to bring social work into public welfare on a national scale, the profession had to accept a relief function, with all of the negative associations attached to investigations and means tests. Counseling had to be adapted to relief giving, not an easy task. The profession could not control the definition of its commodity; public sector social work was tainted.

Neither could the profession control who was considered a social worker and which social workers provided the service, as demand in the economic crisis far outstripped the supply of trained personnel. Correcting these difficulties required a considerable expenditure of energy and time on narrow professional considerations.

The continued dominance of the private agency casework ideal in the public sector perpetuated a dual social work market in which the private sector was viewed as superior to the public, and graduate education as the standard for the profession—an old dilemma. The private sector was closer to an elite group of philanthropic sponsors, who could and did assert control over the nature of charitable service and, when they did, greater emphasis was placed on status than on service and on individual treatment rather than environmental reform.

A significant number of social workers challenged this treatment focus during the Depression years, joining with the labor movement and other progressive groups to protest inequitable political and economic arrangements. Social action was reaffirmed as part of the ideology of social work. Marion Hathway maintained, "Either we accept professional responsibility in relation to the environment and follow the road to the control of forces which threaten to destroy the human personality or we admit that the problems are insoluble and become, in the oft-quoted words of Roger Baldwin, 'merely stretcher-bearers of industry'" (E. L. Brown, 1942: 186). Professionalization proved more conducive to stretcher bearing once the emergency died down, as social workers responded to the strictures of their sponsors, public and private.

Organized social work's drive for self-preservation destined it to remain a small, fairly closed club, consistent with its elitist origins, when it might have expanded its ranks dramatically and gained political strength from its mass base. Presented with the alternative, social workers shied away from unionization as too narrow and too radical. As subsectors of social work—group work and community organization—organized themselves to attain professional recognition, the profession resisted accepting them as legitimate social work specialties. Unification of an expanded profession was delayed until these subgroups could bring their specializations into conformity with a politically "neutral" helping process. A potential cost of social work's exclusionary policies may well have been its slow progress toward certification and licensing.

The profession's tenacious resistance to undergraduate professional education in the 1930s and 1940s was still another facet of its defensiveness. In forcing a postponement of the inevitable, social work may have sacrificed an opportunity to improve the quality of the services which the public had defined as social work and which the profession was stuck with, like it or not. Clients may well have benefited from better-trained personnel, and social work's standing in the public's eye may have been raised.

Under the extreme conditions of the Depression and World War II, more social workers went further in their analysis of America's problems than they had ever done before and further in pushing back the boundaries of social reform. At the same time, a persistent undercurrent of professional self-interest tempered their social activism, limited their vision, and eventually became an overriding preoccupation. As social work entered the 1950s, it was in harmony with the dominant currents of American life—the Cold War, economic prosperity, suburbanization and its social implications, and the transformation to a service economy.

THE ALTRUISTIC ENTERPRISE IN THE 1980S

The growth of professional social work accelerated rapidly between the mid-1950s and the mid-1980s with the continued expansion of government spending for social welfare. Between 1960 and 1983, social welfare expenditures in the public sector, including education, rose from $52.3 billion to $641.7 billion, representing more than 55% of all government spending for that year and about 19% of the GNP in current dollars, up from 10.6% in 1955 (NASW, 1977; NASW, 1987). The voluntary social welfare sector expanded as well, though to a lesser degree. As approximated by private philanthropic allocations in the fields of health, education, and welfare, between 1960 and 1984 these allocations rose from $4.03 billion to $28.5 billion, a gain in absolute dollars but a drop in proportion to public expenditures for the same period (NASW, 1987). Fueled in part by governmental funds, occupational professionalization and the growth of services went well beyond the sphere of social work, heralding a major shift from a goods-producing to a service economy, the coming of a "post-industrial society" (Bell, 1973).

The growth of the public service sector has had a significant impact on the political economy of professional social work and social welfare. With regard to the broader social welfare picture, the enactment of legislation for major social programs over the past 25 years, such as Medicare and Medicaid, SSI, Title XX, and the Community Mental Health Act, seems indicative of fairly widespread nonpartisan acceptance of many features of the welfare state as a minimum requirement to ensure social protection and maintain the quality of life. In the 1970s and 1980s, however, conservatives have vigorously debated the definitions and levels of these minimum requirements. As higher wages and increased services (in cash and kind) raised the real income of the working class, conservatives reaped political capital by focusing on the burden of high taxes and the need for a balanced budget. Still, seven years of assault on the welfare state by the Reagan administration—severe funding cutbacks for human resource programs, devolution of authority and responsibility to the states, and a strong push for privatization—has neither balanced the budget, nor managed to overcome a solid core of resistance to further destruction of the social safety net.

Further, some economists have treated social service spending as an important "countercyclical" tool for stabilizing the economy. Thus, the public social welfare sector, as a massive transfer payment system, has served as (1) a stimulant to the economy; (2) a mechanism for reducing inflation by making higher levels of unemployment more tolerable, and (3) a means for directing the flow of subsidy payments to selected sectors of the economy (e.g., housing, health, food, industry) (Horesji, 1977). From a political perspective, the welfare system has also served as a means to control the marginal work force and to cool civil unrest (Piven & Cloward, 1971). The Reagan administration has devalued this tool, however, so that massive cutbacks in social programs have raised the numbers of persons in poverty to 1965 levels. Women, children, and minorities of color have been hit the hardest.

The flexibility of the social service sector budget as a countercyclical mechanism, and the demand for greater efficiency in the face of resource scarcity, has required the introduction of large-scale information and accountability systems and planning/managerial expertise—"the rationalization of social services" (Hirschhorn, 1978). Unfortunately, this rationalization has been weighted towards meeting short-term political-economic exigencies rather than long-term investments in creating an educated, technically skilled, and physically healthy workforce.

Were the government to invest vigorously in "human capital," newly productive groups would emerge to compete over resources and control of different parts of the economy. Threatening as that might be, if services do not "transform production, marketing, and job allocation" in any real sense, that is, if they are really only stop-gap measures, then "services become unproductive, wasteful, and irrational," leading to "the development of underdevelopment" at the core of the American economy (Hirschhorn, 1978: 165). The stubborn rise in the incidence of homelessness throughout the nation and the creation of a large, potentially permanent black underclass (Wilson, 1978) illustrate this point.

With regard to the professionalization of social work, the expansion of the social welfare sector in the last 25 years has involved extensive growth in the social service work force, well beyond comparable growth in the general civilian labor force and other professional, technical, and kindred workers. Between 1960 and 1980 the number of social service employees rose from 218,000 to 383,000 persons, and has pretty much stabilized since then (Hopps & Pinderhughes, 1987). As in the past, the supply of professional social workers could not keep pace with the market demand, despite federal funding to support social work education. This supply-demand situation probably represents the single most persistent problem which aspiring social workers have had to face since their earliest efforts at professionalization. It helps to account for much of social work's difficulty in establishing occupational control, hence its uncertain status. Of the approximately 400,000 social service workers in the labor force, many of whom the public identifies as social workers, only some 200,000 are estimated to have professional social work degrees (MSW or BSW), and only half of these actually belong to NASW (Hopps & Pinderhughes, 1987).

In the 1970s, social service workers began to be identified as "human service workers," a broadened category intended to include professional social workers as well as employees with a wide range of educational backgrounds and levels of achievement, from high school to advanced degrees, working in such fields as education, housing, health and mental health, criminal justice, child welfare, recreation, rehabilitation, child care, counseling of all sorts, and more. It is almost as though the late twentieth-century postindustrial economy is reproducing in massive numbers the same inchoate array of service workers as the earlier twentieth-century industrial economy produced, and from which social workers have been struggling to establish their own distinctive competence. In 1983, an estimated 12% percent of the U.S. labor force worked in the human service field (Khinduka, 1987). This investment of billions of dollars, involving millions of consumers and providers, encompassing some 2,000 different careers, places human services in the ranks of a major American industry (Ibid.).

The impetus for the development of many of these human service jobs came from the federal government through a variety of support programs. For example, during the 1960s and 1970s, in response to staffing shortages, and out of a desire to respond to and blunt the thrust of community-based social action organizations, the government encouraged and even required the participation of nonprofessional community residents on boards of newly formed or reconstituted community agencies (Gilbert, 1970; Moynihan, 1969; Marris

& Rein, 1967). These positions frequently became avenues for upward job mobility in human service agencies. Government further promoted the training and utilization of community residents in direct service positions as "paraprofessionals" (Austin, 1978; Pearl & Riessman, 1965; Sobey, 1970). Consequently between 1960 and 1970, the number of non–college educated, untrained social service workers increased from 11,580 to 41,887, or from 10% to 19% of the total social service work force (Siegel, 1975: 10).

Since the early 1960s, changes in thinking about the needs of the mentally ill, such as the need for deinstitutionalization, and staff shortages spawned a whole network of programs offering associate degrees at community colleges to train mental health workers. About half of all personnel providing direct service in the mental health field today are estimated to be paraprofessionals (Khinduka, 1987). More than 400 colleges, universities, and technical institutes currently offer certificates, associate, baccalaureate, and master's degrees for human service practitioners (Beilin & Wimberly, 1984). A Council for Standards in Human Service Education, now in existence, speaks to the future development of standardization and certification in this area (Ibid.).

The burgeoning of a modern human services industry has hampered social work's ability to attain occupational control in several obvious ways. First, in a market situation where demand is continuously outstripping supply, employers often prefer to accept less-qualified employees; the standards of service go down. Second, the demand stimulates market competition. Older professionalized groups see new opportunities, and new groups emerge as well. (The privatization of public services encouraged by the Reagan administration does not change this situation.) And while the public may grant licensure to aspiring occupations, this does not ensure commodity control, as similar service commodities may be substituted, if necessary, to meet the demand and keep the costs down. Consequently, while 45 states now regulate social work through some sort of registration, certification, or licensure process (NASW News, September 1987), the competition over social work's domain has intensified, not only from other groups with some degree of professional recognition, such as nurses, psychologists, and community planners, but also from many less-recognized occupational groups, such as substance abuse counselors, who are slowly moving toward certification, and emerging groups, such as patient advocates and hospice workers.

In 1958, Nathan Cohen wrote, "Unless the community is ready to see the value of social welfare services and pay for them through taxes and voluntary contributions, the role and status of the professional social worker will not change significantly" (346). But, even if social workers could convince the public of their distinctive competency—and a recent "independent analysis of social work jobs in the Maryland State Department of Human Resources found that workers with MSW degrees significantly outperform workers who lack the graduate social work degree" (*NASW News,* September 1987: 11)—to the extent that social work services are tied to public and voluntary agencies, the collective costs for their provision and their association with "the undeserving poor" would militate against professional acceptance. Moreover, the cost of fully professionalizing today's human service industry would probably be prohibitive. One consequence for professional social work has been a new form of domain erosion, the declassification, in some states, of social work positions in the public sector—namely, the lowering or removal of educational standards and requirements so that positions can be filled by non-MSW or non-BSW applicants (Khinduka, 1987; Hopps & Pinderhughes, 1987). Data are not yet available to determine the full extent of declassification. Another consequence has been the low salaries paid to social workers compared to other professionals (see Hopps & Pinderhughes, 1987.) It could be argued that in the field of public assistance, the separation of income maintenance from social services, which has allowed for a lowering of educational standards for eligibility workers, has been yet another consequence of the pressure to keep service costs down.

Stimulated by a Departmental Task Force on Social Work Education and Manpower within the U.S. Department of Health, Education, and Welfare, during the mid-1960s the social work enterprise began to respond to "the gap in social work manpower" by considering the recognition of the BSW degree as a professional classification (Baer & Federico, 1978). In 1970, NASW finally implemented a 1969 national membership referendum to provide regular membership to baccalaureate-degree holders from undergraduate programs meeting CSWE criteria (Ibid.) Between 1967 and 1975 federal funds from various Social Security Act amendments supported BSW education for thousands of undergraduates in hundreds of schools (Ibid.). CSWE established standards for accreditation of baccalaureate programs in 1973 and began implementation the following year. At the same time, NASW also developed a six-level differential classification scheme for the social service field, beginning with two preprofessional levels, the Social Service Aide (maturity and life experience) and the Social Service Technician (AA degree in social services or other baccalaureate degree), and four professional levels, starting with the Social Worker (BSW), and the Graduate Social Worker (MSW), and then the Certified Social Worker (ACSW), and the Social Work Fellow (doctorate or ACSW plus two years of specialized experience). (Associate of Arts programs are no longer viewed as part of social work education and tend to operate under the "human services" rubric mentioned earlier.)

Recognition of the BSW as the professional entry degree was probably the single most significant change in the internal structure of the social work enterprise in the last 25 years. Some would argue that it has represented a form of deprofessionalization, a lowering of standards, so long resisted by the social work enterprise. And, although the evidence is not in, certainly the availability of BSW professionals would seem to undercut the value of MSWs in the postindustrial employment market and serve to depress salaries.

While BSWs have not flocked to membership in the professional association, the sheer number of accredited BSW programs (over 350 in 1988 versus 95 MSW programs) has changed the balance of power in CSWE deliberations. Recognition of the BSW degree has forced curriculum revisions to try to eliminate redundancy, and has sharpened the debate about the meaning of generic practice and advanced practice. This differentiation is critical if the MSW-level professionals hope to claim higher salaries. Ironically, the recent development of the one-year master's program for BSW degree holders, spurred by enrollment declines and market competition, would appear to weaken claims to specialized expertise by the advanced practitioner because it suggests a sizable overlap between the BSW and the MSW curriculum. In effect, one year of the two-year MSW program is covered at the undergraduate level.

In retrospect, it is difficult not to wonder, once again, about the historical shortsightedness of social work's exclusive membership and recognition policies. Had bachelor's-level programs been accepted and accredited in the 1930s and 1940s, social work's credentialing apparatus would have been well in place and much better prepared to meet the postwar demand for human service workers with social work personnel.

Although the social work enterprise remained preoccupied with issues pertinent to professionalization throughout the postwar era, the political turmoil of the 1960s—the social movements for peace, civil rights, women's liberation, an end to poverty, welfare reform, and the government's expansion of the welfare state—did shake it from its absorption with matters of "function" for a short time. By and large, social workers came too little and too late to the social "cause" battles of the times. But when they did, the community organization/social reform wing of social work grew from less than 2% of the postgraduate social work student body before 1960 to about 10% in 1970, or about 1,300 students (Gilbert & Specht, 1977; Gurin, 1970). Forty-eight social work programs offered one- or two-year concentrations in community organization in 1969 (Gurin, 1970). The social ferment in and around social work pushed the enterprise, as in the 1930s, to reexamine its commitment to helping the disadvantaged and correcting social injustices through institutional reform. With the return to social equilibrium and conservatism in the mid-1970s and 1980s, social workers again turned to their preoccupation with "function," initiating a new cycle of emphasis on individually oriented clinical social work (née social casework).

In the 1980s, dissatisfaction with the lack of professional recognition, low salaries, poor working conditions in large public bureaucracies, the desire for autonomous professional practice, and the availability of third-party payments have stimulated a marked increase in private and proprietary social work practice. Estimates of the number of part-time private practitioners run between 10,000 and 30,000; for full-time practitioners, the figures are 4,000–10,000 (Barker, 1987). Whether this growth trend will continue is highly uncertain, as competition from other professions is also increasing, while insurance companies are beginning to cut back on their coverage. Nor is it clear that an emphasis on private clinical practice would strengthen the professionalization of social work in the long run. First, there is the question of whether private practice is really social work practice, with an emphasis on the "social" that makes social work unique, or just another form of psychotherapy. Second, professional social work, like it or not, is tied to the institution of social welfare. The political and economic tasks necessary for recognition would thereby seem to call for organizing and coalition development, inclusive rather than exclusive strategies, in order to influence the flow of resources to social welfare services through the political process. In this sense, social workers and their clients share a common interest, as do social workers and other human service workers at all levels. Moreover, if a conservative political leadership continues to press for privatization and to invest less in human development, social workers in the 1990s may find, like their predecessors in the 1930s and 1960s, that organizing militant protective associations of human service workers—a union model—and forming alliances with poor and working-class movements for redistributive justice, will more effectively bring them the recognition and rewards they have sought so assiduously.

Notes

CHAPTER THREE

1. The Association for the Improvement of the Condition of the Poor (AICP) was founded in New York City in 1843 by Robert Hartley in the aftermath of the devastating panic of 1837. The AICP first developed the concept of friendly visiting by upper-class volunteers (predominantly women) and the use of these volunteers to conduct investigations into the conditions of both families and their environments. In 1853, the AICP released one of the first and most famous products of these investigations, a report on tenement housing in New York City, which appealed to the "enlightened" elite to take action to remediate the dreadful conditions in the city's slums. In form, philosophy, staff composition, and activities, therefore, the AICP was clearly the antecedent of the more sophisticated Charity Organization Societies of the late nineteenth century.

2. Attacks on women social work leaders reached their peak in 1918 during the Senate's debate over the Sheppard-Towner bill, the first piece of legislation to emerge directly from the efforts of the Children's Bureau, created in 1912. The bill, ultimately enacted into law in 1921, established for the first time federally funded maternal and child health centers throughout the United States. Although the program was terminated by Congress at President Hoover's behest in 1929, its effects were dramatic in reducing the level of infant and maternal mortality, especially in rural areas. Nevertheless, when the bill was first introduced, conservative opponents questioned both the patriotism and the sexuality of its drafters in the Bureau.

CHAPTER FOUR

3. For example, Richmond described the relationship of the COS with churches as a partnership, and stressed the collegial ties between the COS and teachers, physicians, nurses, the police, and the courts; yet she cast the relationship of the COS with unions in less equal and less sympathetic terms (Cf. Richmond, *Friendly Visiting among the Poor*, 1899: 29–31).

4. Richmond argued that because of the complexity of many families' problems, "charity will be most successful . . . which so arranges its work

as to avoid overcrowding any one worker with too many details. The most successful continuous work will usually be done by volunteers acting under intelligent leadership, and with a trained paid agent [as a supervisor]" (Richmond, 1901:111). She cited the Boston Associated Charities, which limited the caseload of a trained agent—assisted by a group of volunteers—to 125 new families per year. Previously, she had argued for smaller caseloads for these volunteers (three to five families) and a reduced requirement of one visit per week (Richmond, 1902).

5. While Devine's suggestion appeared to complement Richmond's approach to social work practice and to offer potential solutions to problems of professional development within social work, those solutions of more radical reformers like Robert Hunter challenged some of her basic assumptions and, consequently, drew harsh criticism. Although Hunter's book, *Poverty* (1904), was applauded by social work activists like Florence Kelley and Edith Abbott and, in many ways, was the precursor to modern social scientific analyses of social problems, Richmond criticized the "irresponsible way in which both figures and authorities are treated throughout the volume." Significantly, she felt that the book's main flaw was that its author "purposefully ignored the personal causes of poverty," and gave a distorted view not only of the sources of poverty but of the potential solutions for the problem. "The personal and social causes of poverty are as intimately associated as the elements of the air, and the author who proposes to discuss only one of these elements should make this fact clear on his title page" (Richmond review, *International Journal of Ethics*, 1905: 506–7).

6. The research of the Industrial Studies Department and the Committee on Women's Work under Mary van Kleeck might be considered an important exception, but even here impartial investigation rather than social action was the primary objective.

7. The equivalent value in 1987 would have been about $21 million in grants for the same period.

8. The exceptions were two book projects on settlements by Robert Woods and Albert Kennedy, the *Handbook of Settlements* (1910) and *The Settlement Horizon* (1922).

9. The library of the New York School, which was started by the COS, augmented by the State Charities Aid Association's library, and operated jointly by the school and the Russell Sage Foundation (RSF), was moved physically into the Foundation building in 1913. When the school's quarters became cramped, the foundation designed a new wing to accommodate the school's needs. From 1931 until it took over the Carnegie mansion in 1951, the school was housed in the first five floors of the tax-exempt RSF building at Lexington Avenue and Twenty-second Street. RSF staff lectured at the school and vice-versa, their libraries were shared, RSF published many of the books used at the school, and it helped to place the school's students in jobs.

10. The committee members were Mary Richmond, Chair; Robert deForest; Edward Devine; John M. Glenn; Paul U. Kellogg (editor of the jour-

nal *Survey*); Ernest P. Bicknell (general superintendent of the Chicago Bureau of Charities); and Joseph Logan (secretary of the Atlanta Associated Charities).

11. See the letter from John Glenn to McLean, dated March 1, 1909, for a glimpse into the RSF's ongoing concerns about maintaining control over the COS movement (Ormsby, 1969: 46).

12. The American Association for Organizing Family Social Work went through two more name changes over the years. It was renamed the Family Welfare Association of American in 1936. Since 1946, it has been called the Family Service Association of America.

Chapter Five

13. Robert deForest persuaded millionaire John S. Kennedy to provide the critical endowment for founding the school with a minimum operating budget of $10,000 per year. In 1911, Kennedy contributed another $1,000,000 to the school's endowment fund. Between 1907 and 1912 the Bureau of Social Research was established at the school through a grant from the RSF. The foundation also later granted the school an additional $250,000 for its endowment fund.

14. In a confidential report (1911), John Glenn summarized this overall impact: (1) the retention of more high-quality students in the second year of training programs (during which they emphasized casework techniques); (2) the attraction of new teachers with considerable reputations to the schools; (3) the "realization of the *importance and advantage of careful study of social conditions by the case method*" (emphasis added), including personality as well as the environment, through greater contact with the COS to the mutual benefit of Schools and agencies; (4) improvement of teaching and student standards; (5) strengthening of community/school ties; (6) publication of a wide variety of socioeconomic, social policy-related and medicosocial studies; and (7) the placement of 75% of all fellows (1907–11) in COS executive or supervisory positions (Glenn, November 27, 1911, Richmond Papers).

15. The creation of Red Cross Home Service Institutes by Homer Folks during World War I, for example, further stimulated interest in social work education just as the work which the Red Cross did with servicemen and their families stimulated interest in family casework in general.

Chapter Eight

16. The group was mainly based in state hospitals and community clinics in Massachusetts and New York, with seeds planted in other geographic areas and fields of specialization, e.g., in Baltimore's Phipps Clinic and in

the State Psychopathic Hospital at Ann Arbor, Michigan, or in the visiting teachers and child guidance/delinquency prevention fields.

17. Local foundations included: the Amherst H. Wilder Charity in St. Paul; the Michigan Children's Fund in Detroit and Grand Rapids; the Martha Beeman Foundation in Niagara Falls; the Bemis-Taylor Foundation in Colorado Springs; and the Buhl Foundation in Pittsburgh (Coon, 1938: 229)

18. The White-Williams Foundation in Philadelphia also strongly stimulated the introduction of a psychiatric approach into school social work in the 1920s (Lubove, 1965: 102).

CHAPTER TEN

19. At the annual meeting of the Exchange, May 18, 1918, the nominating committee was composed of Arthur Kellogg, NY, chair; Ida Cannon, Boston; Alfred Fairbank, St. Louis; Gertrude Vaile, Denver; and Edith Abbott, Chicago. They proposed the following board members, who were subsequently elected: NY—Richard H. Edwards, Charles A. Beard, John M. Glenn, Alexander Kohut, Mary Vida Clark, Porter R. Lee, James S. Cushman, William Breed, Margaret Byington, Philip P. Jacobs; Boston—Robert A. Woods, Eva W. White, C. C. Carstens; Atlanta—Joseph C. Logan; Dallas—Elmer Scott; Chicago—S. P. Breckinridge, Edna Foley, William T. Cross; Washington—Mary van Kleeck; Philadephia—Karl de Schweinitz; Cleveland—Belle Sherwin; Denver—Gertrude Vaile; California—Jessica Peixotto; and Minneapolis—Frank J. Bruno (SWHA, NSWE, Minutes, 1918).

20. According to Buell, the most influential members of this committee were Claire Tousley, "who had the confidence of two people who were at the top of the social work structure of that day—Mr. John Glenn, who was director of the Russell Sage Foundation, and Mrs. John M. Glenn, who was president and one of the most influencial factors of what was then called the American Association for Organizing Family Social Work"; Frances Taussig, director of the United Hebrew Charities; and Veronica O. Wilder, of the staff of New York COS (Buell, 1967: 13–14).

21. At the Providence meeting of the AASW a year later (June 1922), several different names for the association were considered, including the National Association of Social Workers, which was rejected because it excluded Canadians. In a correspondence from Paul Beisser, who served as AASW Research Secretary from 1921 to 1923, to Brad Buell, he recalls an impassioned plea by Arthur Guild for the name of "The American Association of Socizians." This suggestion was squelched by the response on the floor from Grace Childs whom Buell primed and had recognized. "Grace's lisp in her constantly repeated reference to 'Socizians' brought down the house and buried Arthur's move completely" (SWHA, Buell folder, Beissel correspondence, March 13, 1967).

22. Two settlement workers did get elected to the Council, Frances In-

gram (Neighborhood House, Louisville) and Franklin C. Wells, Jr. (Union Settlement, N.Y.C.).

23. In commenting on Bradley Buell's oral history recalling these times, Frances Taussig wrote to Buell, "It's hard for me to believe that it's 45 years since it all happened. That was just two years after I got to New York from Chicago—where, by the way, I got to respect and admire, with all their faults and prejudices, three characters whom you left out of your dramatis personae of people who were influential in those times—the two Abbotts and Sophonisba Breckinridge. And some New Yorkers—not including me— would be a bit shocked at seeing no mention of Lilian (Lillian) Wald as an important force"(Taussig correspondence, February 24, 1967). Buell replied on March 9 that he did not recall that any of these persons were active in the AASW's formation. "I knew both the Abbots and Miss Breckinridge, . . . and I don't recall that they were very active in the A.A.S.W. affair. However I could be completely wrong about this and their place as early pioneers is undisputed. The same is true of Lillian Wald, of course, and historians would be properly shocked at my failure to mention her. . . . I can't recall that she was active in A.A.S.W. (Buell correspondence, March 9, 1967; Social Work Archives, Univ. of Minnesota, Buell folder).

24. Buell's account of how he went about formulating membership qualifications lends an instructive touch of the ordinary to the esoteric sociology of professionalization:

> I remember one day I got a brilliant idea. I said to myself these other professional societies must have gone through this same thing. I looked up in the yellow book of the telephone directory and found the officers and directors of the Medical Society, the Bar Association, and the Engineering Society. I went up and talked with them, even with the guy who was secretary of the Association of Court Stenographers. All of them understood the problem which I was posing, no question about it. Actually, as I recall, I got the most help from the fellow who was the secretary of the Engineering Society, because this was newer than either the Bar Association or the Medical Society. But they all said essentially the same thing. "What you have to do first," they said, "is blanket in everybody that really thinks of himself as a professional in this field. Then, having done that, you have to work gradually to improve your professional capacity, to improve your professional education, and to establish more and more specific requirements."(SWHA, Buell, 1967: 23; Oral History)

25. Members had to be at least 25 years old and have four years of practical experience in "social organizations of recognized standing" and "an educational background warranting expectation of success and progress in the profession of social work." Academic and professional training equivalents were set up to substitute for part of the experience requirement, but less than a year of social work experience was not allowed. Junior members had to be college graduates, at least 21 years old, with a year's supervised expe-

rience in a recognized social agency. Satisfactory completion of one year of training in an approved school of social work could be substituted for the year of supervised experience (AASW Constitution, June 28, 1922). A proposal for associate membership, a category of dues-paying, but non-voting laypersons, was rejected by the AASW membership in 1922.

26. On a more personal level, Buell viewed van Kleeck as highly ambitious and the behind-the-scenes engineer of NSWE's split from the Intercollegiate Bureau and its transition to the AASW. Buell wrote,

> Mary van Kleeck was an extremely able woman. I am not sure about her family background, but with the name "van Kleeck" you can be sure it was old New York. She was a contemporary of Frances Perkins. She had a very masculine mind, was a keen analyst, and had a driving ambition for power that was her eventual undoing. If anyone were to write the life of Mary van Kleeck it would be a tragic story, because she moved from positions over the years that had great potentialities, further and further down the line until she became the front for little leftist groups. Nothing she ever tried to dominate quite came off.

As Buell saw it, van Kleeck opposed the "independence" policy because she feared a loss of personal influence which stemmed from her control over RSF grants to the association. Buell's description indicates that the conflict became rather bitter and ultimately cost him his job. His position was compromised when he naively left a folder of notes and memoranda on plans for the Providence meeting in which he had "engineered" the passage of the resolution of self-support. Graham Taylor allegedly went through his desk and brought the folder to van Kleeck. From that time on Buell was considered disloyal, and the controversy allegedly degenerated to attacks on him personally (SWHA, Buell, 1967: 9, 28, Oral History).

27. Accounts of the formation of the Association of Professional Training Schools of Social Work in 1919 disagree over the number of charter members. Some (e.g., Hollis & Taylor, 1952; Bruno, 1957; Lubove, 1965) say there were 17; some (e.g., Meier, 1915; *Encyclopedia of Social Work*, 1977: 290) say 15. We follow the listing of charter members provided by James Hagerty (1931: 52, 53). These were as follows: The New York School of Social Work, the Boston School of Social Work, the Chicago School of Civics and Philanthropy, the St. Louis School of Social Work, the Richmond School of Social Work, and the Pennsylvania School of Social Work. The following universities and colleges were also represented at the organizing conference: Bryn Mawr College, Carnegie Institute of Technology, Smith College, University of Chicago, University of Minnesota, Ohio State University, University of Pittsburgh, University of Toronto, and Western Reserve University. Note that Chicago institutions were represented twice. The Chicago School of Civics and Philanthropy affiliated with the University of Chicago in 1920.

28. A study by Syndor H. Walker (Univ. of North Carolina, Chapel Hill, 1928) found 35 institutions with organized social work curricula in 1928.

Hagerty (1931: 52, 53) listed 28 members of the association in 1931 plus an additional 8 non-member schools with social work courses.

29. Accounts vary as to the actual number: Esther Lucile Brown (1942: 31) and Hagerty (1931) indicate there were fifteen; Hollis and Taylor (1951: 14) say twenty.

CHAPTER ELEVEN

30. Along with Chicago and New York, Boston also did not have a developed Community Chest until the mid-1930s. Trolander omits Boston from her argument that non-Chest cities sustained more reform involvement during the 1920s than Chest cities. If the level of social activism was low among Boston settlements during this period, as it seems to have been, and Chest control was not the explanation, what accounts for this situation? Our speculation, which needs to be systematically investigated, is that over the years the Boston agencies had been much more interested in education and cultural arts, the predilection of leaders such as Albert Kennedy and Robert Woods, and their aristocratic supporters, and this pattern had continued even without federation control.

31. That settlement workers were concerned about the impact of the new mass society on the quality of life was also reflected, for example, in the agenda of troublesome questions that were considered by settlement workers in preparation for the Third International Conference of Settlements in 1929. On the one hand these concerned the effects on society and the individual of: "the 'mechanization' of industry which tends to reduce the workers' opportunity for self-expression or the exercise of creative faculties; the 'mechanization' and 'mass production' of ideas, pleasures, tastes and standards through the press, wireless, commercialized amusements, advertisements, the supply of goods on hire purchase, etc.; the influence of modern transport facilities on community life, separation of work and home life and of employment and employees, development of dormitory suburbs." On the other hand they concerned the effects of: "the growth of opportunity for education and self-development through increased facilities, the press, wireless, easy travel, etc.; the rising standard of living conditions and the spread of knowledge in regard to conditions in other countries; the rising standard of working conditions; the change in the position of women" (Wald, 1928).

32. Prohibition so divided the settlement and general social work leadership that the 1928 presidential election found Lillian Wald, John L. Elliott, and Paul Kellogg active as Alfred Smith supporters, while Jane Addams, Sophonisba Breckenridge, and Mary McDowell supported Herbert Hoover.

CHAPTER THIRTEEN

33. See also Abraham Epstein's account of how "the poor support [ed] the poor," in *Insecurity: A Challenge to America*, 182–84.

CHAPTER FOURTEEN

34. In November 1932 the Federal Action Conference was dissolved and the Steering Committee moved back within the formal structure of AASW as the Committee on Federal Action on Unemployment to take better advantage of the access to local AASW chapters. In 1933 it became the Committee on Federal Action in Social Welfare, and in April 1934 it reemerged as the Division of Government and Social Work when AASW adopted a new structure to conform to changes on the national scene.

35. The nine states (and the District of Columbia) that did not receive FERA funds for sending relief workers to schools of social work were: Massachusetts, Connecticut, Rhode Island, New York, Pennsylvania, Delaware, New Jersey, Maryland, and Ohio. These states already had many social workers and some had training programs of their own (J. Brown, 1940: 283).

36. The other four members of the Committee were: Harry Hopkins as head of FERA; Henry Wallace, Secretary of Agriculture; Henry Morgenthau, Jr., Secretary of the Treasury; and Homer Cummings, Attorney General.

37. Dr. Witte was Altmeyer's former economics professor at the University of Wisconsin. Witte, in turn, assembled an array of technical experts, including another former student, Wilbur Cohen, who 30 years later became Secretary of HEW.

38. The old-age and unemployment insurance provisions of the act were landmarks in American social policy, but the public assistance provisions most directly affected social work. These titles provided federal subsidies to state programs of cash assistance for the needy aged, the needy blind, and dependent children, and funds for the development of various services in the area of public health, child welfare, and care and rehabilitation of the disabled. The grants to states opting to participate were to be provided on a matching basis according to a percentage formula for each category of assistance. The act also established the federal Social Security Board (SSB), to set standards and oversee the new programs. Participating states were required to submit to the board for approval programs that will "be in effect in all political subdivisions of the State, and if administered by them, be mandatory upon them," will "provide for financial participation by the State," and will either "provide for the establishment or designation of a single State agency to administer the plan" or "to supervise the administration of the plan" (Social Security Act, Title I, sec. 2, p. 1).

39. Fred M. Vinson, a leading member of the House Ways and Means Committee, stated with regard to the SSB, "No damned social workers are going to come into my State to tell our people whom they shall hire" (Altmeyer, 1966: 36).

CHAPTER FIFTEEN

40. The information about the Rank and File Movement in this chapter draws heavily from the outstanding, original work of Jacob Fisher, editor of

Social Work Today, early Rank and File leader, author and chronicler of the movement. No historian interested in this aspect of social work can escape the influence of Fisher's writings on the topic. Porter R. Lee, Director of the New York School of Social Work, recognized Fisher's unique insight and ability in 1936 by inviting him to lead a student seminar on rank and file developments. Subsequently the New York School published Fisher's account of the Movement, *The Rank and File Movement in Social Work, 1931–1936,* (NY: June 1936). In his foreword to this 40-page piece, Porter Lee wrote: "Mr. Fisher has been intimately associated with the rank and file movement and is one of its intellectual leaders. His opinions and principles are clear and may even be regarded as militant, but the present pamphlet is, we believe, a production of remarkable objective scholarship."

41. In 1967 Jacob Fisher responded to a series of questions about the Rank and File Movement from John Earl Haynes who was researching the Rank and File Movement for the paper he eventually published. Fisher's recollections offer additional insight into the state of mind of many young social workers at the time (letter from Jacob Fisher to John Earl Haynes, May 20, 1967, as reproduced in Alexander, 1977: 209).

How early what you call the "rank and file attitude" emerged I don't know. The 1932 and 1933 articles in the JSSQ you cite are I believe the first published on the subject. The underlying dissatisfaction didn't arise overnight; on the other hand I doubt whether there was any articulated dissent prior to 1932. Nobody, or almost nobody, believed in 29, 30, or 31 that the depression would last as long as it did. Social workers were guided in their thinking by the experience of the 1914 and 1921–22 recessions—not only on how to meet the needs of the unemployed but also in looking ahead to better days soon. By the end of 31 or thereabouts some of us began to feel we were in the middle of the beginning of something unique and it was then that ideas about the desirability of changes in the welfare system and indeed in the economy as a whole began to circulate among us. You must remember that we were not only social workers but also members of the book and magazine reading public and influenced by the reporting in and the editorial positions taken by such journals of opinion as The Nation, the New Republic, and the New Masses. As one hope after another about the end of the depression proved illusory receptivity sharpened to suggestions for fundamental changes in the system.

42. Some authors (Haynes, 1975; Glazer, 1961; Spano, 1982) have attached much significance to the influence of Jewish radicalism on the inception and Marxist bent of the Rank and File Movement, because Jewish social workers were among the first proponents of rank and file organizations in New York and elsewhere, and because a disproportionate number of Jews belonged to the Communist Party in the 1920s and 1930s. This emphasis runs the risk of characterizing the Rank and File Movement in social work as a Jewish phenomenon. As such it minimizes the formative

impact of broader social, political, and economic forces as well as the substantial contributions of the many non-Jews who led and supported progressive action and whose radicalism then also needs to be explained.

We have suggested that the attraction of social workers to the political left and to the labor movement was a function of their economic plight, their role as "dirty workers" in the relief agencies, and the larger transformation of social work from a small agency craft to a social service industry.

It should also be noted in passing that Spano (1982: 52) misquotes Glazer as saying that "out of a population of 4,500,000 American Jews there were roughly 50,000 Jews in the Communist Party." Glazer (1961: 130) indicated that at its peak the Party "rose only briefly above 50,000" members, some large percentage of whom were of Jewish origin. CP membership also fluctuated enormously during its major growth period of 1930–50, as only the most devoted militants were willing to surrender their lives to the party discipline of the Stalinist era (Howe & Coser, 1957: 528–29; Glazer, 1961: 101).

43. See also, the "Common Goals of Labor and Social Work," given at another session of the same NCSW, and the discussion afterwards reproduced in *SWT,* October 1934.

44. The NCC's accomplishments at the Montreal meetings, where the group was officially recognized as an associate member, included action on Negro discrimination, interviews of FERA representatives on the Administration's relief plans, and sponsorship of five well-attended sessions which continued their reform agenda. (For a listing of these sessions, see Alexander, 1977: 88–89.)

CHAPTER SIXTEEN

45. For simplicity we will use the later AASSW abbreviation or name instead of the American Association of Professional Schools of Social Work or AAPSW.

46. The AASW changes in membership set forth in 1929 were the following. (See Chapter 10, note 25, for a comparison with 1922 requirements.)

Junior Membership, effective after March 1, 1930

1. Minimum age of twenty-one years.
2. Completion of at least two years' work in an approved college.
3. Three additional years of general education, technical training or employment in an approved agency. This requirement might be satisfied in either one of the two following ways:

    a. Completion of two additional years' work in an approved college plus one year's work in an approved school of social work.

    b. Three years spent in some combination of: attendance at an approved college, attendance at an approved school of social work, or employment in an approved agency, provided that the applicant has satisfactorily completed:

Fifteen semester hours of social or biological science in an approved school of social work or college;
Ten semester hours of approved technical social work courses;
Three hundred hours of supervised field work in connection with technical social work courses.

4. Employment at the time of application in an approved agency.

Full Membership, effective July 1, 1933.

1. Completion of at least two years' work in an approved college.
2. Five additional years of general education, technical training or employment in an approved agency. This requirement might be satisfied in either one of the two following ways.

   a. Graduation from an approved college plus one year in an approved school of social work, plus two years of employment in an approved agency.

   b. Five years spent in some combination of: attendance at an approved college, attendance at an approved school of social work, or employment in an approved agency, provided, however, that the applicant has satisfactorily completed:

   Twenty semester hours of social and biological science in an approved college or school of social work.
   Twenty-four hours of approved technical social work courses.
   Two years of employment in an approved agency.

3. (Substitute for requirements 1 and 2) Graduation from a four-year college plus completion of a two-year graduate course in an approved school of social work shall be regarded as fulfilling requirements 1 and 2.

47. Between 1930 and 1934, the National Membership Committee (NMC) of the AASW and its various subcommittees met regularly to consider standards for approving technical social work courses, social agencies, and field experiences. As part of its boundary-defining process, it also carefully screened application appeals for junior and senior (or "full") membership, trying to find and apply objective criteria for admission or rejection. These reviews led to many important decisions and conclusions, such as the agreement that occupational therapy was not social work but an allied field (SWHA, NASW, b6, f#48, 49); that applicants could get credit for a one-year course of training in public health nursing, but not for bedside nursing, up to July 1, 1933 (SWHA, NASW, b6, f#50); and that it would brook no discrimination against Negroes as members of the AASW despite local chapter difficulties. In the latter case, which pertained to Wiley A. Hall, the executive secretary of the Urban League in Richmond, Va., the

NMC had received an inquiry from the Richmond, Va., Chapter of AASW as to "whether a chapter has the right to exclude Negro members of the national association from chapter membership." To its credit, the committee noted, "Mr. West wrote that the N.M.C. makes no distinction between Negro and white applicants for membership and that any member of the National Association is eligible to chapter membership on payment of chapter dues" (SWHA: NASW, b6, f#49: 10).

48. Historically, Mary Richmond had mentioned private practice as early as 1917 in *Social Diagnosis* and in 1922 in "What is Social Casework?" The AASW had considered the idea in 1926 but set it aside until standards could be established. The American Association of Psychiatric Social Workers (AAPSW) did likewise in 1927 (French, 1940). And in 1936, a professional social worker named Steiner (1936; 1938) in fact began a private practice in New York (Levenstein, 1964).

CHAPTER 17

49. As it later turned out, for various reasons the mail vote did not put Section 6 to rest. In October 1944 a new NMC, discovering that the largest number of admissions under Section 6 since 1939–40 had been only 28, decided to retain the provision without restrictions (SWHA, National AASW Board Meeting, Appendix B, October, 1944).

References

BOOKS AND DISSERTATIONS

Abbott, Edith. 1940. *Public Assistance: American Principles and Policies.* Vol. 2. Chicago: University of Chicago Press. Reprint. 1966. New York: Russell and Russell.

Adams, Elizabeth Kemper. 1921. *Women Professional Workers.* New York: Macmillan.

Adams, Henry H. 1977. *Harry Hopkins: A Biography.* New York: Putnam.

Addams, Jane. 1893a. *Philanthropy and Social Progress.* New York: Thomas Crowell.

———. 1902. *Democracy and Social Ethics.* New York: Macmillan.

———. 1910. *Twenty Years at Hull House.* New York: Macmillan.

———. 1912a. *A New Conscience and an Ancient Evil.* New York: Macmillan.

Aldrich, Howard E. 1979. *Organizations and Environments.* Englewood Cliffs, NJ: Prentice-Hall.

Alexander, Leslie B. 1977. *Organizing the Professional Social Worker: Union Development in Voluntary Social Work, 1930–1950.* Unpublished Ph.D. dissertation, The Graduate School of Social Work and Social Research, Bryn Mawr College.

Altmeyer, Arthur Joseph. 1966. *The Formative Years of Social Security.* Madison: University of Wisconsin Press.

American Association of Group Workers. 1947. *Toward Professional Standards: Selected Papers for the Years 1945 and 1946.* New York: American Association of Group Workers.

American Association of Social Workers. 1929. *Social Case Work: Generic and Specific* (A Report of the Milford Conference, New York) Reprint. Washington, DC: NASW, Classic Series, 1974.

———. 1936. *This Business of Relief.* New York: American Association of Social Workers.

Austin, Michael J. 1976. *Professionals and Paraprofessionals.* New York: Human Sciences Press.

Axinn, June, and Herman Levin. 1983. *Social Welfare: A History of the American Response to Need* (2nd ed.). New York: Harper and Row.

Baer, Betty L., and Ronald Federico. 1978. *Educating the Baccalaureate Social Worker: Report of the Undergraduate Social Work Curriculum Development Project.* Cambridge, MA: Ballinger.

Banner, Lois. 1979. *Women in Modern America: A Brief History.* New York: Harcourt Brace Jovanovich.

Bell, Daniel. 1973. *The Coming of Post-Industrial Society.* New York: Basic Books.

Bender, Thomas. 1975. *Toward an Urban Vision.* Baltimore: Johns Hopkins University Press.

Berkowitz, Edward, and Kim McQuaid. 1980. *Creating the Welfare State: The Political Economy of Twentieth Century Reform.* New York: Praeger.

Bledstein, Burton J. 1976. *The Culture of Professionalism: The Middle Class and the Development of Higher Education in America.* New York: W. W. Norton.

Blumberg, Dorothy R. 1966. *Florence Kelley: The Making of a Social Pioneer.* New York: Augustus Kelley.

Boyer, Paul. 1978. *Urban Masses and Moral Order in America, 1820–1920.* Cambridge: Harvard University Press.

Brace, Charles Loring. 1872. *The Dangerous Classes of New York and Twenty Years Work Among Them.* New York: Wynkoop and Hallenbeck.

Brock, William. 1965. *The Character of American History* (2nd ed.). New York: Harper and Row.

Brody, David. 1980. *Workers in Industrial America: Essays on the 20th Century.* New York: Oxford University Press.

Brooks, Thomas R. 1964. *Toil and Trouble: A History of American Labor.* New York: Delacorte.

Brown, Esther Lucile. 1935, 1936, 1942. *Social Work as a Profession.* New York: Russell Sage Foundation.

Brown, Josephine Chapman. 1940. *Public Relief: 1929–1939.* New York: Henry Holt and Company.

Bruno, Frank J. 1948, 1957. *Trends in Social Work, 1874–1956.* New York: Columbia University Press.

Cabot, Richard. 1915. *Social Service and the Art of Healing.* New York: Moffatt Yard.

Cannon, Ida M. 1952. *On the Social Frontier of Medicine: Pioneering in Medical Social Service.* Cambridge: Harvard University Press.

Carlton, Iris. 1982. *A Pioneer in Social Work: George Edmund Haynes.* Unpublished Ph.D. dissertation, School of Social Work and Community Planning, University of Maryland.

Chambers, Clarke A. 1963. *Seedtime of Reform: American Social Service and Social Action, 1918–1933.* Minneapolis: University of Minnesota Press.

———. 1971. *Paul U. Kellogg and the Survey: Voices for Social Welfare and Social Justice.* Minneapolis: University of Minnesota Press.

Chambers, John Whiteclay, II. 1980. *The Tyranny of Change: America in the Progressive Era, 1900–1917.* New York: St. Martin's.

Cohen, Nathan E. 1958. *Social Work in the American Tradition*. New York: Dryden.

Commager, Henry Steele (ed.). 1967. *Lester Ward and the Welfare State*. Indianapolis: Bobbs Merrill.

Coon, Horace. 1938. *Money to Burn: What the Great American Philanthropic Foundations Do with Their Money*. New York: Longmans, Green.

Costin, Lela B. 1983. *Two Sisters for Social Justice*. Urbana: University of Illinois Press.

Davis, Allen. 1967. *Spearheads for Reform: The Social Settlements and the Progressive Movement, 1890–1914*. New York: Oxford University Press.

Davis, Phillip (ed.). 1915. *The Field of Social Service*. Boston: Small, Maynard.

Devine, Edward. 1904. *The Principles of Relief*. New York: Macmillan.

Dewey, John. 1916. *Democracy and Education: An Introduction to the Philosophy of Education*. New York: Macmillan.

Dillick, Sidney. 1953. *Community Organization for Neighborhood Development—Past and Present*. New York: Women's Press, Whiteside, and William Morrow.

Dinnerstein, Leonard, Roger L. Nichols, and David M. Reimers. 1979. *Natives and Strangers: Ethnic Groups and the Building of America*. New York: Oxford University Press.

Duffus, Robert Luther. 1938. *Lillian Wald: Neighbor and Crusader*. New York: Macmillan.

Ehrenreich, John H. 1985. *The Altruistic Imagination: A History of Social Work and Social Policy in the United States*. Ithaca, NY: Cornell University Press.

Epstein, Abraham. 1936. *Insecurity: A Challenge to America* (rev. ed.). New York: Random House.

Epstein, Beryl Williams. 1948. *Lillian Wald, Angel of Henry Street*. New York: J. Messner, 1948.

Etzioni, Amitai (ed.). 1969. *The Semi-professions and Their Organization: Teachers, Nurses and Social Workers*. New York: Free Press.

Ewen, Stuart. 1976. *Captains of Consciousness: Advertising and the Social Roots of the Consumer Culture*. New York: McGraw-Hill.

Felt, Jeremy. 1965. *Hostages of Fortune: Child Labor Reform in New York State*. Syracuse: Syracuse University Press.

Fink, Arthur E. 1942. *The Field of Social Work* (rev. ed., 1949). NY: Henry Holt.

Fisher, Jacob. 1936a. *The Rank and File Movement in Social Work: 1931–1936*. New York: New York School of Social Work.

———. 1980. *The Response of Social Work to the Depression*. Cambridge, MA: Schenkman.

Fisher, Robert. 1984. *Let the People Decide: Neighborhood Organizing in America*. Boston: J. K. Hall and Twayne.

Folks, Homer. 1902. *The Care of Destitute, Neglected and Delinquent Children.* New York: Macmillan.

Follett, Mary P. 1918. *The New State.* New York: Longmans, Green.

Frederickson, George M. 1965. *The Inner Civil War: Northern Intellectuals and the Crisis of the Union.* New York: Harper and Row.

Freidson, Eliot. 1970a. *Profession of Medicine.* New York: Dodd, Mead.

————. 1970b. *Professional Dominance: The Social Structure of Medical Care.* New York: Atherton Press.

French, Lois Meredith. 1940. *Psychiatric Social Work.* New York: Commonwealth Fund.

Furner, Mary O. 1975. *Advocacy and Objectivity: A Crisis in the Professionalization of American Social Science, 1865–1905.* Lexington: University of Kentucky Press.

Galbraith, John Kenneth. 1967. *The New Industrial State* (rev. ed., 1971). New York: New American Library.

Gilbert, James. 1970. *Work without Salvation: American Intellectuals and Industrial Alienation, 1880–1910.* Baltimore: Johns Hopkins University Press.

Gilbert, Neil. 1970. *Clients or Constituents.* San Francisco: Jossey-Bass.

Glazer, Nathan. 1961. *The Social Basis of American Communism.* New York: Harcourt, Brace and World.

Glenn, John, Lilian Brandt and F. Emerson Andrews. 1947. *The Russell Sage Foundation.* 2 vols. New York: Russell Sage Foundation.

Goldmark, Josephine. 1953. *Impatient Crusader: Florence Kelley's Life Story.* Urbana: University of Illinois Press.

Gurin, Arnold. 1970. *Community Organization Curriculum in Graduate Social Work Education: Report and Recommendations.* New York: Council on Social Work Education.

Gutman, Herbert. 1976. *Work, Culture and Society in Industrializing America.* New York: Vintage.

Hagerty, James E. 1931. *The Training of Social Workers.* New York: McGraw-Hill.

Handlin, Oscar (ed.). 1959. *Immigration as a Factor in American History.* Englewood Cliffs, NJ: Prentice-Hall.

Harris, Neil, David Rothman, and Stephen Thernstrom. 1969. *The History of the United States: Source Readings,* Vol. 2. New York: Holt, Rinehart and Winston.

Haskell, Thomas. 1977. *The Emergence of Professional Social Science.* Chicago: University of Illinois Press.

Hawley, Ellis W. 1979. *The Great War and the Search for a Modern Order: A History of the American People and Their Institutions, 1917–1933.* New York: St. Martin's.

Hershkowitz, Leo. 1978. *Tweed's New York: Another Look.* New York: Anchor.

Hobsbawm, Eric J. 1964. *The Age of Revolution, 1789–1848.* New York: Mentor.

Hofstadter, Richard. 1955. *The Age of Reform.* New York: Vintage.
———. 1959. *Social Darwinism in American Thought.* Boston: Beacon.
———. 1960. *The American Political Tradition.* New York: Vintage.
Holden, Arthur C. 1922. *The Settlement Idea: A Vision of Social Justice.* New York: Macmillan.
Hollis, Ernest V., and Alice L. Taylor. 1951. *Social Work Education in the United States.* New York: Columbia University Press.
Hopkins, Harry L. 1936. *Spending to Save: The Complete Story of Relief.* New York: W. W. Norton.
Horesji, John E. 1977. *Working in Welfare: Survival Through Positive Action.* Iowa City: University of Iowa School of Social Work.
Howe, Irving. 1976. *World of Our Fathers.* New York: Harcourt Brace Jovanovich.
Howe, Irving, and Lewis Coser. 1957. *The American Communist Party: A Critical History (1918–1957).* Boston: Beacon.
Huggins, Nathan I. 1971. *Protestants Against Poverty: Boston's Charities, 1870–1900.* Westport, CT: Greenwood Press.
Hunter, Robert. 1904. *Poverty.* New York: Grosset and Dunlap.
Hymowitz, Carol, and Michaele Weissman. 1978. *A History of Women in America.* New York: Bantam.
Jeffrys-Jones, Rhodri. 1978. *Violence and Reform in American History.* New York: New Viewpoints.
Johnson, Terence J. 1972. *Professions and Power.* London: Macmillan.
Jones, John Finbar, and John Middlemist Herrick. 1976. *Citizens in Service: Volunteers in Social Welfare during the Depression, 1929–1941.* Ann Arbor: Michigan State University Press.
Karp, Abraham J. 1976. *Golden Door to America.* New York: Penguin.
Karpf, Morris J. 1931. *The Scientific Basis of Social Work: A Study in Family Case Work.* New York: Columbia University Press.
Kasson, John. 1976. *Civilizing the Machine: Technology and Republican Values in America, 1776–1900.* New York: Grossman.
Keller, Morton. 1977. *Affairs of State: Public Life in Late 19th Century America.* Cambridge: Harvard University Press.
Kessler-Harris, Alice. 1982. *Out to Work: A History of Wage-earning Women in the United States.* New York: Oxford University Press.
Kessner, Thomas. 1977. *The Golden Door: Italian and Jewish Immigrant Mobility in New York City: 1880–1915.* New York: Oxford University Press.
Kolko, Gabriel. 1963. *The Triumph of Conservatism.* Chicago: Quadrangle.
———. 1976. *Main Currents in Modern American History.* New York: Harper and Row.
Kurzman, Paul A. 1974. *Harry Hopkins and the New Deal.* Fairlawn, NJ: R. E. Burdick.
Larson, Magali Sarfatti. 1977. *The Rise of Professionalism.* Berkeley: University of California Press.

Lee, Porter R. 1937. *Social Work as Cause and Function.* New York: Columbia University Press.

Lee, Porter R., and Marion E. Kenworthy. 1929. *Mental Hygiene and Social Work.* New York: Commonwealth Fund.

Leiby, James. 1978. *A History of Social Welfare and Social Work in the United States.* New York: Columbia University Press.

Leighninger, Leslie Hartrich. 1981. *The Development of Social Work as a Profession, 1930–1960.* Unpublished Ph.D. dissertation, School of Social Welfare, University of California-Berkeley.

———. 1987. *Social Work: Search for Identity.* Westport, CT: Greenwood Press.

Levenstein, Sidney. 1964. *Private Practice in Social Casework.* New York: Columbia University Press.

Levine, Daniel. 1971. *Jane Addams and the Liberal Tradition.* Madison: State Historical Society of Wisconsin.

Liebman, Arthur. 1979. *Jews and the Left.* New York: John Wiley.

Lindeman, Eduard C. 1936. *Wealth and Culture: A Study of One Hundred Foundations and Community Trusts and Their Operations During the Decade 1921–1930.* New York: Harcourt, Brace.

———. 1952. *The New York School of Social Work: An Interpretive History.* New York: Columbia University Press.

Linn, James Weber. 1935. *Jane Addams.* New York: D. Appleton Century.

Lloyd, Gary A. 1971. *Charities, Settlements and Social Work: An Inquiry into Philosophy and Method, 1890–1915.* New Orleans: Tulane University Press.

Lowry, Fern (ed.). 1939. *Readings in Social Case Work, 1920–1938.* New York: Columbia University Press.

Lubove, Roy. 1962. *The Progressives and the Slums.* Pittsburgh: University of Pittsburgh Press.

———. 1965. *The Professional Altruist: The Emergence of Social Work as a Career, 1880–1930.* Cambridge: Harvard University Press.

———. 1968. *The Struggle for Social Security, 1900–1935.* Cambridge: Harvard University Press.

Lunt, Sally Herman. 1974. *The Profession of Social Work: The History of Education for Social Work, with Special Reference to the School for Social Workers (Boston, 1904).* Unpublished Ph.D. dissertation, Graduate School of Education, Harvard University.

Maddow, Ben. 1979. *A Sunday between the Wars: The Course of American Life, 1865–1917.* New York: W. W. Norton.

Manchester, William. 1975. *The Glory and the Dream: A Narrative History of America, 1932–1972.* New York: Bantam Books.

Marris, Peter, and Martin Rein. 1967. *Dilemmas of Social Reform.* London: Routledge and Kegan Paul.

Matthaei, Julie. 1982. *An Economic History of Women in America: Women's Work, the Sexual Division of Labor and the Development of Capitalism.* New York: Schocken.

McMillen, Wayne. 1945, 1951. *Community Organization for Social Welfare*. Chicago: University of Chicago Press.

Meier, Elizabeth. 1954. *A History of the New York School of Social Work*. New York: Columbia University Press.

Moynihan, Daniel Patrick. 1969. *Maximum Feasible Misunderstanding*. New York: Free Press.

Munson, Carlton (ed.). 1978. *Social Work Education and Practice: Historical Perspectives*. Houston: Jovon.

National Association of Social Workers. 1970. *The Encyclopedia of Social Work*. New York: NASW.

———. 1977. *The Encyclopedia of Social Work*. New York: NASW.

———. 1987. *The Encyclopedia of Social Work*. Silver Spring, MD: NASW.

Nevins, Allan, and Henry Steele Commager. 1976. *A Short History of the United States* (rev. ed.). New York: Knopf.

O'Grady, John. 1931. *Catholic Charities in the United States: History and Problems*. Washington: National Conference of Catholic Charities.

Olson, Thomas L. 1972. *Unfinished Business: American Social Work in Pursuit of Reform, Community, and World Peace, 1939–1950*. Unpublished Ph.D. dissertation, University of Minnesota.

O'Neill, William. 1969. *Everyone Was Brave: The Rise and Fall of Feminism in America*. Chicago: Quadrangle.

Ormsby, Ralph. 1969. *A Man of Vision: Francis H. McLean, 1869–1945*. New York: Family Service Association of America.

Osthaus, Carl. 1976. *Freedman, Philanthropy and Fraud: A History of the Freedmen's Saving Bank*. Urbana: University of Illinois Press.

Pacey, Lorene M. (ed.). 1950. *Readings in the Development of Settlement Work*. New York: Association Press.

Pearl, Arthur, and Frank Riessman. 1965. *New Careers for the Poor*. New York: Free Press.

Peterson, Florence. 1947. *Survey of Labor Economics*. New York: Harper.

Piven, Frances, and Richard A. Cloward. 1971. *Regulating the Poor: The Functions of Public Welfare*. New York: Random House.

———. 1977. *Poor People's Movements*. New York: Pantheon.

Poulantzas, Nicos. 1976. *Classes in Contemporary Capitalism*. New York: Humanities Press.

Pray, Kenneth L. M. 1949. *Social Work in a Revolutionary Age*. Philadelphia: University of Pennsylvania Press.

Proceedings. Vols. 1929 through 1948. National Conference of Social Work. Chicago: University of Chicago Press, and New York: Columbia University Press.

Queen, Stuart. 1922. *Social Work in the Light of History*. Philadelphia: J. B. Lippincott.

Reynolds, Bertha Capen. 1934. *Between Client and Community: A Study in Social Responsibility in Social Case Work*. Northhampton, MA: Smith College Studies in Social Work, Vol. 5 (1) Reprint. NASW Classic Series, Silver Spring: MD, 1982.

————. 1963. *An Uncharted Journey.* New York: Citadel.

Rich, Margaret E. 1956. *A Belief in People: A History of Family Social Work.* New York: Family Service Association of America.

Richmond, Mary Ellen. 1899a. *Friendly Visiting among the Poor.* Philadelphia: Society for Organizing Charity.

————. 1911. *First Steps in Social Services Treatment: A Textbook for Caseworkers.* New York: Russell Sage Foundation.

————. 1917. *Social Diagnosis.* New York: Russell Sage Foundation.

Riis, Jacob. 1890. *How the Other Half Lives: Studies among the Tenements of New York.* New York: Macmillan.

Robinson, Virginia O. 1930. *A Changing Psychology in Social Case Work.* Chapel Hill: University of North Carolina Press.

Rosen, Sumner M., David Fanshel, and Mary E. Lutz (eds.). 1987. *Face of the Nation, 1987: Statistical Supplement to the 18th Edition of the Encyclopedia of Social Work.* Silver Spring, MD: National Association of Social Workers.

Ross, Edyth L. 1978. *Black Heritage in Social Welfare: 1860–1930.* Metuchen, NJ: Scarecrow.

Ross, Murray G. 1955. *Community Organization: Theory and Principles.* New York: Harper.

Rubinow, I. M. 1913. *Social Insurance with Specific Reference to American Conditions.* New York: Columbia University Press.

Salmond, John. 1983. *A Southern Rebel: The Life and Times of Aubrey Willis Williams, 1890–1965.* Chapel Hill: University of North Carolina Press.

Schlesinger, Arthur M., Jr. 1957. *The Crisis of the Old Order: 1919–1933.* Boston: Houghton Mifflin.

Seager, Henry Rogers. 1910. *Social Insurance: A Program of Social Reform.* New York: Columbia University Press.

Seymour, Helen. 1937. *When Clients Organize.* Chicago: American Public Welfare Association.

Siegel, Sheldon. 1975. *Social Service Manpower Needs: An Overview to 1980.* New York: Council on Social Work Education.

Simkhovitch, Mary. 1917. *City Workers World.* New York: Macmillan.

————. 1938. *Neighborhood: My Story of Greenwich House.* New York: Norton.

Sobey, Francine. 1970. *The Nonprofessional Revolution in Mental Health.* New York: Columbia University Press.

Social Security Act. August 14, 1935, Public-271–74th Congress, pp. 1–32.

Social Work Year Book, 1929. 1930. New York: Russell Sage Foundation.

Spano, Rick. 1982. *The Rank and File Movement in Social Work.* Washington, D.C.: University Press of America.

Starr, Paul. 1982. *The Social Transformation of American Medicine.* New York: Basic Books.

Steele, Evelyn, and H. K. Blatt. 1946. *Careers in Social Service.* New York: E. P. Dutton.

Steiner, Jesse F. 1925. *Community Organization: A Study of Its Theory and Current Practice.* New York: Century.

Stewart, William Rhinelander. 1911. *The Philanthropic Work of Josephine Shaw Lowell.* New York: Macmillan.

Strong, Josiah. 1898. *The Twentieth Century City.* New York: Macmillan.

Swanberg, W. A. 1976. *Norman Thomas: The Last Idealist.* New York: Scribner.

Symes, Lillian, and Travers Clement. 1972. *Rebel America: The Story of Social Revolt in the United States.* Boston: Beacon.

Terkel, Studs. 1970. *Hard Times: An Oral History of the Depression.* NY: Avon.

Tocqueville, Alexis de. 1945. *Democracy in America.* Ed. Phillips Bradley. 2 vols. New York: Knopf.

Toren, Nina. 1972. *Social Work: The Case of a Semi-profession.* Beverly Hills, CA: Sage.

Trattner, Walter I. 1979. *From Poor Law to Welfare State: A History of Social Welfare in America* (2nd ed.). New York: Free Press.

Trolander, Judith. 1975. *Settlement Houses and the Great Depression.* Detroit: Wayne State University Press.

Tufts, James. 1923. *Education and Training for Social Work.* New York: Russell Sage Foundation.

United Way of America. 1972. *1971–72 Directory.* Alexandria, VA: United Way of America.

———. 1977. *People and Events: A History of the United Way.* Alexandria, VA.: United Way of America.

U.S. Department of Commerce, Bureau of the Census. 1944. *Statistical Abstract of the United States, 1943.* Washington, D.C.: U.S. Government Printing Office.

van Kleeck, Mary. 1936. *Creative America: Its Resources for Social Security.* NY: Covici Friede.

Veblen, Thorsten. 1899. *The Theory of the Leisure Class: An Economic Study of Institutions.* New York: Funk and Wagnalls.

Wade, Louise C. 1964. *Graham Taylor: Pioneer for Social Justice, 1851–1938.* Chicago: University of Chicago Press.

Wald, Lillian. 1915. *The House on Henry Street.* New York: Holt, Rinehart and Winston.

Walker, Robert (ed.). 1976. *The Reform Spirit in America.* New York: Putnam.

Walker, Syndor H. 1928. *Social Work and the Training of Social Workers.* Chapel Hill: University of North Carolina Press.

Ward, Lester. 1974. *Pure Sociology and Applied Sociology.* New York: Arno.

Warner, Amos. 1894. *American Charities.* New York: Thomas Crowell.

Warner, Amos, Stuart Queen, and Ernest Baldwin. 1929. *American Charities and Social Work* (4th ed.). New York: Thomas Crowell.

Watson, Frank D. 1922. *The Charity Organization Society Movement in the United States.* New York: Macmillan.

Waxman, Chaim I. 1977. *The Stigma of Poverty: A Critique of Poverty Theories and Policies.* New York: Pergamon.

Weinstein, James. 1969. *The Corporate Ideal in the Liberal State, 1900–1918.* Boston: Beacon.

Whitman, Walt. 1877. *Democratic Vistas.* Reprinted in Richard D. Heffner, *A Documentary History of the United States.* New York: Mentor, 1956.

Wiebe, Robert. 1967. *The Search for Order: 1977–1920.* New York: Hill and Wang.

Wilensky, Harold L., and Charles N. Lebeaux. 1958, 1965. *Industrial Society and Social Welfare.* New York: Free Press.

Williamson, Margaretta. 1929. *The Social Worker in Group Work.* New York: Harper.

Wilson, William Julius. 1978. *The Declining Significance of Race.* Chicago: University of Chicago Press.

Wise, Winifred. 1935. *Jane Addams of Hull House.* New York: Harcourt Brace Jovanovich.

Witmer, Helen L. 1942. *Social Work: An Analysis of a Social Institution.* New York: Rinehart.

Woodroofe, Kathleen. 1962. *From Charity to Social Work in England and the United States.* London: Routledge and Kegan Paul.

Woods, Robert. 1922. *The Settlement Horizon: A National Estimate.* New York: Russell Sage Foundation.

Woods, Robert, and Albert Kennedy. 1910. *Handbook of Settlements.* Boston: National Federation of Settlements.

Zinn, Howard. 1980. *A People's History of the United States.* New York: Harper and Row.

ARTICLES, MINUTES, CORRESPONDENCE

"A Program of Social Work." 1908. Editorial, *Charities and the Commons, 21,* October 3.

Abbott, Edith. 1936. "Public Welfare and Politics." *Proceedings of the National Conference of Social Work.* Chicago: University of Chicago Press, 27–45.

Adler, Herman. 1932. "The Need of Trained Personnel in Public Welfare Services: Defining Public Welfare Work in Professional Terms." *Social Service Review,* 6 (3), September, 429–36.

Addams, Jane. 1893b. "The Subjective Necessity for Social Settlements." In *Philanthropy and Social Progress.* New York: Thomas Crowell.

———. 1895. "The Settlement as a Factor in the Labor Movement." In *Hull House: Maps and Papers.* New York: Thomas Crowell.

———. 1899. "The Subtle Problem of Charity." *Atlantic Monthly, 83,* February.

———. 1908. "Women's Conscience and Social Amelioration." In Charles

Stelze (ed.), *Social Applications of Religion*. Cincinnati: Jennings and Graham.

———. 1912b. "The House of Dreams." In *The Spirit of Youth and the City Streets*. New York: Macmillan.

Alexander, Leslie B. 1972. "Social Work's Freudian Deluge: Myth or Reality?" *Social Service Review*, 46(4), December.

Alexander, Leslie B., and Milton D. Speizman. 1980. "The Union Movement in Voluntary Social Work." *Social Welfare Forum, 1979*, National Conference on Social Welfare. New York: Columbia University Press.

Almy, Frederic, et al. 1912. "Public Pensions to Widows." *Proceedings*, National Conference of Charities and Correction. Ft. Wayne, IN: Ft. Wayne Printing.

American Association for Organizing Family Social Work. 1920. "Expenditures and Salaries of Case Workers." *The Family*, 1 (1) March, and 1(2), April.

———. 1921. "Shall the Associated Charities Change Its Name?" *Newsletter* #14. New York.

American Association of Social Workers. *The Compass*, 1(2), February 1921; 1 (3), March 1921; 1(4) April 1921; 1(5) May 1921; 1(6) June 1921; 1(7), September 1921; 2(3), March 1922; 7(6), February 1926; 7 (9), May 1926; 7(11) July-August 1926; 10(11) August 1929; 11(3) November 1929; 11(7) March 1930.

Anderson, Joseph P. 1945. "Social Work as a Profession." *Social Work Yearbook, 1945*. New York: Russell Sage Foundation.

Andrews, Janice. 1987. "Social Work Public Image Building: 'East Side/West Side' Revisited." *Social Service Review*, 61 (3), September.

Anonymous. 1907. "Individual Self-Service: The Primary Impulse of Social Service." *The Public*, 10, October 26.

Antler, Joyce. 1976. "Medical Women and Social Reform: A History of the New York Infirmary for Women." *Women and Health*, 1(4), July-August.

Atherton, Lewis. 1975. "Morality on the Middle Border." In Thomas Frazier (ed.), *The Private Side of American History: Readings in Everyday Life*, Vol. 2. New York: Harcourt Brace Jovanovich.

Ayres, Philip W. 1901. "The Summer School in Philanthropic Work." *Charities*, 6(9), March 2. [See also *Charities*, 7(2), July 13, and 7(5), August 3.]

Baldwin, Roger N. 1922. "The Immorality of Social Work." *The World Tomorrow*, February.

Bane, Frank. 1930. "Public Welfare, Local Agencies." In Fred S. Hall (ed.), *Social Work Year Book, 1929*. New York: Russell Sage Foundation.

Banner, Lois. 1973. "Religious Benevolence as Social Control: A Critique of an Interpretation." *Journal of American History*, 60(1).

Barker, Robert L. 1987. "Private and Proprietary Services." In *Encyclopedia of Social Work*, Vol. 2, 324–29. Silver Spring, MD: National Association of Social Workers.

Barnett, Samuel. 1906. "The Settlements: Education By Permeation." *Charities and the Commons*, March.

Bartlett, Harriet. 1976. "Early Trends." In Neil Gilbert and Harry Specht (eds.), *The Emergence of Social Welfare and Social Work*, Itasca, IL: Peacock Publishers.

Baum, Howell S. 1978. "Legitimation Crisis in Education." *Journal of Educational Thought*, 12(3), 159–75.

Beck, Joseph E. 1930. "The High Cost of Poor Personnel." *Survey*, 65(4), November 15.

Beckelman, Moses W. 1933. "Protective Aspects of the Program of the American Association of Social Workers." *Jewish Social Service Quarterly*, June.

Becker, Dorothy G. 1961. "The Visitor to the New York City Poor, 1843–1920." *Social Service Review*, 35(1), March.

———. 1964. "Exit Lady Bountiful: The Volunteer and Professional Social Work." *Social Service Review*, 38(1), March.

———. 1968. "Social Welfare Leaders as Spokesmen for the Poor." *Social Casework*, 49(2), February.

Beilin, Anne L., and Janie Wimberly, 1984. "Hard Times and Human Services: An Overview of Today's BSW and MSW Competition." Paper delivered at CSWE Annual Program Meeting, Detroit, March 13.

Beisser, Paul T. 1967. Correspondence to Bradley Buell, March 13, Social Welfare History Archives, University of Minnesota.

Ben-David, Joseph. 1964. "Professions in the Class System of Present-Day Societies." *Current Sociology*, 12(3), 247–98.

Benjamin, Paul L. 1930. "The Last Straw." *Survey*, 65(4), November 15.

Bershtel, Sara, and Allen Graubard. 1983. "The Mystique of the Progressive Jew." *Working Papers*, 10 (2), March/April, 18–25.

Bishop, Samuel H. 1901. "A New Movement in Charity." *Charities*, 7 (20), November 16.

———. 1903. "The Personal Equation in Friendly Visiting." *Charities*, 11, October.

Bitensky, Reuben. 1973. "The Influence of Political Power in Determining the Theoretical Development of Social Work." *Journal of Social Policy*, 2(2), April.

Bolin, Winifred D. Wandersee. 1973. "Feminism, Reform and Social Service: A History of Women in Social Work." Minneapolis: Minnesota Resource Center for Social Work Education, July.

Boroff, David. 1975. "A Little Milk, A Little Honey: Jewish Immigration in America." In Thomas Frazier (ed.), *The Private Side of American History*, Vol. 2. New York: Harcourt Brace & Jovanovich.

Borst, Homer W. 1930. "Community Chests and Relief: A Reply. *Survey*, 65(2), October 15, 74–76.

Brackett, Jeffrey. 1901. "Present Opportunities for Training in Charity Work." *Proceedings*, National Conference of Charities and Correction. Boston: Geo. H. Ellis.

Breckinridge, Sophonisba P. 1932. "Report of the Committee on Personnel Standards in Public Social Work." *The Compass*, *13*(10), June, 14–15.

Bremner, Robert. 1968. "The Prelude: Philanthropic Rivalries in the Civil War." *Social Casework*, *49*(2), February.

———. 1980. "Scientific Philanthropy, 1873—1893." In Frank Breul and Steven Diner (eds.), *Compassion and Responsibility: Readings in the History of Social Welfare in the United States*. Chicago: University of Chicago Press.

Briehl, Walter. 1936. "Environment and Neurosis." *Social Work Today*, *4*(1), October.

Brooks, John Graham. 1894. "The Future Problem of Charity and the Unemployed." *Annals of the American Academy of Political and Social Science*, 5, July.

———. 1901. "Some Problems of the Family." *Proceedings*, National Conference of Charities and Correction. Boston: Geo. H. Ellis.

Brown, E. Richard. 1979. "He Who Pays the Piper: Foundations, the Medical Profession and Medical Education." In Susan Reverby and David Rosner (eds.), *Health Care in America: Essays in Social History*. Philadelphia: Temple University Press.

Brown, Esther Lucile. 1932. "Social Work Against a Background of Other Professions." *The Compass*, *13*(9), May, 8–11.

Bruno, Frank J. 1933. "Social Work Objectives in the New Era." Presidential address, *Proceedings of the National Conference of* Social Work. 3–19, Chicago: University of Chicago Press.

———. 1944. "Twenty-Five Years of Schools of Social Work." *Social Service Review*, *28*(2), June.

Buder, Stanley. 1971. "Pullman." In Thomas Frazier (ed.), *The Underside of American History*, (1st ed.) Vol. 2. New York: Harcourt Brace & Jovanovich.

Buell, Bradley J. 1923. "Memorandum to Members of the American Association of Social Workers re: Three-Year Program–1923–1924–1925." April 30. Social Welfare History Archives, University of Minnesota.

———. 1966. "Oral History." May; edited January 1967. Social Welfare History Archives, University of Minnesota.

The Bulletin of the Association of Federation Workers. 1933. "Federation Embarks on New Economies"; "Salaries Go Down"; "The EWB—a Boomerang"; "Why Are Teachers Better Paid than Social Workers?"; "The Drift to Public Social Work"; "Workers' Councils." New York City, March.

Carnegie, Andrew. 1899. "Wealth." In Richard D. Heffner, *A Documentary History of the United States*. New York: Mentor, 1956.

Chambers, Clarke A. 1986. "Women in the Creation of the Profession of Social Work." *Social Service Review*, 60 (1), March.

Chambers, Clarke A., and Andrea Hinding. 1968. "Charity Workers, the Settlements and the Poor." *Social Casework*, *49*(2), February.

Clague, Ewan. 1933. "Social Work and the NRA." *The Compass*, *14*(10), July.

———. 1936. "The Social Security Act as a Relief Measure." In *This Business of Relief*, American Association of Social Workers, New York.

Clark, Clifford. 1970. "Religious Beliefs and Social Reform in the Gilded Age." *New England Quarterly*, March.

Colcord, Joanna C. 1930. "Facing the Coming Winter." *Survey*, *65*(4), November 15, 206–8.

———. 1943. "Social Work and the First Federal Relief Programs." *Proceedings*, National Conference of Social Work. New York: Columbia University Press.

Committee of the Case Workers Group of the Chicago Chapter. 1933. "The Practitioners' Movement." *The Compass*, *14*(10), July.

The Compass. 1929. "Questions for the Council"; "The Association Adopts the Proposed Membership Requirements." *10*(11), August.

———. 1930. "What Effect Is Unemployment Having on the Profession?" *12*(3), November.

———. 1931. "Economic Depression Affecting Social Work Jobs," *12*(9), May.

———. 1931. "Standards of Training"; "The Value of High Membership Standards," *12*(11), July.

———. 1931. "Social Work Salaries During Periods of Depression"; "Social Workers and Federal Legislation for Relief"; "Demand and Supply in Social Work," *13*(2), October.

———. 1931. "The Federal Relief Question," *13*(3), November.

———. 1931. "A Statement by the Commission on Unemployment," *13*(4), December.

———. 1932. "New Federal Relief Bills"; "A Chapter Tries Soliciting," *13*(6), February.

———. 1932. "Qualifications of Members," *13*(7), March.

———. 1932. "The Salary Question," *13*(8), April.

———. 1932. "New Personnel in Social Work," *13*(11), July.

———. 1933. "Analyzing the Membership," *14*(6), February.

———. 1933. "Unemployment Among Social Workers," *14*(10), July.

———. 1933. "New Membership Record"; "Certification Adopted in California"; "Social Workers in the Census"; "Certification–Why Have It?" *15*(1), September.

———. 1933. "The Case for the Practitioners' Movement," *15*(2), October.

———. 1934. "The Conference on Governmental Objectives for Social Work." *15*(6), March.

———. 1937. "Community Studies of Social Work Personnel," *18* (5), February.

———. 1940. "Arguments About Membership Policy and Requirements," *21*(7), April.

Constitution and By-laws, National Association of Schools of Social Administration, adopted April 22, 1944, Social Welfare History Archives, University of Minnesota (Maxted Papers, Box 1, folder #2).

Conway, Jill. 1969. "Jane Addams: An American Heroine." *Daedalus*, *93*, Spring.

———. 1971–72. "Women Reformers and American Culture, 1879–1930." *Journal of Social Work*, *5*, Winter.

Cook, Blanche Wiesen. 1979. "Female Support Networks and Political Action: Lillian Wald, Crystal Eastman and Emma Goldman." In Nancy Coit and Elizabeth Pleck (eds.), *A Heritage of Our Own: Towards a Social History of American Women*. New York: Free Press.

Council on Social Work Education, 1952. *Bi-laws* Approved at Constitutional Convention, New York, January 28, Social Welfare History Archives, University of Minnesota (Maxted Papers, Box 3, folder #26).

Coyle, Grace L. 1935. "Group Work and Social Change." *Proceedings*, National Conference of Social Work. Chicago: University of Chicago Press.

———. 1937. "Social Group Work." *Social Work Yearbook*. New York: Russell Sage Foundation.

———. 1940. "Social Work at the Turn of the Decade." *Proceedings*, National Conference of Social Work. New York: Columbia University Press.

———. 1944. Correspondence to Clara Kaiser, August 25, Social Welfare History Archives, University of Minnesota (NASW Coll., Box 2, folder #12).

———. 1947. "On Becoming Professional." In *Toward Professional Standards*. New York: American Association of Group Workers.

Cumbler, John. 1980. "The Politics of Charity: Gender and Class in Late 19th Century Charity Policy." *Journal of Social History*, *14*(1), Fall.

Davies, Stanley P. 1932a. "Report of the National Membership Committee." *The Compass*, *13*(10), June, 15–16.

———. 1932b. "Working Toward One Professional Standard—Public and Private." *Social Service Review*, *4*(3), September, 429–37.

———. 1933. "The Association of Social Workers in a Changing World." *The ompass*, *14* (9), June.

Davis, Allen. 1980. "Raymond Robins: The Settlement Worker as Municipal Reformer." In Frank Breul and Steven Diner (eds.), *Compassion and Responsibility: Readings in the History of Social Welfare in the United States*. Chicago: University of Chicago Press.

Davis, Cameron J. 1901a. "The Purposes of Organized Charity." *Charities*, *6*(12), March 23.

———. 1901b. "The Relation of the Church to Dependent Families." *Charities*, *7*(21), November 23.

Dawes, Anna. 1893. "The Need for Training Schools for a New Profession." *Proceedings*, International Congress of Charities, Corrections and Philanthropy, Baltimore.

Day, Florence R. 1937. "Changing Practices in Case Work Treatment."

The Family, March. Reprinted in Fern Lowry (ed.) *Readings in Social Case Work: 1920–1938,* 330–43. New York: Columbia University Press, 1939.

Dean, Vera Micheles. 1940. "Implications of the European Situation for the United States." *Proceedings,* National Conference of Social Work. New York: Columbia, University Press.

Deardoff, Neva R. 1925. "The Place of a Professional School in Training for Social Work." American Academy of Political and Social Science, *Annals, 121,* September.

deForest, Robert. 1901. "Justice, Not Charity." *Charities,* 7(21), November 23.

———. 1904. "The Federation of Organized Charities." *Charities, 12,* January 2.

Devine, Edward. 1897. "Does Charity Make Paupers?" New York *World,* December 20.

———. 1898. "The Practice of Charity." *Proceedings,* National Conference of Charities and Correction. Boston: Geo. H. Ellis.

———. 1901. "Principles and Methods in Charity." *Proceedings,* National Conference of Charities and Correction. Boston: Geo. H. Ellis.

———. 1908. "The New View in Charity." *Atlantic Monthly, 92,* December.

Dunham, Arthur. 1940. "The Literature of Community Organization." *Proceedings,* National Conference of Social Work. New York: Columbia University Press.

Evans, Glendower. 1889. "Scientific Charity." *Proceedings,* National Conference of Charities and Correction. Boston: Geo. H. Ellis.

The Family. 1924. "Editorial." *5*(3), May.

Felt, Jeremy. 1974. "Children at Work." In Thomas Frazier (ed.), *The Underside of American History* (2nd ed.) Vol. 2. New York: Harcourt Brace Jovanovich.

Field, Martha Heineman. 1980. "Social Casework Practice During the Psychiatric Deluge." *Social Service Review, 54*(4), December.

Fisher, Jacob. 1934. "Social Work and Liberalism." *Social Work Today, 1*(2), May–June.

———. 1935. "Rank and File Challenge: The First National Convention of Rank and File Groups in Social Work." *Social Work Today, 2*(5), April.

———. 1936b. "The Rank and File Movement, 1930–1936." *Social Work Today, 3*(5), February.

———. 1936c. "The AASW Takes Its Stand." *Social Work Today, 3*(7), April.

———. 1937. "New Goals in Employment Practices." *Social Work Today, 4*(7), April.

———. 1937. "It Just Doesn't Belong!" *Social Work Today, 4*(8), May.

———. 1937. "Trade Unionism in Social Work." *Social Work Yearbook, 1937.* New York: Russell Sage Foundation.

Fitch, John A. 1938. "Security in Social Work." *Survey, 74*(8), August, 259–60.

———. 1940. "The Nature of Social Action." *Proceedings,* National Conference of Social Work. New York: Columbia University Press.

Flexner, Abraham. 1915. "Is Social Work a Profession?" *Proceedings,* National Conference of Charities and Correction. Chicago: Hildmann.

Folks, Homer. 1893a. "College Graduates in Benevolent Work." *Proceedings,* International Congress of Charities, Corrections and Probation, Chicago, 1893.

———. 1893b. "Family Life for Dependent Children." *Proceedings,* International Congress of Charities, Corrections and Probation, Chicago.

———. 1897a. "The Care of Delinquent Children." *Proceedings,* National Conference of Charities and Correction. Boston: Geo. H. Ellis.

———. 1897b. "Does Charity Make Paupers? "New York *World,* December 20.

———. 1897c. "Reform and Public Charities." *The Outlook,* March 6.

———. 1898a. "Distinctive Features of American Child-Saving Work." *Proceedings,* International Congress of Arts and Science, St. Louis.

———. 1898b. "The Separation of Families in Order that Parents May Be Self-Supporting." Unpublished paper, 1898.

———. 1901a. "The Care of Needy Families in Their Homes." *Charities,* 7(20), November 16.

———. 1901b. Excerpt from speech on being named Commissioner of Public Charities of the City of New York (and press comments). *Charities,* July–December.

———. 1911. "The Prevention of Insanity." *Review of Reviews,* May.

———. 1912a. "Millions for Care and Cure–Nothing for Prevention." Unpublished paper delivered at New York State Mental Hygiene Conference, New York, November 14.

———. 1912b. "Prevention of Insanity." *Proceedings,* National Conference of the American Public Health Association, Washington, D.C., September 20, 1912.

———. c.1909–12. Unpublished address, Poughkeepsie, New York.

———. 1913. "Aftercare of the Insane." *State Hospital Bulletin.* Utica, NY, November.

———. 1915. Unpublished remarks at American Association for Organizing Charity.

Folks, Homer, and Everett S. Elwood. 1915. "Why Should Anyone Go Insane? Some Facts as to the Extent, Causes and Prevention of Insanity." New York: State Charities Aid Association.

Frankel, Leo. 1901. "Unusual Forms of Relief." *Proceedings,* National Conference of Charities and Correction. Boston: Geo. H. Ellis.

Furner, Mary O. 1980. Review of Thomas Haskell, *The Emergence of Professional Social Science. American Journal of Sociology,* 85(5), March.

Gans, Herbert. 1964. "Redefining the Settlements for the War on Poverty." *Social Work,* 9(4), October.

George, Henry. 1973. "City and Country." In Ann Cook, Marilyn Gittel, and

Herb Mack (eds.), *City Life, 1865–1900: Views of Urban America*. New York: Praeger.

———. 1976. "Progress and Poverty." In Robert Walker (ed.), *The Reform Spirit in America*. New York: Putnam.

Gettleman, Marvin. 1963. "Charity and Social Classes in the United States, 1874–1900, I." *American Journal of Economics and Sociology, 22*(3).

———. 1975. "Philanthropy as Social Control in Late 19th Century America: Some Hypotheses and Data on the Use of Social Work." *Societas, 5*, Winter.

Gilbert, Neil, and Harry Specht. 1977. "Social Planning and Community Organization Approaches." In *Encyclopedia of Social Work*, Seventeenth Issue, Vol. 2. Washington, D.C.: National Association of Social Workers, 1412–1424.

Ginsberg, Sonia. 1933. "Experiences in Protective Organization for Social Workers in New York City." *Jewish Social Service Quarterly*, June.

Goldsmith, Samuel A. 1931. "Registration of Social Workers." *Social Service Review, 5*(4), December 1931, 582–95.

Granger, Lester B. 1945. "Negroes." *Social Work Year Book*. New York: Russell Sage Foundation, 280–89.

Greenwood, Ernest. 1957. "Attributes of a Profession." *Social Work, 2*(3), July, 44–55.

Grinker, Roy R., Helen MacGregor, Kate Selan, Annette Klein, and Janet Kohrman. 1961. "The Early Years of Psychiatric Social Work." *Social Service Review, 35*(2), June.

Gurin, Arnold. 1971. "Social Planning and Community Organization." *Encyclopedia of Social Work*, 1324–37. Washington, D.C.: National Association of Social Workers.

Gutman, Herbert. 1974. "Industrial Workers Struggle for Power." In Thomas Frazier (ed.), *The Underside of American History* (2nd edition), Vol. 2. New York: Harcourt Brace Jovanovich.

Gutridge, A. W. 1903. "The Volunteer Worker." *Proceedings*, National Conference of Charities and Correction. Boston: Geo. H. Ellis.

Hall, Peter Dobkin. 1974–75. "The Model of Boston Charity: A Theory of Charitable Benevolence and Class Development." *Science and Society, 38*, Winter.

Hamilton, Dona Cooper. 1984. "The National Urban League and New Deal Programs." *Social Service Review, 58*(2), June.

Hamilton, Gordon. 1939. "Basic Concepts in Social Case Work." *Proceedings of the NCSW, 1937*. Reprinted in Fern Lowry (ed.), *Readings in Social Case Work, 1920–1938*, 155–171. New York: Columbia University Press.

Harper, Ernest B. 1945. Correspondence to Maxted, June 23. Social Welfare History Archives (Maxted Papers, Box 1, folder #6).

———. 1948. "Accomplishments and Aims of the National Association of Schools Administration." *Annual Proceedings*, NASSA, at the National

Conference of Social Work, Atlantic City, N.J., April 19–20. Social Welfare History Archives (Maxted Papers, Box 1, folder #3).

———. 1948. Correspondence to Moore, January 10. Social Welfare History Archives (Maxted Papers, Box 1, folder #9).

———. 1948. Correspondence to Cape, February 17. Social Welfare History Archives (Maxted Papers, Box 1, folder #9).

———. 1952. Correspondence to Maxted, February 2. Social Welfare History Archives (Maxted Papers, Box 3, folder #16).

Hart, Helen. 1931. "The Changing Function of the Settlement Under Changing Conditions." *Proceedings*, National Conference of Social Work, 1931. Reprinted in Lorene M. Pacey (ed.), *Readings on the Development of Settlement Work*. New York: Association Press, 1950.

Haynes, John Earl, 1975. "The 'Rank and File Movement' in Private Social Work." *Labor History*, 16, Winter, 78–98.

Hendry, Charles E. 1947. "All Past Is Prologue.'" In *Toward Professional Standards*. New York: American Association of Group Workers.

Hill, Octavia. 1900–1901. "'The Need for Thoroughness in Charity Work." London: Society for Organizing Charity.

Hill, Ruth, Mildred B. Hoodin, and Merlin M. Paine. 1930. "Should We Limit Intake?" Survey, 64(2), April 15, 98–99.

Hirschhorn, Larry. 1978. "The Political Economy of Social Service Rationalization." *Contemporary Crises 2* January, 63–81. Amsterdam, The Netherlands: Elsevier Scientific Publishing Company. Reprinted in Richard Quinney (ed.), *Capitalist Society: Readings for a Critical Sociology*. Homewood, IL: Dorsey Press, 1979.

Hodson, William. 1934. "The Social Worker in the New Deal." *Proceedings*, National Conference of Social Work. Chicago: University of Chicago Press, 3–11.

Hoey, Jane. 1952. Correspondence to Steininger, January 3. Social Welfare History Archives (Maxted Papers, Box 3, folder #16).

Hopkins, Harry L. 1933. "The Developing National Program of Relief." *Proceedings*, National Conference of Social Work. Chicago: University of Chicago, 65–71.

Hopps, June Gary and Elaine B. Pinderhughes. 1987. "Profession of Social Work: Contemporary Characteristics." *Encyclopedia of Social Work*, Vol. 2, 351–65. Silver Spring, MD: National Association of Social Workers.

Hoy, William Alexander. 1904. "Social Uplift in American Cities: A Study of Its Means and Some Ways for Strengthening Them." *The Outlook*, March 26.

Hubbard, Ray S. 1929. "Child Protection." In Fred S. Hall, ed., *Social Work Year Book, 1929*. New York: Russell Sage Foundation.

Illich, Ivan. 1977. "Disabling Professions." In Ivan Illich et al. *Disabling Professions*. London: Marion Boyars.

Jarrett, Mary. 1919. "The Psychiatric Thread Running Through All Social

Case Work." *Proceedings*, National Conference of Social Work. Chicago: University of Chicago Press.

Jeter, Helen R. 1933. "Salaries and Professional Education of Social Workers in Family Welfare and Relief Agencies in Chicago." *Social Service Review*, 7(2), June.

Johnson, Arlien. 1943. "Social Work as a Profession." *Social Work Yearbook, 1943*. New York: Russell Sage Foundation.

———. 1945. "Community Organization." *Social Work Yearbook, 1945*. New York: Russell Sage Foundation.

Johnson, Fred R. 1930. "Public Agencies for Needy Families." *Social Work Year Book 1930*. New York: Russell Sage Foundation.

Kahn, Dorothy C. 1946. "Operation Crossroads for Social Work." *The Compass*, 27(8), June, 23–25.

Kaiser, Clara A. 1953. "Group Work Education in the Last Decade." *The Group*. 15(5), June.

Kann, Kenneth. 1976. "The Big City Riot of 1877." Unpublished paper delivered at the annual conference of the American Historical Association, Washington.

Keller, John. 1901. "Problems of the Almshouse." *Charities*, 7(21), November 23.

Kellogg, Charles. 1893. "Charity Organization in the United States." *Proceedings*, National Conference of Charities and Correction. Boston: Geo. H. Ellis.

Kellogg, Reverend D. O. 1880. "The Objectives, Principles and Advantages of Association in Charities." *Journal of Social Science, 12*.

Kelly, April. 1906. "The Settlements: Their Lost Opportunity." *Charities and the Commons, 12*, March.

Kelso, Robert W. 1930. "An Alibi for the Indifferent." *Survey*, 65(4), November 14.

———. 1931. "Alms and the Case Worker." *Survey*, 65(12), March 15.

Khinduka, S. K. 1987. "Social Work and the Human Services." *Encyclopedia of Social Work*, Vol. 2, 681–95. Silver Spring, MD: National Association of Social Workers.

King, Edith Shatto. 1918. "Wanted–Social Workers." *Survey, 40*.

Kingsbury, F. J. 1895. "The Tendency of Men to Live in Cities." *Journal of Social Science, 32*, November.

Klein, Philip. 1924. "Professional Service and Salaries in Public Welfare Departments." American Academy of Political and Social Science, *Annals, 120*, May.

Kunitz, Stephen. 1974. "Professionalism and Social Control in the Progressive Era: The Flexner Report." *Social Problems, 22*, October.

Kusmer, Kenneth. 1973. "The Function of Organized Charity in the Progressive Era: Chicago as a Case Study." *Journal of American History*, 60(3), December.

Lane, Robert P. 1939. "Community Organization: A Preliminary Inquiry into its Nature and Characteristics." *Proceedings*, National Conference of Social Work. New York: Columbia University Press.

———. 1940. "Report of Groups Studying the Community Organization Process." *Proceedings*, National Conference of Social Work, New York: Columbia University Press.

Lee, Porter. 1915a. "Some Necessary Re-adjustments in Casework." *Charity Organization Bulletin*, 6, n.s.

———. 1915b. "The Professional Base of Social Work." *Proceedings*, National Conference of Charities and Correction. Chicago: Hildmann Printing.

———. 1929. "Social Work as Cause and Function." Presidential address to National Conference of Social Work. Reprinted in Porter Lee, *Social Work as Cause and Function, and Other Papers*. New York: Columbia University Press, 1937, 3–24.

Leiby, James. 1962. "How Social Workers Viewed the Immigrant Problem, 1870–1930." In *Current Issues in Social Work as Seen in Historical Perspective*. New York: Council on Social Work Education.

———. 1968. "State Welfare Institutions and the Poor." *Social Casework*, 49(2), February.

Lenroot, Katharine F. 1940. "American Childhood Challenges American Democracy." *Proceedings*, National Conference of Social Work. New York: Columbia University Press.

Lerner, Max. 1940. "Making a Democracy Work." *Proceedings*, National Conference of Social Work. New York: Columbia University Press.

Levin, Herman. 1969. "Volunteers in Social Work: The Challenge of their Future." *Social Work*, 14, January.

Levy, Joseph H. 1934. "New Forms of Organization Among Social Workers." *Proceedings*, National Conference of Social Work. Chicago: University of Chicago Press.

"Licensure Law Enacted: Two Others Are Revised." 1987. *NASW News*, September. Silver Spring, MD: National Association of Social Workers.

Lies, Eugene. 1901. Comment in question and answer session, *Proceedings*, National Association for Organizing Charity, Cleveland.

Lindeman, Eduard C. 1924. "The Social Worker and His Community." *Survey*, April 15.

———. 1934. "Basic Unities in Social Work." *Proceedings*, National Conference of Social Work. Chicago: University of Chicago Press.

Lodge, Clarence. 1901. "The Report of the Committee on Institutional Care of Destitute Adults." *Charities*, 7(2), November 23.

Lowell, Josephine Shaw. 1889. "The Economic and Moral Effects of Public Outdoor Relief." *Proceedings*, National Conference of Charities and Correction. Boston: Geo. H. Ellis.

Lundberg, Emma O. 1930. "Mothers' Aid." *Social Work Year Book, 1929*. New York: Russell Sage Foundation.

Lurie, Harry L. 1937. "Organization, Support of Social Work." *Social Work Today*, 4(8), May.

Lynd, Staughton. 1961. "Jane Addams and the Radical Impulse." *Commentary*, 32, July.

MacLeish, Archibald. 1961. "Jane Addams and the Future." *Social Service Review*, 35(1), March.

Maher, Amy G. 1931. "The Employment of Women." *Social Service Review*, 5(1), March.

Marcus, Victoria. 1933. Organization Committee of Social Work Discussion Group, Correspondence to Mr. Winters, Committee on Cooperation, AASW, July 22, Cleveland, Ohio, and report entitled "Social Work Discussion Group." Social Welfare History Archives (National Association of Social Workers Collection, Box 22, folder #253).

Markowitz, David, and David Rosner. 1979. "Doctors in Crisis: Medical Education and Medical Reform During the Progressive Era, 1895–1915." In Susan Reverby and David Rosner, eds., *Health Care in America, Essays in Social History*. Philadelphia: Temple University Press.

Maxted, Mattie Cal. 1945. "The Need for Undergraduate Trained Social Workers in Arkansas." Annual Meeting of the National Association of Schools of Social Administration, January 26. Social Welfare History Archives (Maxted Papers, Box 1, folder #3).

———. 1945. Correspondence to Harper, June 15. Social Welfare History Archives (Maxted Papers, Box 1, folder #6).

———. 1951. Memo to NASSA members, c. July. Social Welfare History Archives (Maxted Papers, Box 2, folder #15).

———. 1952. Correspondence to Whatley, January 11. Social Welfare History Archives (Maxted Papers, Box 3, folder #16).

McMillen, Wayne A. 1929. "Some Statistical Comparisons of Public and Private Family Social Work." *Proceedings*, National Conference of Social Work. Chicago: University of Chicago Press.

———. 1930. "Taxes and Private Relief Funds." *Survey Midmonthly*, November.

———. 1937. "Trade Unions for Social Workers." *Social Work Today*, 4(7), April, 7–9.

———. 1944. "Community Organization—A Process in Social Work." *Social Service Review*, 18(1), March.

Mead, George Herbert. 1907. "The Social Settlement: Its Basis and Function." *University Record*, October 28.

Mills, C. Wright. 1943. "The Professional Ideology of Social Pathologists." *American Journal of Sociology*, 49, September.

Minutes of NASSA meeting. 1942. Southwestern regional conference, April 3. Social Welfare History Archives (Maxted Papers, Box #1, folder #1).

Minutes, Second Annual Meeting, NASSA. 1944. Des Moines, Iowa, April 22, 23. Social Welfare History Archives (Maxted Papers, Box #1, folder #3).

Minutes, First meeting of Incorporators. 1948. National Council on Social Work Education, Inc., New York, January 14. Social Welfare History Archives (Maxted Papers, Box #1, folder #9).

Minutes of Executive Committee. 1944. AASW, July 28, 29. Social Welfare History Archives (NASW Collection, Box 2, folder #18).

Minutes of National Board, and Appendix B. 1944. AASW, October 5–7. Social Welfare History Archives (NASW Collection, Box 2, folder #12).

Minutes of National Membership Committee. 1930. AASW, October 26. Social Welfare History Archives (NASW Collection, Box 6, folder #48).

Minutes of National Membership Committee. 1931. AASW, March 28. Social Welfare History Archives (NASW Collection, Box 6, folder #49).

Minutes of National Membership Committee. 1931. AASW, November 7. Social Welfare History Archives (NASW Collection Box 5, folder #50).

Minutes of National Membership Committee. 1932. AASW, May 15. Social Welfare History Archives (NASW Collection, Box 6, folder #50).

Minutes of National Membership Committee. 1933. AASW, April 15. Social Welfare History Archives (NASW Collection, Box 6, folder #51).

Minutes of National Membership Committee, 1935. AASW, April 6. Social Welfare History Archives (NASW Collection, Box 6, folder #52).

Minutes of National Membership Committee. 1935. AASW, June 9. Social Welfare Archives (NASW Collection, Box 6, folder #52).

Minutes of National Membership Committee, Subcommittee on Section 6. 1935. AASW, December 7. Social Welfare History Archives (NASW Collection, Box 6, folder #52).

Minutes of Joint Meeting of Representatives of the Social Work Forum and the AASW. 1937. Cleveland, Ohio, Saturday, July 15. Social Welfare History Archives (NASW Collection, Box 22, folder #253).

Moore, Wilbert E. 1949. "Unions in Social Work." Social Work Yearbook, 1949, 10, 517–21. New York: Russell Sage Foundation.

Morgenthau, Mrs. Hans. 1913. "Training of Club Leaders at the Henry Street Settlement." 1st Intercity Settlement Conference of New York Association of Settlements and the Boston Social Union, New York, March 29–31.

"MSWs Do a Better Job, New Study of Maryland Social Services Shows." 1987. NASW News, September. Silver Spring, MD: National Association of Social Workers.

Nacman, Martin. 1977. "Social Work in Health Settings: A Historical Review." Social Work in Health Care, 2(4), Summer.

National Coordinating Committee. 1935a. "Rank and File Speak: A Summary of the Proceedings of the First National Convention of Rank and File Groups in Social Work." New York. Social Welfare History Archives (Fisher Papers, Box #1).

———. 1935b. "A Permanent National Coordinating Committee." Report of the Constitutional Committee of the NCC, October 1. Social Welfare History Archives (Fisher Papers, Box #1).

———. 1936. "Summary of Sessions Held; The 1936 Platform of the N.C.C." February. Social Welfare History Archives (Fisher Papers, Box #1).

National Membership Committee. 1942. "Report to AASW Board and Appendices 9 and 10." October 9. Social Welfare History Archives (NASW Collection, Box 6, folder #57).

———. 1943. "Report on Special Study of Membership Standards." February. Social Welfare History Archives (NASW Collection, Box 7, folder #60).

National Social Workers Exchange. 1918. Minutes of Annual Meeting. May 18. Social Welfare History Archives (NASW Collection, Box 1, folder #2).

———. 1921. Minutes of Annual Meeting. June 27. Social Welfare History Archives (NASW Collection, Box 1, folder #2).

Newstetter, W. I. 1935. "What Is Social Group Work?" *Proceedings*, National Conference of Social Work. Chicago: University of Chicago Press, 1935.

New York State Board of Charities. 1917. "Field Work Manual." *Eugenics and Social Welfare Bulletin*, 10, Albany, New York.

Nilson, Linda Burzotta, and Murray Edelman. 1976. "The Symbolic Evocation of Occupational Prestige." Discussion Papers, Inst. for Research on Poverty, University of Wisconsin-Madison, May, #348–76.

Olds, Victoria. 1963. "The Freedmen's Bureau: A 19th Century Social Welfare Agency." *Social Casework*, 44, May.

O'Neill, William. 1971. "Feminism as a Radical Ideology." In Thomas Frazier (ed.), *The Underside of American History: Other Readings* (1st ed.) Vol. 2. New York: Harcourt Brace Jovanovich.

Paine, Robert Treat. 1901. "Personal Service." *Proceedings*, National Conference of Charities and Correction. Boston: Geo. H. Ellis.

Palmer, Bryan. 1975. "Class, Conception and Conflict: The Thrust for Efficiency, Managerial Views of Labor and the Working Class Rebellion, 1903–1922." *Review of Radical Political-economy*, 7(2), Summer.

Pettit, Walter W. 1933. "Membership Problems and Activities: Report of the National Membership Committee, May 1, 1932–June 1, 1933." *The Compass*, 14(10), July, 9–11.

Popple, Philip R. 1978. "Community Control of Social Work Education: A Historical Example." *Journal of Sociology and Social Welfare*, 5(2), March.

———. 1981. "Social Work Practice in Business and Industry, 1875–1930." *Social Service Review*, 55 (3), June.

Porterfield, Austin. 1942. Correspondence to Maxted, March 4. Social Welfare History Archives (Maxted Papers, Box 1, folder #1).

Powers, H. H. 1895. Review of Amos Warner's *American Charities. Annals of the American Academy of Political and Social Science*, January.

Pray, Kenneth L. M. 1945. "Social Work and Social Action." Reprinted in Kenneth L. M. Pray, *Social Work in a Revolutionary Age, and Other Papers*. Philadelphia: University of Pennsylvania, 1947.

———. 1947. "When Is Community Organization Social Work Practice?" Reprinted in Kenneth L. M. Pray, *Social Work in a Revolutionary Age, and Other Papers*. Philadelphia: University of Pennsylvania, 1947.

"The Problem of the Exceptional Clause." 1938. American Association of Social Workers, May 26, New York. Social Welfare History Archives (NASW Collection, Box 7, folder #58).

Pullman, Rev. James M. 1901. "The Requirements for Social Service." *Charities*, 6(25) June 22.

Rabinowitz, Clara. 1936. "Discussion: Case Workers and Environmental Change." *Social Work Today*, 4(1), October.

Rapone, Anita. 1983. "Women's Work: Offices and Opportunity." *American Historical Association Perspectives*, 21(1), January.

Rauch, Julie. 1975. "Women in Social Work: Friendly Visitors in Philadelphia, 1880." *Social Service Review*, 49(2), June.

———. 1976. "The Charity Organization Movement in Philadelphia." *Social Work*, 21(1), January.

Reisch, Michael, and Stanley Wenocur. 1984. "Professionalization and Voluntarism in Social Welfare: Changing Roles and Functions." In Florence S. Schwartz (ed.), *Voluntarism and Social Work Practice: A Growing Collaboration*. Lanham, MD: University Press of America.

"Report of Committee on Practitioners' Movement." 1933. Northern California Chapter, AASW. Social Welfare History Archives (NASW Collection, Box 22, folder #253).

"Report of Conference with Representatives of Group Work, Community Organization, Public Welfare, Probation and Parole." 1945. AASW, January. Social Welfare History Archives (NASW Collection, Box 2, folder #18).

"Report of the Joint Committee on Accrediting." 1946. Chicago, April 26–27. Social Welfare History Archives (Maxted Papers, Box 1, folder #3).

"The Responsibility and Contribution of Social Workers in Unemployment Crises." 1930. *The Compass*, 12(4), December, 2.

Reynolds, Bertha. 1935. "Social Case Work: What Is It? What Is Its Place in the World Today?" *The Family*, December. Reprinted in Fern Lowry (ed.), *Readings in Social Case Work, 1920–1938*, 136–47. New York: Columbia University Press, 1939.

———. 1938. "Re-Thinking Social Case Work." *Social Work Today*, 5(7), April; 5(8), May; 5(9), June.

———. 1945. "Labor and Social Work." *Social Work Year Book, 1945*, 8, 230–34. New York: Russell Sage Foundation.

Rhoades, Lawrence J. 1980. "Society Experienced Major Change in the Turbulent '30's." *Footnotes*, American Sociological Society, 8(4), April.

Rich, Margaret E. 1937. "Social Case Work." *Social Work Year Book, 1937*. New York: Russell Sage Foundation.

Richmond, Mary Ellen. 1896a. "Criticism and Reform in Charity." *Charities Review*, 5(4), February.

———. 1896b. "The Friendly Visitor: General Suggestions to Those that Visit the Poor." Philadelphia: Society for Organizing Charity.

———. 1896c. "The Need for a Training School in Applied Philanthropy."

Proceedings, National Conference of Charities and Correction. Boston: Geo. H. Ellis.

———. 1896d. "The Training of Charity Workers." Philadelphia Society for Organizing Charity, *Bulletin.*

———. 1896e. "The Work of a District Agent." Richmond Archives, Columbia University.

———. 1899a. "Attitude of a Working Woman." Philadelphia: Society for Organizing Charity.

———. 1899b. "The Profession and Practice of Begging," Unpublished speech, Philadelphia. Richmond Archives, Columbia University.

———. 1901a. "Charitable Cooperation." *Proceedings*, National Conference of Charities and Correction. Boston: Geo. H. Ellis.

———. 1901b. "The Message of the Associated Charities." *Proceedings*, National Conference of Charities and Correction. Boston: Geo. H. Ellis.

———. 1901c. "Some Methods of Charitable Cooperation." *Proceedings*, National Conference of Charities and Correction. Boston: Geo. H. Ellis.

———. 1902. "General Suggestions to Those Who Visit the Poor." New York: Charity Organization Society.

———. 1903. "How Can Social Workers Aid Housing Reform?" New York: Russell Sage Foundation.

———. 1905. "First Principles in the Relief of Distress." *Charities and the Commons.*

———. 1906. "Industrial Conditions and the Charity Worker. " New York, December, Richmond Archives, Columbia University.

———. 1907. "Where Realism and Idealism Meet." *Annals*, American Society for Organizing Charity, Richmond Archives, Columbia University.

———. 1912. "The Relation of Output to Intake." *Charity Organization Bulletin*, New Series, 3(9), August.

———. 1914. "First Steps in Social Casework." Kennedy Lectures, New York School of Social Work.

———. n.d. "The Importance of Training." Richmond Archives, Columbia University.

———. n.d. "What is Charity Organization?" Richmond Archives, Columbia University.

Robinson, Virginia. 1937. "Is Unionization Compatible with Social Work?" *The Compass*, 28(8), May, 5–9.

Rosen, Irwin (with Jacob Fisher). 1933. "Feasibility of a National Protective Organization for Social Workers." *Jewish Social Service Quarterly*, June.

Rowe, Helen. 1947. "Report of the Central Committee." In *Toward Professional Standards*, American Association of Group Workers. New York: Association Press.

Ruchames, Louis. 1969. "Jewish Radicalism in the United States." In Peter I. Rose, ed., *The Ghetto and Beyond: Essays on Jewish Life in America*. New York: Random House.

Saveth, Edward N. 1980. "Patrician Philanthropy in America: The Late 19th and Early 20th Century." *Social Service Review,* 54(1), March.

Schuyler, Louisa Lee. 1915. "43 Years Ago, or the Early Days of the SCAA, 1872–1915." Address to the Annual Meeting of the New York State Charities Aid Association.

Siegel, Mary. 1935. "Case Work: A Realistic Approach." *Social Work Today,* 2(7), July.

Simkhovitch, Mary. 1926. Remarks at the Annual Meeting of the American Society for Organizing Family Social Work, 1926.

Skocpol, Theda, and John Ikenberry. 1982. "The Political Formation of the American Welfare State in Historical and Comparative Perspective." Paper presented at the annual meeting of the American Sociological Association, San Francisco.

Smith, Zilpha Drew, et al. 1899. Notes of 3rd Annual Meeting of Agents Who Train Agents, Boston, October 19.

Social Service Review. 1941. "Notes and Comment: Recent Statistics from the Professional Schools." 15(2), June, 337–41.

Social Work Today. 1936. "Political Action and Social Work: A Symposium." 3(9), June.

———. 1936. Editorial, "Social Work's Stake in the Election." 4(1), October, 4.

———. 1937. "A Re-evaluation of Social Work."4(5), March.

———. 1937. Editorial, "We Support the President." 4(7), April, 3.

———. 1937. "An Appeal for Spain"; "Facing the War Issue." 4(8), May.

———. 1937. "Don't Buy Japanese Goods." 5(2), November.

———. 1938. Editorial, 5(9), June, 4.

———. 1939. Editorial, "The New Deal is Our Deal." 6(9), June, 38.

———. 1940. "Meeting Social Need: A Peace Program." 7(4), January.

Solomon, Maida H. 1926. "Report of the President." Section on Psychiatric Social Work of the American Association of Hospital Social Workers, June. Social Welfare History Archives (NASW Collection, Box #69, folder 7659).

Somers, Mary Louise. 1976. "Problem-Solving in Small Groups." In Robert W. Roberts and Helen Northern (eds.), *Theories of Social Work with Groups.* New York: Columbia University Press.

Speizman, Milton. 1968. "The Radicals and the Poor." *Social Casework,* 49(2), February.

Springer, Gertrude. 1931. "The Challenge of Hard Times." *Survey,* 66(8), July 15, 380–85.

———. 1934. "Rising to a New Challenge." *Survey,* 70(6), June, 179–80.

Springer, Gertrude, and Helen Cody Baker. 1934. "The National Conference at Work." *Survey,* 70(6), June, 181–89.

State Charities Aid Association. 1917. "Memorandum of the Work of Mrs. William B. (Gertrude Stevens) Rice," New York.

Steiner, Lee. 1936. "Hanging Out a Shingle." *Newsletter of the American Association of Psychiatric Social Workers,"* 6, 1–8.

————. 1938. "Casework as a Private Venture." *The Family, 19.*

Stinchcombe, Arthur L. 1965. "Social Structure and Organizations." In James G. March (ed.), *Handbook of Organizations.* Chicago: Rand McNally.

Strong, Josiah. 1973. "Why the City Grows." In Ann Cook, Marilyn Gittell, and Herb Mack (eds.), *City Life, 1865–1900: Views of Urban America.* New York: Praeger.

Sumner, William Graham. 1969. "The Absurd Effort to Make the World Over." In Neil Harris, David Rothman, and Stephen Thernstrom, *The History of the United States: Source Readings,* Vol. 2. New York: Holt, Rinehart, Winston.

Survey. 1930. "Should Salaries Be Cut?" 65(4), November 15.

Swift, Linton B. 1930a. "Family Welfare Societies." *Social Work Year Book, 1930.* New York: Russell Sage Foundation.

————. 1930b. "Community Chests and Relief." *Survey,* 64(12), September 15, 502–03, 525, 527.

————. 1936. "Private Agencies and Public Welfare." In *This Business of Relief,* New York: American Association of Social Workers.

Sytz, Florence. 1936. "Personnel for Social Welfare Services." In *This Business of Relief,* AASW, New York.

Taylor, Graham. 1906. "Whither the Settlement Movement Tends?" *Charities and the Commons, 12,* March.

Thelen, David. 1969. "Social Tensions and the Origins of Progressivism." *Journal of American History, 56.*

Thernstrom, Stephen, and Peter B. Knights. 1970. "Men in Motion: Some Data and Speculations About Urban Population Mobility in 19th Century America." *Journal of Interdisciplinary History, 1* (1).

Thompson, Reverend James. 1843. "Manual for Friendly Visiting Among the Poor." New York: Association for the Improvement of the Condition of the Poor.

Titmuss, Richard. 1969. "War and Social Policy." In *Essays on the Welfare State.* Boston: Beacon.

Trecker, Harleigh B. 1944. "Group Work: Frontiers and Foundations—in Wartime." *The Compass, 25*(3), March.

Tucker, William Jewett. 1903. "The Progress of the Social Conscience." *Atlantic Monthly, 116*(3).

Turner, C., and M. N. Hodge. 1970. "Occupations and Professions." In John Archer Jackson (ed.), *Professions and Professionalization,* 17–50. London: Cambridge University Press.

Ufford, Walter. 1901. Comment in *Proceedings,* National Conference of Charities and Correction. Boston. Geo. H. Ellis.

U.S. Bureau of the Census. 1975. *Historical Statistics of the United States from Colonial Times to 1970, Vol. I.* U.S. Dept. of Commerce, September, 140, Series D 233–683, "Detailed Occupation of the Economically Active Population: 1900–1970."

U.S. Department of Labor. 1981. Bureau of Labor Statistics, "Consumer

Price Index, January 1913-November 1981," All Urban Consumers. U.S. City Average, (1967 = 100), December 22.

Vaile, Gertrude. 1915a. "An Experiment in Trying to Grade District Visitors." *Proceedings*, National Conference of Charities and Correction. Chicago: Hildmann Printing.

———. 1915b. "An Experiment with Mother's Pensions." *Vassar Miscellany*, January 22.

———. 1915c. "Principles and Methods of Outdoor Relief," June, Vaile Archives, Columbia University.

———. 1940. "Family Case Work and Public Assistance Policy." *The Family, 21*, December.

———. n.d. "The Denver Bureau of Public Welfare." Vaile Archives, Columbia University.

———. n.d. "Memories of G. V. and the Old West Side." Vaile Archives, Columbia University.

Vandiver, Susan. 1980. "A Herstory of Women in Social Work." In Elaine Norman and Arlene Mancuso (eds.), *Women's Issues and Social Work Practice*, Itasca, IL: Peacock.

van Kleeck, Mary. 1933. "A Planned Economy as a National Economic Objective for Social Work." *The Compass, 14*(8), May, 20–24.

———. 1934. "Common Goals of Labor and Social Work." *Social Work Today, 1*(3), October, 4–8.

———. 1934. "Our Illusions Regarding Government." *Proceedings*, National Conference of Social Work. Chicago: University of Chicago Press, 473–85.

———. 1940. "Social Work in the World Crisis." *Social Work Today, 7*(6), March.

Wald, Lillian. Wald Collection, Columbia University Libraries. 1928. "Suggested Subjects for Study Preparatory to the Third International Conference of Settlements." Correspondence to Lillian Wald from Lionel F. Ellis.

Wallach, Rita Teresa. 1903. "The Settlements of New York City." Lillian Wald Archives, Columbia University Libraries.

Warner, Beverly. 1903. "The Social Settlement and Charity Organization Problem." *Proceedings*, National Conference of Charities and Correction. Boston: Geo. H. Ellis.

Washington, Forrester B. 1934. "The Negro and Relief." *Proceedings*, National Conference of Social Work, Chicago: University of Chicago Press.

Watson, Goodwin. 1938. "Therapy and/or Social Change." *Social Work Today, 5*(4), January.

Watts, Phyllis A. 1964. "Casework Above the Poverty Line: The Influence of Home Services in World War I on Social Work." *Social Service Review, 38*(3), September.

Weisz-Buck, Elizabeth. 1982. "The Public Economy and the Feminist Economy: The Work of Elizabeth Abbott, 1908–1928." Paper delivered at the annual meeting of the American Historical Association, Washington, D.C.

West, Walter. 1932. "Registration or Certification of Social Workers." *The Compass*, *13*(9), May, 6–7.

———. 1933. "The Association Program: Annual Report of the Executive Secretary." *The Compass*, *14*(9), June, 9–15.

Wetzel, H. E. 1952. Correspondence to Maxted, February 16. Social Welfare History Archives (Maxted Papers, Box 3, folder #16).

White, Clyde R. 1943. "A Strategy for Social Workers." *The Compass*, *25*(1), November, 21–23.

White, Gaylord. 1911. "The Social Settlements After 25 Years." *Harvard Theological Review*, *12*, January.

———. 1915. "Some Tentative Suggestions for the Development of Settlement Work." April 12.

White, George Cary. 1959. "Social Settlements and the Immigrant Problem." *Social Service Review*, *30*(11), March.

Whitfield, Stephen J. 1980. Book Review of *Jews and the Left* by Arthur Liebman, *Transaction/Society*, July/August, 83–86.

Wilder, Veronica O. 1922. "Our Salaries." *Family*, *3*(1), March.

Willard, Dudley W. 1930. "Public Welfare, State Agencies." *Social Work Year Book, 1929*. New York: Russell Sage Foundation.

Williams, Aubrey. 1936. "The Works Progress Administration." In *This Business of Relief*, New York: American Association of Social Workers, 1936.

Wilson, Gertrude. 1976. "From Practice to Theory: A Personalized History." In Robert W. Roberts and Helen Northern (eds.), *Theories of Social Work with Groups*. New York: Columbia University Press.

Woods, Robert. A. 1899. "University Settlements: Their Point and Drift." *Quarterly Review of Economics*, *14*, November.

———. 1901. "The Social Settlement Movement After 16 Years." *The Congregationalist*, February 2.

———. 1905. "Social Work: A New Profession." *International Journal of Social Ethics*, *16*, October.

———. 1923. "The Settlements: Foothold of Opportunity." In *The Neighborhood in Nation-Building*. Boston: Houghton-Mifflin. Reprinted in Lorene M. Pacey (ed.), *Readings in the Development of Settlement Work*. New York: Association Press, 1950.

Zainaldin, Janil S., and Peter L. Tyor. 1979. "Asylum and Society: An Approach to Industrialization and Change." *Journal of Social History*, *13*(1), Fall.

Archival Sources

Archives of the Association for the Improvement of the Condition of the Poor (AICP), 1842–1916. Community Service Society of New York.

Archives, Department of Health, City of New York, 1880–1906. Columbia University Libraries.

Archives, New York Charities Organization Society (COS), 1898–1917. Columbia University Libraries.

Archives, New York State Charities Aid Association (SCAA), 1818–1917. Community Service Society of New York.

Baltimore Charity Organization Society. Mary Richmond Papers. Columbia University Libraries.

Boston School of Social Work. Columbia University Libraries.

Bradley Buell Papers. Social Welfare History Archives, University of Minnesota.

Buffalo Charity Organization Society. Columbia University Libraries.

Jacob Fisher Papers. Social Welfare History Archives, University of Minnesota.

Homer Folks Papers. Columbia University Libraries.

Goucher College Libraries. Baltimore, Maryland.

Mattie Cal Maxted Papers. Social Welfare History Archives, University of Minnesota.

National Association of Social Workers Collection. Social Welfare History Archives, University of Minnesota.

National Child Labor Committee, *Proceedings*. New York: Arno Press, 1974.

National Federation of Settlements. Lillian Wald Papers. Columbia University Libraries, New York Public Library.

New York School of Social Work. Columbia University Libraries.

New York State Civil Service. New York Public Library.

Philadelphia Society for Organizing Charity—Reports and *Monthly Register*. Mary Richmond Papers. Columbia University Libraries.

Mary Richmond Papers. Columbia University Libraries.

Russell Sage Foundation. Mary Richmond Papers. Columbia University Libraries.

Social Welfare History Archives (SWHA), University of Minnesota.

United States Department of the Census, 1904, 1930. Washington, D.C., Library of Congress.

University of Pennsylvania School of Social Work. Philadelphia.

Gertrude Vaile Papers. Columbia University Libraries.

Lillian Wald Papers. Columbia University Libraries and New York Public Library.

Index

Note on the Authors

Stanley Wenocur is an Associate Professor in the School of Social Work and Community Planning at the University of Maryland. He has published articles in journals such as the *Social Service Review, Social Policy, Social Work*, and the *Journal of Sociology and Social Welfare*. Professor Wenocur has delivered a number of papers dealing with community organization, the voluntary sector, resource development for non-profit organizations, and urban poverty, and has served as a research and organization development consultant on several social service projects in Maryland and Washington, D.C.

Michael Reisch is Director of the Department of Social Work Education and Professor of Social Work and Public Administration at San Francisco State University. Working from a background in law, social history, and social work, Professor Reisch has published numerous papers dealing with the history and political economy of social welfare, social work, advocacy, administration, and social policy in such journals as *Social Service Review, Social Casework, Administration in Social Work*, and the *Journal of Sociology and Social Welfare*. He has served as a consultant to human service organizations in New York, Maryland, Washington, D.C., and California, and as a campaign manager and political consultant to local, state, and Congressional candidates.